Fr.

Mo

S

D0420521

1985

The Gospel of Jesus

EDIZIONI ISG ISTITUTO S. GAETANO

STRADA MORA, 57 - 36100 VICENZA - TEL. 31912 - 24534 - C.C.P. 28/19746

Original title: IL VANGELO DI GESÙ
Copyright © 1977 by Istituto S. Gaetano - Vicenza (Italy)

English edition produced in collaboration
with St. Paul Publications, Slough, England,
and copyrighted © 1979 by Istituto S. Gaetano - Vicenza (Italy)

Introductory and explanatory notes translated by Kent White, M.A.

The Bible text in this publication is from the
Revised Standard Version of the Bible - Catholic Edition,
copyrighted © 1965 and 1966 by the
Division of Christian Education of the National Council
of the Churches of Christ in the U.S.A. and used by permission.

Nihil obstat: M. J. Byrnes, ssp, stl

Imprimatur: F. Diamond, v.g., Northampton

Printed in Italy by Tipolitografia Istituto S. Gaetano - Vicenza

THE GOSPEL OF JESUS has been published in the following languages:
English, Italian, French, Portuguese, Spanish, Czech, Malagasy.
All editions copyright © by Istituto S. Gaetano - Vicenza (Italy)

Preface

The present volume sets out to be a new edition, thoroughly revised and, in my judgment, improved, of **The Gospel of Jesus.** This work, which appeared in its first edition ten years ago and was very soon enriched with colour, received a welcome beyond all expectation, as is proved by numerous reprints and by its translation into various languages. This successful publication, backed up by many letters testifying to its usefulness, has confirmed the value of the enterprise and has encouraged the MIMEP group and its skilful collaborators of the Istituto S. Gaetano of Vicenza to adhere to the format of a "unified Gospel", chosen for reasons which in the Preface to the first edition I expressed thus: "It has an extremely practical aim, the encouraging of the young, the very young, and indeed everybody, to read the four gospels for themselves. They are not easy to read as we know by experience: books of the gospels are widely distributed among Christian families, but they are not read. This book does not take their place, but it provides the necessary background for reading them with profit."

The difficulty which arises from having four different accounts of the acts and sayings of Jesus has — since the appearance in the second century of Tatian's **Diatessaron** which was circulated for centuries in both east and west, and translated in the Middle Ages into the emerging European languages (Tuscan, Venetian, German, Dutch) — encouraged the production of 'harmonies of the gospels' which relate in a single narrative without repetition the content of the four gospel stories. The popularity of these publications and their continual revision shows that they met a need which was felt.

But this book is not a 'harmony', for it avoids mingling phrases belonging to different gospels. It has rather the character of an anthology, in which each individual fact is recorded in the words of one evangelist alone. This new edition emphasizes the respect which is due to the words of the Gospel and to the characteristics of each evangelist.

In order to achieve this aim, and following the advice of biblical experts, the authors have tried to keep each story, as far as possible, in the context in which it has been set by the evangelist, in accordance with theological and pastoral rather than chronological considerations. Therefore the new edition has rejected a strictly chronological account of the order of events (a method much criticized by biblical scholars and in fact impossible) and has divided the material into 'periods' which are sometimes merely 'aspects' of Jesus' ministry (e.g. the preaching at Jerusalem, which is deduced from John's gospel). Really, these periods, only broadly speaking chronological, follow the scheme of the individual evangelists, thus making it easier to keep each incident in the context desired by the original writer.

Other improvements are more obvious: more numerous notes, and these theological as well as historical, revision of the illustrations not so much as to make the work more attractive, but — as I wrote in the first edition — "principally to give the reader a constantly renewed feeling of being faced with concrete reality, rooted in history and accurately sited. The work of our salvation is not only a doctrine; it is also a historical reality."

Mgr. ENRICO GALBIATI
Doctor in Biblical Sciences

Contents

PALESTINE
IN THE TIME
OF JESUS

GEOGRAPHICAL AND HISTORICAL BACKGROUND

I - The geography of Palestine in the time of the gospels

Palestine, at the centre of the region which we call the Middle East, is the country in which the great events of the Bible took place. It is like a passage-way between Asia and Africa, and its situation is the cause of its ancient and troubled history. Here it was that, about 1200 B.C., the Hebrew people settled, when God, in fulfilment of his promise, led them there; here it was that Jesus lived; and hence Christianity spread throughout the world.

Palestine is a strip of territory 250 kilometres long and 80 kilometres wide. Its principal geographical feature is the *valley of the river Jordan* which runs from north to south dividing the whole region into two. It is a narrow, deep valley whose course runs almost entirely below sea-level. The Jordan rises on Mount Hermon and very soon forms the Lake of Gennesaret (already at a level of — 212 metres) whence it winds its tortuous way until it empties itself into the Dead Sea (394 metres below the level of the Mediterranean, and the lowest point of the earth's surface). Since it has no outlet, the level of the Dead Sea is kept down by evaporation; its waters thus remain so salty that no fish can live there. Thence it derives its name. The Lake of Gennesaret on the other hand is full of fish. From the valley, on either

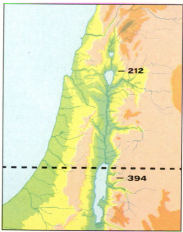

side, rise *two mountainous regions* like two plateaux. The western massif has an average height of 700 metres and in places reaches 1000 metres. From the mountains flow a number of intermittent streams which swell in the winter and dry up in the summer. The only ones worthy of mention are the Kishon which crosses the Plain of Esdraelon and debouches into the Mediterranean, and the Kedron which flows from Jerusalem to the Dead Sea.

The plateau to the east of the Jordan has an average height of 800 metres with some hills reaching 1200 metres. It is deeply furrowed by the valleys of three tributaries of the Jordan, the Yarmuk, the Jabbok and the Arnon.

Like other subtropical countries, Palestine has really no more than two *seasons*; the winter or rainy season from November to April and the summer which is completely dry from May to October. The favourable winds are from the west, bringing rain in winter and cool refreshment in summer: those from the east and south-east are hot and stifling, often laden with fine sand which can even blot out the sun.

In the coastal plain and mountain massif the *climate* is thus that of southern Europe, a Mediterranean climate with infrequent days of cold and snow. Corn and barley, vines, olives and figs, common in Biblical times, grow there. For modern times we must add oranges, lemons and grape-fruit. In the deep, shut in, Jordan valley, however, there is a tropical climate in which bananas and dates ripen.

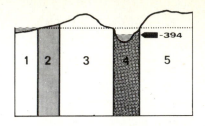

Section of Palestine at the latitude of the Dead Sea: (1) the Mediterranean; (2) the coastal plain; (3) the western mountainous region; (4) the depression of the Dead Sea; (5) the Transjordanian plateau.

Sketch of the climatic zones of Palestine.

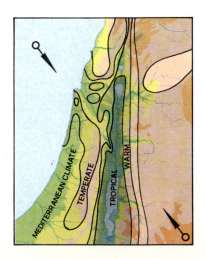

Towards the south, about the level of Beersheba, begins the Sinai Desert. Towards the east, 50 km. beyond the Jordan one is already in the Syro-Arabian Desert.

In the time of Jesus Palestine was divided into *provinces*. To the west of the Jordan were:
Galilee (to the north),
Samaria (in the middle),
Judaea (to the south).
Beyond the Jordan stretched Peraea and the Decapolis.
The principal *towns* with which the gospel story is concerned are:
in Galilee: Nazareth, Cana, Capernaum;
in Samaria: Sychar;
in Judaea: Bethlehem, Jericho, Bethany and above all Jerusalem, the holy city, and the centre of religious and national life.

Palestine divided into provinces.

Jerusalem is situated in a mountainous district about 700 m. above sea-level. The old city is bounded on the east by the valley of the Kedron and on the west and south by that of the Hinnom or Gehenna which flows into the Kedron. The city is built on two hills separated by a trough which also opens out to the south-east at the junction of the two other valleys. It is a very ancient city which was already inhabited in prehistoric times.

Then it occupied only the rocky spur of the lower part of the eastern hill (Ophel). Having been conquered by David in about 1000 B.C., it became the political and religious capital of the Israelitish people.

Jerusalem from the air. The perimeter of the walls in Jesus' day is marked in white.

11

Site of the Tower of Antonia
on the north-west corner
of the esplanade

Mount of Olives

Garden of Gethsemane

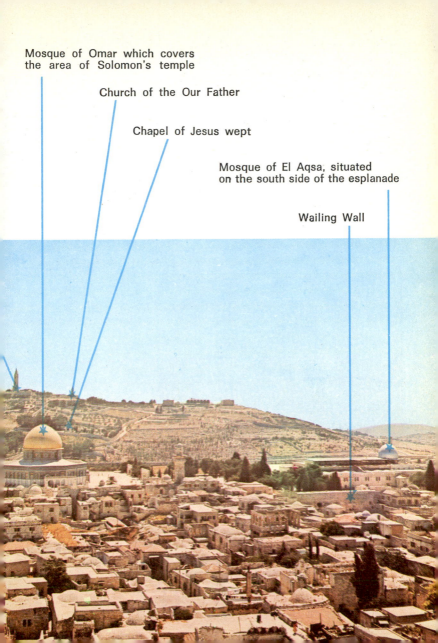

Mosque of Omar which covers
the area of Solomon's temple

Church of the Our Father

Chapel of Jesus wept

Mosque of El Aqsa, situated
on the south side of the esplanade

Wailing Wall

The city spread first towards the north, always on the eastern hill, on the top of which — Mount Zion — Solomon built his great temple; then it extended also to the west, occupying the southern part of the western hill (now mistakenly called Zion). Jerusalem was destroyed in 586 B.C. but was rebuilt, particularly by Nehemiah's efforts, in the fifth century B.C. A few years before the birth of Jesus, Herod the Great enlarged and very greatly embellished both the city and the temple.

Jerusalem was to have a fundamental importance in the story of Jesus; here, in the official religious capital of the nation, he was to be killed. A short while before his death he was to foretell the destruction of the holy city (which took place in 70 A.D.).

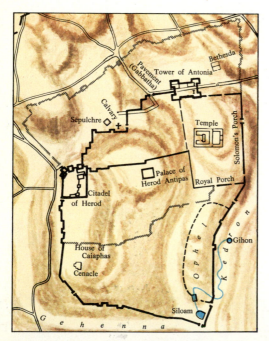

Diagrammatic plan of the city of Jerusalem at the time of Jesus.

II · The political and religious situation

With the destruction of Jerusalem in 586 and the Exile in Babylon, the ancient people of Israel lost its independence. From that time it remained under the suzerainty of the empires which followed one another in the Orient: from the Babylonian to the Persian and then to the Hellenistic Greek of Alexander the Great. When Alexander died his empire was divided into four kingdoms: Palestine passed first to Egypt and afterwards to Syria. Then (167 B.C.) erupted the religious revolt of the Maccabees, which with a series of successful battles followed by skilful diplomacy, supported by the Romans, succeeded in winning even political independence. But in 63 B.C. Palestine passed under the direct control of Rome. Some ten years later the ambitious and astute *Herod (the Great)*, guaranteeing his absolute loyalty to Rome, secured for himself the rule of the whole of Palestine. It was in the last years of his reign, while Caesar Octavius Augustus was Emperor of Rome, that Jesus was born at Bethlehem.

On the death of Herod the Great, the kingdom was divided between his four sons. Judaea and Samaria were given to Archelaus, but later, when he was deposed on account of his cruelty, they passed under the direct administration of Rome, which governed the two provinces by means of procurators. One of these was *Pontius Pilate* who held office from 26 to 36 A.D. Galilee and Peraea fell to the second son,

A coin of Herod the Great, with inscription in Greek OF KING HEROD.

Divisions of Palestine at the death of Herod the Great:
Ethnarchate of Archelaus
Ethnarchate of Herod Antipas
Kingdom of Philip

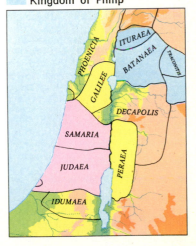

Herod Antipas. His territories were the scene of the preaching of John Baptist (on the banks of the Jordan) and of Jesus (in Galilee). The Decapolis, a federation of ten Hellenistic towns, retained its independence under Roman supervision, whereas the territories to the northeast of the Lake of Gennesaret were allotted to the prudent Philip, third son of Herod the Great.

Meanwhile Augustus had died at Rome (14 A.D.) and been succeeded by his son Tiberius. During his reign Jesus suffered the death penalty, during Pontius Pilate's procuratorship of Judaea.

In the last centuries before Christ, the Jews, although without political independence, were firmly united and very conscious of being different from other people. It was a difference on the religious level: they believed in one only God, and had made the Law of Moses the basis of their very lives, they were distinguished by circumcision and the keeping of the sabbath, and they were looking forward to a mighty action by God which would re-establish his people. The true centre for all the Jews, even if they were dispersed among the cities of the Empire, was always Judaea with Jerusalem and the Temple. This whole phenomenon was called *Judaism.*

Within Judaism however there were various streams:

The Pharisees recognized not only the written Law but also, and above all, the oral traditions which interpreted it and applied it pedantically to every detail of life. They kept it faithfully, but theirs

The precious inscription on stone, the only one that has come down to us, in which Pontius Pilate is named. It was found at Caesarea in 1961. The inscription reads (translated) "(Pon)tius Pilate (Pref)ect of Judea (gives this temple) in honour of Tiberius."

16

was a religiosity which was almost entirely external. Jesus frequently denounced their pride and hypocrisy.

With the Pharisees the Gospel often associates the *Scribes*, i.e. the Doctors of the Law, for the majority of these teachers followed the principles of the Pharisees.

The *Sadducees* on the other hand did not admit any oral tradition and of the Scriptures they retained only the Pentateuch, the first five books of the Bible. Consequently they denied the more recent doctrines, especially the resurrection of the dead. The Sadducees, mainly aristocrats or temple priests, formed a real political party which collaborated with the Roman rulers of the country.

At the other extreme, politically speaking, were the *Zealots*: fervent nationalists, they recognized no authority other than God's, and advocated armed struggle against the Romans.

There was also another sect, called *Essenes*, organized in individual communities, devoted to common prayer, the study of the Law, and work. The important discoveries made from 1947 onwards at Qumran, a site to the north-west of the Dead Sea, have brought to light the existence of a sort of monastic community with special doctrines and a strong internal organization.

General view of the excavations carried out in the district of Qumran.

Holy Place

Holy of Holies   Court of the men

Court of the priests   Court of the women

Balustrade

Solomon's Porch   Courtyard
of the Gentiles

Pinnacle

Tower of Antonia

Royal Porch

Reconstruction of the Temple at Jerusalem
as it probably was in Jesus' time

III - Jewish religious institutions

A) THE TEMPLE AND THE PRIESTHOOD

The Romans always respected the religious organization of the Jewish people, as indeed did Herod the Great and his sons. In Jesus' time this was centred in the Temple and the priesthood.

The *Temple at Jerusalem* was the one place where sacrifice might lawfully be offered to God. It was built by Solomon in the tenth century B.C., destroyed by the Babylonians in 586 B.C., reconstructed by Zerrubabel 70 years later, reached the peak of magnificence with the work of Herod the Great and was dedicated four years before Jesus was born. Its embellishment was not completed until 64 A.D., but a few years later, in 70, it was razed to the ground by the armies of Titus.

Herod's Temple was erected on the wide level space to the north-east of Jerusalem and was reached by means of underground stairways. Splendid porticoes adorned its four sides: the Royal Porch and that named after Solomon were famous. The south-eastern corner, known as the Pinnacle of the Temple, overhung the valley of the Kidron. At the opposite corner rose the Tower of Antonia, a palace-fortress, from which a garrison of King Herod's or the Roman Procurator's troops controlled movement in the Temple, particularly on the occasions when it was crowded with pilgrims. In the middle of the level esplanade a great rectangular balustrade bounded the inner space reserved to the Israelites. Entrance to this was forbidden to Gentiles on pain of death. They had to remain in the area between the porticoes and the balustrade (Court-yard of the Gentiles). This space was always cluttered up with the stalls of the vendors of doves, kids, etc. and of the money-changers.

Beyond the balustrade rose the imposing edifice of the Temple with its successive courts, those of the women, of the men and of the priests, in which the altar of burnt offering was set up. In the centre was the Sanctuary, divided into two compartments; first the *Holy Place*, with the altar of incense, the table of the shew-bread and the golden seven-branched candlestick: then, shut off by a heavy curtain, the *Holy of Holies*, which in Solomon's time had contained the Ark of the Covenant with the tables of the Law but, in Jesus' day, was empty: into it, where God was present, the High Priest, alone, entered once a year, on the solemn Day of the Atonement (Yom Kippur).

In the Temple were offered *sacrifices* to God. They were of several kinds of which the most important was the burnt offering in which the whole of the victim was burnt in acknowledgement and worship of God.

In the period of Judaism sacrifices were offered in the Temple at Jerusalem only. But in every town or village of any consequence the religious life of the Jews had its focus in the *Synagogue* where the scrolls of the Bible were kept. These were read and expounded to the faithful. The readings and common prayers were directed by a "ruler," but the exposition could be given by a member of the congregation.

It must be recorded that the Samaritans, for ethnic and historical reasons, had set up another temple, in opposition to the one at Jerusalem, on Mount Gerizim. At the time of Jesus that had already been destroyed, but the Samaritans continued to offer their sacrifice on its site. Jesus was to bring a completely new approach to this matter. Christ was to be the new and living temple: with his sacrifice all men would have access to God without let or hindrance, and the worship of the Father would be carried out "in spirit and in truth."

The Jewish priesthood, to which members of the tribe of Levi alone were admitted, had at its head the *High Priest*. During Jesus' time, the High Priest was for a long while Annas (or Ananias), whose influence was so great that he was able to have the office conferred in succession on his five sons and his son-in-law, Caiaphas, under whom Jesus was condemned.

Under the High Priest supreme authority in Judaism was exercized by the *Sanhedrin*. This was a sort of executive council, under the presidency of the High Priest and made up of 71 members divided into three groups:

a) the *Chief Priests*, i.e. the High Priests no longer in office and the heads of the priestly families,

b) *the Elders of the People*, i.e. laymen belonging to the aristocratic families.

These two groups tended to hold the Sadducean position.

c) the *Scribes*, or Doctors of the Law, who, as we have said, tended to lean towards Pharisaism.

The Sanhedrin had very wide judicial and executive powers in both religious and civil affairs, to which the Romans set a limit in only a few matters, e.g., it had not the power to inflict the death penalty in Judaea.

Capernaum. Architectural ornament with Jewish symbols in a synagogue.

B) MEASUREMENT OF TIME, AND FESTIVALS

The *day* was considered to begin in the evening and to end at sunset. So the sabbath rest had to start on Friday evening, which was called the *Preparation*. The other days of the week until the sabbath were known by their numbers: the "first day of the week" was that which we call Sunday, and so on.

To tell the *hours* of the day, reference was usually made to the four principal hours: the *first* (6 a.m.), *third* (9), *sixth* (noon) and *ninth* (3 p.m.), the two following hours being included in each case. The *night* was divided into four *watches* (the word refers to the sentries' turn of duty) of three hours each.

The *month* was calculated from observation of the phases of the moon and consisted of 29 or 30 days starting from the new moon.

The *year* was made up of twelve lunar months, but every two or three years a thirteenth month was added so as to re-establish agreement with the cycle of seasons (i.e. the solar year). That was necessary because the festivals, though fixed according to the lunar months, were also connected with the agricultural seasons.

The *festivals* were seven, of which the chief are mentioned in the Gospel. The *Passover* was the first of the seven days of *Unleavened Bread*, from 15 to 22 Nisan (i.e. from full moon in the first month, March-April); it commemorated the exodus of Israel from Egypt. On the night between 14 and 15 Nisan the paschal lamb was eaten and for seven days the food was unlea-

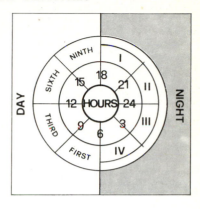

Diagram of the measurement of hours by day and night.

Diagram of the days of the week.

WEEK						
DAY I	II	III	IV	V	VI	SAT.
SUN.	MON.	TUES.	WED.	THURS	FRI.	SAT.

vened bread; on the 16th was made the offering of the first sheaves of barley, with which the harvest began.

Seven weeks after Passover came *Pentecost*, the fiftieth day (generally 6 Sivan), on which were offered the first loaves of bread made from the corn of the new harvest. This day, called also the "Feast of Weeks," was considered in some Jewish circles to commemorate the proclamation of the Law on Mount Sinai.

The third great feast was that of *Tabernacles*, six months after Passover, from 15 to 22 Tishri (September-October): "the last day of the Feast" was kept with special solemnity. This feast, originally called "of the Harvest" later served as a memorial of Israel's sojourn in the desert, in tents, on the long journey to the Promised Land. So, during the eight days of the festival, people were required to live in booths improvised from branches of trees.

The Gospel also mentions the Feast of the *Dedication* of the Temple, which fell on 25 Chislev (November-December) and lasted eight days. It had been instituted by Judas Maccabeus in 164 B.C. to commemorate the reconsecration of the Temple after its desecration by Antiochus Epiphanes, about which we read in the first book of the Maccabees.

The penitential solemnity of the *Atonement* (Yom Kippur) on 10 Tishri was the only day on which the High Priest entered the Holy of Holies. The other festivals were the civil *New Year,* or Feast of Trumpets on 1 Tishri, and the Feast of *Purim* (i.e. Lots) on 14-15 Adar (February-March) in commemoration of the Jews' escape from massacre in the reign of Ahasuerus (Xerxes), told in the book of Esther.

The festivals, their last days and all *sabbaths* in the year required the most rigorous abstention from all work and travel.

The diagram gives the names of the months (Babylonian in origin) used by the Jews in Jesus' time, their correspondence with our calendar, and the dates of the Jewish festivals.

I Nisan	March-April	15 Passover	
		15-22 Unleavened Bread	
II Iyyar	April-May		
III Sivan	May-June	6 Pentecost	
IV Tammuz	June-July		
V Ab	July-August		
VI Elul	August-September	1 Civil New Year	
VII Tishri	September-October	10 Day of Atonement	
VIII Marche-shvan	October-November	15-22 Tabernacles	
IX Chislev	November-December	25 Dedication of the Temple (8 days)	
X Tebeth	December-January		
XI Shebat	January-February		
XII Adar	February-March	14-15 Purim (Lots)	
(XIII Ve-Adar)			

IV - Chronology of the life of Jesus

Before the Christian era years were generally reckoned from the *foundation of the city of Rome*, or from the election of the emperor. With the establishment of Christianity they began to be reckoned from the *birth of Jesus.* An error in calculation by Dionysius the Younger (who in the sixth century introduced the present method of dating) made the birth of Christ coincide with the Roman year 754, whereas further studies have since ascertained that Jesus was actually born in 747 or 748, that is six or seven years earlier than Dionysius had supposed.

From this results the curious fact that the Christian calendar which we now use, instead of starting from the birth of Christ, actually started six or seven years after it. This explains why the date of the birth of Jesus is today reckoned to be 6 or 7 B.C.

As regards the public ministry of Jesus, it is generally held to have lasted little more than two years, in view of certain indications in the fourth gospel, which seems the most accurate on this score and speaks of three different Passovers (chapters 2,6 & 11-19). So, in all probability Jesus began his public ministry towards the beginning of 28 A.D.; his death occured on the eve of the Passover of 30 A.D.

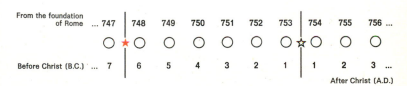

From the foundation of Rome ...	747	748	749	750	751	752	753	754	755	756 ...
Before Christ (B.C.) ...	7	6	5	4	3	2	1	1	2	3 ...

After Christ (A.D.)

The white star shows the beginning of the present era, in the year 754 "of the foundation of Rome," called also 1 A.D., mistakenly held to have been the date of the birth of Jesus. The coloured star on the other hand points approximately to the real date of the birth of Christ.

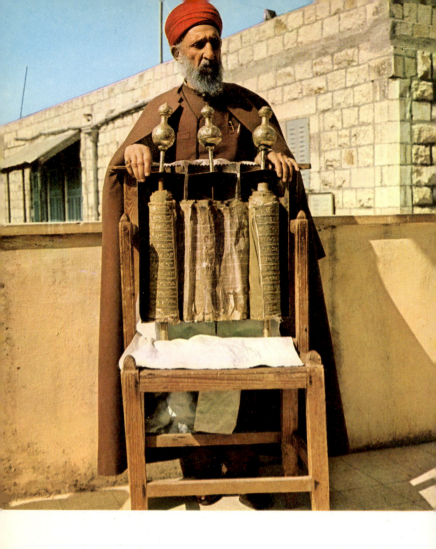

Samaritan priest with a copy of the Pentateuch in the form of scrolls, written in Samaritan characters, derived from the ancient Phoenician alphabet.

V - The books of the Old and New Testaments

The gospels often refer to phrases of the Old Testament. In this book they are printed in italics and the reference is nearly always given in the notes.* It is therefore necessary for the reader to have a clear, even if elementary, knowledge of the Bible and the books of which it is composed.

In fact the *Bible* or *Holy Scripture* is not a single book, but a collection of various books which were written under divine inspiration and contain God's message to mankind.

Some of these books were written *before* Jesus came and constitute the *Old Testament*; others were written *after* his coming and make up the *New Testament*.

The books of the Old Testament are:

THE PENTATEUCH, or THE LAW: Genesis, Exodus, Leviticus, Numbers, Deuteronomy;

HISTORICAL BOOKS: Joshua, Judges, Ruth, Samuel, Kings, Chronicles, Ezra, Nehemiah, Tobit, Judith, Esther, Maccabees;

WISDOM or INSTRUCTIONAL BOOKS: Job, Psalms, Proverbs, Ecclesiastes (or Qoheleth), Song of Songs, Wisdom, Ecclesiasticus (or Sirach);

PROPHETICAL BOOKS: the four major prophets: Isaiah, Jeremiah, with Lamentations and Baruch, Ezekiel, Daniel; the twelve minor prophets: Hosea, Joel, Amos, Obadiah, Jonah, Micah, Nahum, Habbakuk, Zephaniah, Haggai, Zechariah, Malachi.

The books of the New Testament are:

HISTORICAL BOOKS: the four Gospels and the Acts of the Apostles.

INSTRUCTIONAL BOOKS: the letters of Paul: Romans, I & II Corinthians, Galatians, Ephesians, Philippians, Colossians, I & II Timothy, Titus, Philemon. The letter to the Hebrews. The other letters called "catholic": the letters of James, two of Peter, that of Jude, and three of John.

THE PROPHETIC BOOK: the Apocalypse (Revelation).

Of these the most important are the gospels because they present to us the person of Jesus Christ, the Son of God, his example and his teachings. Jesus is the centre and climax of the Scriptures.

* The psalms are quoted in accordance with the Jewish numbering.

VI - The manuscripts of the Gospel

In ancient times all documents were written by *hand* on papyrus or parchment.

The leaves of *papyrus* were obtained by collecting thin strips of the pith of this plant which grows on marshy ground. *Parchment* was made from the skins of animals by means of a process actually invented at Pergamum (in present-day Turkey) in the second century B.C. Papyrus was inexpensive but perishable, whereas parchment was costly but lasted longer.

The single leaves, whether of papyrus or parchment, were next joined together by one of two methods; either they were stuck together so as to make a long strip "rolled up" on two sticks (hence the name "roll" or "scroll"), or they were bound together along one side so as to form a sort of book (called a "codex"). This second method was cheaper as it allowed of writing on both sides of the leaf.

We do not possess the original manuscripts of the gospels, but *copies*, which however go back to a time very near that of the originals. Their number is enormous, about 4,680; about eighty fragments of papyrus were written between 125 and 250 A.D.; in additon, about 230 codices of parchment contain the whole gospel, and some of them reach as far back as 300 A.D.

Among ancient texts the gospels were by far the most copied and the most widespread, and therefore their text is the surest of all. It was handed on faithfully and accurately through the centuries.

Papyrus fragment no. 52, called Rylands; it is the oldest manuscript of the gospel which has come down to us (from about 120-140 A.D.). It was found in Egypt and contains on each side some verses of chapter 18 of the fourth gospel.

ORIGIN AND VALUE OF THE FOUR GOSPELS

The word *"evangel"* (gospel) comes from Greek and means "joyful news." In the early Church this word did not refer to a book, but to the glad tidings of salvation brought by Jesus Christ by means of his death and resurrection. Therefore, tradition speaks of a single Gospel preached by the apostles.

In the first Christian community it was very soon felt that there was need not only to preach about Jesus' death and resurrection but also about what he had done and taught during his life on earth. For those who had had the extraordinary experience of living with Jesus it was easy to remember certain *acts* which had impressed them, particularly the miracles. In the same way some of his *words* also were unforgettable because of their unusual force, novelty and intensity (e.g. the parables), the more so as Jesus had used contemporary methods of teaching.

These memories were also encouraged by the situation in which the community came to be involved and by the problems which arose: e.g. the missionary preaching to Jews and Gentiles, the liturgical celebration of the Lord's Supper, the controversies with the Jews and the requirements of organization. Naturally the first witnesses remembered the fundamental content of Jesus' teaching rather than the exact words, and similarly they refer to the central core of the acts without trying to state precisely the exact circumstances in which they occurred. Above all, they now spoke of them in the light of the final dénouement, the resurrection, and therefore with a new and deeper understanding. Thus was formed the *Tradition* about Jesus, transmitted by word of mouth in the primitive Church.

Later the first writings began to be circulated, e.g. the story of the Passion, collections of the sayings of Jesus, accounts of miracles or controversies. Finally the evangelists, in different places, times and surroundings, wrote the four gospels (*"versions"*). They chose, arranged and edited the traditional material, bringing into prominence different and complementary characteristics of Jesus.

In all this process towards the final form of our gospels, faith recognizes the action and inspiration of the Holy Spirit.

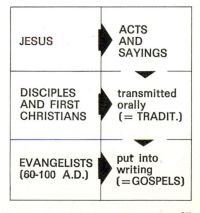

JESUS	ACTS AND SAYINGS
DISCIPLES AND FIRST CHRISTIANS	transmitted orally (= TRADIT.)
EVANGELISTS (60-100 A.D.)	put into writing (=GOSPELS)

The *gospel of Matthew* was, according to the tradition of the Church, the work of the apostle who had been a tax collector. It was written in Aramaic, which was spoken in Palestine at that time, for the Christian community with a Jewish background. That which we have to-day as the first gospel was a new version, coherent and well put together, written in Greek on the basis of Matthew's work, and perhaps about 80 A.D.

The first gospel emphasizes Jesus' role as the Teacher of the Church. It lays great stress on the five great discourses of Jesus which it puts together: the Sermon on the Mount, that for the mission and that in parables, and the discourses about the community and about the expectation of the Last Coming. Writing for the Palestinian Church which had to face Judaism and was troubled by a number of internal difficulties, the evangelist showed his skill as teacher and pastor.

Beginning of the Gospel of Matthew in the Vatican Codex (4th century).

Beginning of the Gospel of Mark in the Vatican Codex (4th century).

The second gospel is attributed by the unanimous tradition of the Church to *Mark*, a disciple of Peter; it was written in Greek, probably in Rome about 70 A.D. Mark brings out the essential features of the Christian message, the mystery of the person of Jesus and, with particular emphasis, the way of the cross. He wrote for Christians who had come from Paganism and were undergoing persecution. His interest lies in incidents rather than in sayings; in this an echo of Peter's testimony is heard.

Luke, disciple and fellow-worker of Paul, took much from the gospel of Mark, but also made use of all the sources of information he could find and fashioned a gospel which, more than any of the others, is something like a biography of Jesus. But the third gospel is only the first part of Luke's work: it is followed by the Acts of the Apostles in which the author tells of the beginnings of the Church, bringing out its essential characteristics and universal mission. The first part (the gospel) brings the story to Jerusalem, whence the second (Acts) takes its beginning. Luke, in addition to being a theologian, was also a historian and a man of letters. He wrote in Greek, after 70 and perhaps about 80 A.D.

The third evangelist pictures Jesus as the Prophet guided by the Spirit, and the Saviour of the world, particularly concerned with the poor and with sinners. Christians, called to a total loyalty to Jesus, find in him a model for their lives.

John wrote his gospel in Greek at Ephesus about 100 A.D. He was the youngest of the apostles and, surviving all the rest by many years, did not copy the traditional teaching of the first three evangelists, but wrote his own personal convictions, taught many times, and deepened over the long years of his apostolate in Asia Minor.

In contemplative and symbolic language he sought to express the human and divine mystery of Christ, the Son of God, the Revelation of the Father and the Giver of Life. On the other hand

Beginning of the Gospel of Luke in the Vatican Codex (4th century).

Beginning of the Gospel of John in the Vatican Codex (4th century).

John gave a whole series of historical notes and a great deal of geographical and topographical information which have been found precise and reliable.

The fourth gospel is the most original and the most profound; it revolves round a number of key ideas: truth, life, light; believing, standing fast, loving; world, judgment, witness.

Other books appeared later claiming to complete or rival the four gospels, but the Church did not recognize them and they are called "apocryphal."

FROM THE CONSTITUTION "DEI VERBUM" OF THE SECOND VATICAN COUNCIL

18 - No one can ignore the fact that of all the Scriptures, even in the New Testament, the Gospels are the most valuable, in that they are the principal witness to the life and doctrine of the Incarnate Word, our Saviour.

The Church has always and everywhere held and still holds that the four Gospels are of apostolic origin. Indeed, what the Apostles preached by Christ's command, was afterwards handed on in writing as a foundation of the faith, by those same men and others of their circle, and is the fourfold gospel of Matthew, Mark, Luke and John.

19 - ... Holy Mother Church has firmly and with absolute constancy held, and continues to hold, that the four gospels, whose historical accuracy she affirms without any hesitation, faithfully hand on what Jesus, the Son of God, really wrought and taught for the salvation of men during his life among them until the day in which he was taken up into heaven (Ac 1, 1-2). After the Lord's Ascension the Apostles passed on to their hearers what he had said and done, with that fuller understanding which they enjoyed from their teaching of the glorious deeds of Christ and from the enlightenment they received from the Spirit of truth. The sacred writers wrote the four Gospels, choosing certain things that were handed down by word of mouth or sometimes in writing, giving some in outline only, explaining others with a view to the situation of the Church, and in short preserving the character of the preaching, so as to depict Jesus with sincerity and truth. Indeed, whether they drew on their own memories or on the testimony of those "who from the beginning were eye-witnesses and ministers of the word", they wrote with the intention of making us know "the truth concerning those things of which we have been informed" (Lk. 1, 2-4).

20 - ... The Lord Jesus was, in fact, as he had promised, with his Apostles (cf. Mt. 28, 20) and sent to them the Holy Paraclete whose task it was to "guide them into all the truth" (Jn. 16, 13).

READER'S GUIDE

The present work can with every right be called the *"Gospel of Jesus,"* for it simply takes the material of the four gospels and arranges it in the probable order of events. The value of such a volume is that it shortens the over abundant material of the gospels so as to render them easier to absorb (sacrificing shades of meaning which the reader as a rule ignores).

After the example of the evangelists we have tried to place every word and act of Jesus in a significant setting, while following the main outlines of a biographical sketch. The public activity of Jesus moves little by little between Galilee and Judaea while the periods at Jerusalem grow longer and more packed with teaching. The dramatic tension grows continually as we can easily see from the gospels of Mark and John. At the same time the disciples and the teaching given to them occupy an increasingly prominent place, a foreshadowing of what was to happen in the Church.

Following this plan we reach an arrangement which is almost biographical, like that of the evangelists and what happened in actual fact. In accordance with the example of the evangelists, there are alternately *narratives*, taken preferably from the gospels of Mark and Luke, and *sayings*, taken from Matthew, whose gospel is built round five well ordered collections of utterances. Only for the complicated discourse about the end of Jerusalem is Luke's version preferred as it is shorter and clearer. Usually the individual evangelists are quoted in sections which are fairly long and homogeneous, so as not to break up the original context of the incidents or words, and in order to make it possible to get an idea, at least on broad lines, of the special viewpoint and characteristics of each evangelist. The section-headings and certain notes help towards this. All that we know of the historical Jesus, we know through the "editorial work" which the several evangelists have undertaken on the mass of material at their disposal.

On the basis of this, the present work sets out to be no more than a new "edition" with its inevitable qualities and disadvantages. It is intended to be a first approach to the Gospel, and a preparation for that deeper reading of the four separate evangelists by which alone it is possible to perceive the plan of each of them and the quality of its execution.

To make it easy for the reader to understand and draw profit from the Gospel, care has been taken to prepare a graphic arrangement of text, notes, maps and illustrations, which, while owing much to the valuable suggestions of other books of this kind, represents in its complete form something which is truly new and original.

Every page of « The Gospel of Jesus » is divided into four parts:

1 The *text* of the four evangelists, arranged in the probable chronological order, provides a continuous story of what Jesus did and said. It is divided into seven parts (see the index) and under numerous headings which make it easier to find and understand the various episodes. Beneath each heading are noted the gospel texts in which the episode is narrated; in heavy type is the reference to the text printed and in brackets the references to parallel passages.

2 The *time* in which the event occurred is shown at the top of the page by two types of diagram:

a) A diagram for the public life of Jesus. For this there is shown on each page the period of his activity to which the passage quoted belongs. The appropriate section is given a coloured background.

b) For the paschal triduum the diagram is more detailed.

3 The *place* where the gospel event took place is shown on the sketch-map by a round black dot (●), or if the place is on a hill by a triangular one (▲). Movements are shown by a continuous red line. The notes are preceded by asterisks which correspond to those beside the verses to which reference is made.

4 The *photographs*, all of which are original, are explained in short captions at the foot of the page on which they appear, and are intended to give the reader a picture of the geographical and historical environment in which Jesus lived.

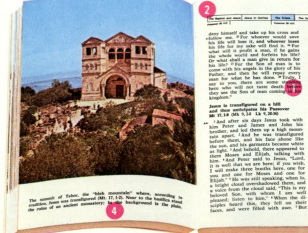

The summit of Tabor, the "high mountain" where, according to tradition, Jesus was transfigured (Mt. 17, 1-2). Near to the basilica stand the ruins of an ancient monastery; in the background is the plain.

The Baptist and Jesus	Jesus in Galilee	The Crisis	The last journey	At Jerusalem
Passover 28 A.D.		Passover 29 A.D.		Passover 30 A.D.

deny himself and take up his cross and *follow me. ²⁵ For whoever would save his life will lose it, **and whoever loses his life for my sake will find it.** ²⁶ For what will it profit a man, if he gains the whole world and forfeits his life? Or what shall a man give in return for his life? ²⁷ For the Son of man is to come with his angels in the glory of his Father, and then he will repay every man for what he has done. ²⁸ Truly, I say to you, there are some standing here who will not taste death before they see the Son of man coming in his kingdom."

Jesus is transfigured on a hill and thus anticipates his Passover
Mt 17, 1-8 (Mk 9, 2-8 Lk 9, 28-36)

** ¹ And after six days Jesus took with him Peter and James and John his brother, and led them up a high mountain apart. ² And he was transfigured before them, and his face shone like the sun, and his garments became white as light. ³ And behold, there appeared to them Moses and Elijah, talking with him. ⁴ And Peter said to Jesus, "Lord, it is well that we are here; if you wish, I will make three booths here, one for you and one for Moses and one for Elijah." ⁵ He was still speaking, when lo, a bright cloud overshadowed them, and a voice from the cloud said, "This is my beloved Son, with whom I am well pleased; listen to him." ⁶ When the disciples heard this, they fell on their faces, and were filled with awe. ⁷ But

* A disciple is someone who follows Jesus by his own path.

** Jesus was on his way to the cross, but it was just by way of the cross that God's glory and victory were to appear. For a moment Jesus allowed the irresolute disciples to catch a glimpse of his glory. That experience meant to them that God confirmed Jesus' status, approved of the way that he had chosen, and invited and encouraged the disciples to follow him.

195

THE GOSPEL OF JESUS

Miniature in a Gospel-book of the twelfth century, portraying the evangelist St Luke in the act of writing under divine inspiration (Milan, Ambrosian Library).

Luke's introduction
Lk 1, 1-4

[1] Inasmuch as many have undertaken
* to compile a narrative of the things
which have been accomplished among
us, [2] just as they were delivered to us
by those who from the beginning were
eyewitnesses and ministers of the word,
[3] it seemed good to me also, having
followed all things closely for some time
past, to write an orderly account for you,
most excellent Theophilus, [4] that you
may know the truth concerning the
things of which you have been informed.

* Here we see how a
gospel originated: ev-
ents took place (the
doings of Jesus) and
then were passed on in
the community by eye-
witnesses and finally
written down by the
evangelist, after careful
consideration, in a cer-
tain order. In Luke's
work we find particul-
arly a direct or indirect
echo of information
whose source was Mary,
the mother of Jesus.

Nazareth, seen from the north. In the centre is the Basilica of the Annunciation. The district where Jesus lived the years of his "hidden life" was until that time a small, unknown and neglected village.

I - THE INFANCY
AND HIDDEN LIFE OF JESUS

The happenings connected with the infancy and hidden life of Jesus were not collected until a comparatively late date in the history of the early Church.

Luke and Matthew chose some of these happenings to show us who he really was. They started with different points of view and therefore chose different episodes; thus Luke was more concerned with the figure of Mary and underlined the joy of the coming of the Saviour of the world; Matthew paid more attention to the figure of Joseph and emphasized the fulfilment of prophecy and also the fate of Jesus in his rejection by his own people.

The two different accounts agree on certain fundamental points: the birth of Jesus by the operation of the Holy Spirit, the virginity of Mary, Joseph's status as legal father, the birth at Bethlehem and the life at Nazareth.

The Temple area at Jerusalem seen from the south-west. Zechariah was officiating in the Temple when he received the promise of the birth of a son (Lk. 1, 8-9). In the background is the Mount of Olives.

Luke's account

Announcement of the birth of John the Baptist
Lk 1, 5-25

5 In the days of Herod, king of Judea, there was a priest named Zechariah, of the division of Abijah; and he had a wife of the daughters of Aaron, and her name was Elizabeth. 6 And they were both righteous before God, walking in all the commandments and ordinances of the Lord blameless. 7 But they had no child, because Elizabeth was barren, and both were advanced in years.

* 8 Now while he was serving as priest before God when his division was on duty, 9 according to the custom of the priesthood, it fell to him by lot to enter the temple of the Lord and burn incense. 10 And the whole multitude of the people were praying outside at the hour of incense. 11 And there appeared to him an angel of the Lord standing on the right side of the altar of incense. 12 And Zechariah was troubled when he saw him, and fear fell upon him. 13 But the angel said to him, "Dot not be afraid, Zechariah, for your prayer is heard, and your wife Elizabeth will bear you a son, and you shall call his name John. 14 And you will have joy and gladness, and many ** will rejoice at his birth; 15 for he will be great before the Lord, and he shall drink no wine nor strong drink, and he will be filled with the Holy Spirit, even from his mother's womb. 16 And he will turn many of the sons of Israel to the

* See what has been said in the Introduction about the Jewish priesthood. Since each class of priests was very numerous, those who had to perform special duties were chosen by lot. The offering of incense was made twice a day, in the morning and before sunset.

** The consecration to God and the prophetic mission of the future baby were described with several references to the Old Testament: to Samson, to Samuel and particularly to the prophecy of Malachi (3, 23-24) which speaks of the future fore-runner as a new Elijah.

Nazareth. The modern basilica built on the site of the Annunciation (Lk. 1, 26-38). It stands on the foundations of earlier shrines, which have existed on this site from the first Christian centuries.

Lord their God, [17] and he will go before him in the spirit and power of Elijah, to turn the hearts of the fathers to the children, and the disobedient to the wisdom of the just, to make ready for the Lord a people prepared."

[18] And Zechariah said to the angel, "How shall I know this? For I am an old man, and my wife is advanced in years." [19] And the angel answered him, "I am Gabriel, who stand in the presence of God; and I was sent to speak to you, and to bring you this good news. [20] And behold, you will be silent and unable to speak until the day that these things come to pass, because you did not believe my words, which will be fulfilled in their time." [21] And the people were waiting for Zechariah, and they wondered at his delay in the temple. [22] And when he came out, he could not speak to them, and they perceived that he had seen a vision in the temple; and he made signs to them and remained dumb. [23] And when his time of service was ended, he went to his home. [24] After these days his wife Elizabeth conceived, and for five months she hid herself, saying, [25] "Thus the Lord has done to me in the days when he looked on me, to take away my reproach among men."

Annunciation to the Virgin Mary of the birth of Jesus, the Son of God
Lk 1, 26-38

* [26] In the sixth month the angel Gabriel was sent from God to a city of Galilee ** named Nazareth, [27] to a virgin betrothed

* "In the sixth month" means the sixth month of Elizabeth's pregnancy.

** Among the Jews at that time marriage was completed in two stages. The first was the "betrothal": with the official marriage contract the two young people were truly married, but they were not yet allowed to live together. With the "marriage feast", which happened about a year afterwards, began the second stage, in which they enjoyed the full privileges of marriage. The Annunciation took place during the first stage, while Mary was "betrothed" to Joseph.

Nazareth. Basilica of the Annunciation. The cave in which the Incarnation of the Word is worshipped. The Latin inscription under the altar reads: "The Word was made flesh — here" (cf. Jn. 1, 14).

to a man whose name was Joseph, of the house of David; and the virgin's name was Mary. ²⁸ And he came to her and said, "Hail, full of grace, the Lord is with you!" ²⁹ But she was greatly troubled at the saying, and considered in her mind what sort of greeting this might be. ³⁰ And the angel said to her, "Do not be afraid, Mary, for you have found favour with God. ³¹ And behold, you will conceive in your womb and bear a son, and you shall call his name Jesus.

* ³² He will be great, and will be called the Son of the Most High; and the Lord God will give to him the throne of his father David, ³³ and he will reign over the house of Jacob for ever; and of his kingdom there will be no end."

³⁴ And Mary said to the angel, "How can this be, since I have no husband?" ** ³⁵ And the angel said to her, "The Holy Spirit will come upon you, and the power of the Most High will overshadow you; therefore the child to be born will be called holy, the Son of God. ³⁶ And behold, your kinswoman Elizabeth in her old age has also conceived a son; and this is the sixth month with her who was called barren. ³⁷ For with God nothing will be impossible." ³⁸ And Mary said, "Behold, I am the handmaid of the Lord; let it be done to me according to your word." And the angel departed from her.

Mary's visit to Elizabeth
Lk 1, 39-45

³⁹ In those days Mary arose and went with haste into the hill country, to a city

* This verse describes the dignity and mission of the future baby who will be the King-Messiah promised by the prophets (2 Sam. 7; Isa. 9, 6).

** The expression calls to mind the presence of God in hallowed places: the son of Mary will be conceived by the mysterious operation of God himself without human intervention.

43

Ain Karim. The village in the Judaean hills to which Mary made her way to visit her cousin Elizabeth (Lk. 1, 39-56). Here a shrine commemorates the Visitation.

of Judah, ⁴⁰ and she entered the house of Zechariah and greeted Elizabeth. ⁴¹ And when Elizabeth heard the greeting of Mary, the babe leaped in her womb; and Elizabeth was filled with the Holy Spirit ⁴² and she exclaimed with a loud cry, "Blessed are you among women, and blessed is the fruit of your womb!

* ⁴³ And why is this granted me, that the mother of my Lord should come to me? ⁴⁴ For behold, when the voice of your greeting came to my ears, the babe in my womb leaped for joy. ⁴⁵ And blessed is she who believed that there would be a fulfilment of what was spoken to her from the Lord."

The song of Mary
Lk 1, 46-56

** ⁴⁶ And Mary said,
"My soul magnifies the Lord,
⁴⁷ and my spirit rejoices
in God my Saviour,
⁴⁸ for he has regarded the low estate
of his handmaiden.
For behold, henceforth all generations
will call me blessed;
⁴⁹ for he who is mighty has done
great things for me,
and holy is his name.
⁵⁰ And his mercy is on those who fear him
from generation to generation.
⁵¹ He has shown strength with his arm,
he has scattered the proud
in the imagination of their hearts,
⁵² he has put down the mighty
from their thrones,
and exalted those of low degree;

* Elizabeth, inspired by the Spirit, understands what has happened in Mary and meets her with the greeting David used when he welcomed the ark in which God was present (2 Sam. 6, 9).

** It is a fairly common tradition in the Bible to express one's feelings towards God in the form of poetry. So, for example, did Hannah, the mother of Samuel (1 Sam. 2). The Magnificat is a sort of "collage" of Old Testament texts, and expresses the joy and gratitude of the poor for what God has done for the salvation of his people.

45

Ain Karim. The church built on the site of the birth of John the Baptist (Lk. 1, 57-60). Fragments of Byzantine mosaic and vases of the Roman and Herodian period have been found on the site.

53 he has filled the hungry
with good things,
and the rich he has sent empty away.
54 He has helped his servant Israel,
in remembrance of his mercy,
55 as he spoke to our fathers,
to Abraham and to his posterity
for ever."
56 And Mary remained with her about
three months, and returned to her home.

The birth of John the Baptist
Lk 1, 57-66

* 57 Now the time came for Elizabeth
to be delivered, and she gave birth to a
son. 58 And her neighbours and kinsfolk
heard that the Lord had shown great
mercy to her, and they rejoiced with her.
59 And on the eighth day they came to
circumcise the child; and they would
have named him Zechariah after his
father, 60 but his mother said, "Not so;
** he shall be called John." 61 And they said
to her, "None of your kindred is called
by this name." 62 And they made signs to
his father, inquiring what he would have
him called. 63 And he asked for a writing
tablet, and wrote, "His name is John."
And they all marvelled. 64 And immediately his mouth was opened and his
tongue loosed, and he spoke, blessing
God. 65 And fear came on all their neighbours. And all these things were talked
about through all the hill country of
Judea; 66 and all who heard them laid
them up in their hearts, saying, "What
then will this child be?" For the hand of
the Lord was with him.

* After the account
of the two annunciat-
ions — of John and of
Jesus — there now
follows that of the two
births.

** John means "God
is gracious."

Ain Karim. Church of St. John the Baptist: the chapel which commemorates the birth of the Forerunner. On the proscenium arch are recorded the first words of the song of Zechariah in Latin (Lk. 1, 68).

The song of Zechariah
Lk 1, 67-80

⁶⁷ And his father Zechariah was filled with the Holy Spirit, and prophesied, saying.

* ⁶⁸ "Blessed be the Lord God of Israel,
for he has visited and redeemed
his people,
⁶⁹ and has raised up a horn
of salvation for us
in the house of his servant David,
⁷⁰ as he spoke by the mouth of his holy
prophets from of old,
⁷¹ that we should be saved from
our enemies,
and from the hand of all who hate us;
⁷² to perform the mercy promised
to our fathers,
and to remember his holy convenant,
⁷³ the oath which he swore to our father
Abraham, ⁷⁴ to grant us
that we, being delivered from the hand
of our enemies,
might serve him without fear,
⁷⁵ in holiness and righteousness before
him all the days of our life.
⁷⁶ And you, child, will be called
the prophet of the Most High;
for you will go before the Lord
to prepare his ways,
⁷⁷ to give knowledge of salvation
to his people
in the forgiveness of their sins,
⁷⁸ through the tender mercy of our God,
when the day shall dawn upon
us from on high
⁷⁹ to give light to those who sit in
darkness and in the shadow of death,

*   This song also, full of biblical references as it is, extols God's mercy and faithfulness. God fulfils his promises, sending a "dawn" which is the Messiah and Saviour; the young John will be the prophet who will prepare the way for him.

Bethlehem. The Judaean village which was Jesus' birthplace, seen from the "Shepherds" Field. Here David, Joseph's ancestor, had been born about a thousand years earlier (Lk. 2, 4).

to guide our feet into the way
of peace."
⁸⁰ And the child grew and became strong
in spirit, and he was in the wilderness
till the day of his manifestation to Israel.

The birth of Jesus
Lk 2, 1-7

¹ In those days a decree went out
from Caesar Augustus that all the world
should be enrolled. ² This was the first
enrolment, when Quirinius was governor
of Syria. ³ And all went to be enrolled,
* each to his own city. ⁴ And Joseph also
went up from Galilee, from the city of
Nazareth, to Judea, to the city of David,
which is called Bethlehem, because he
was of the house and lineage of David,
⁵ to be enrolled with Mary, his betrothed,
who was with child. ⁶ And while they
were there, the time came for her to be
delivered. ⁷ And she gave birth to her
** first-born son and wrapped him in swaddling cloths, and laid him in a manger,
because there was no place for them in
the inn.

The glad tidings to the shepherds
of Christ the Saviour
Lk 2, 8-20

⁸ And in that region there were shepherds out in the field, keeping watch
over their flock by night. ⁹ And an angel
of the Lord appeared to them, and the
glory of the Lord shone around them,
and they were filled with fear. ¹⁰ And
the angel said to them, "Be not afraid;

* According to Orien-
tal practice, in a census,
people had to report
to the native district
of their ancestors. So
Joseph went to Beth-
lehem, the birthplace
of David.

** It does not follow
from the word "first-
born" that other chil-
dren followed. The
word, which can also
be applied to an only
son, recalls the special
provisions of the Jew-
ish Law: the first born
had to be offered in
the Temple and re-
deemed. Luke also em-
phasizes the poverty
into which Jesus was
born.

Bethlehem. The Shepherds' Fields. A cave where the shepherds used to spend their nights. Here an altar records the appearance and message of the angels (Lk. 2, 8-14).

for behold, I bring you good news of a great joy which will come to all the
* people; ¹¹for to you is born this day in the city of David a Saviour, who is Christ the Lord. ¹²And this will be a sign for you: you will find a babe wrapped in swaddling cloths and lying in a manger." ¹³And suddenly there was with the angel a multitude of the heavenly host praising God and saying, ¹⁴"Glory to God in the highest,
   and on earth peace among men with
   whom he is pleased!"

¹⁵When the angels went away from them into heaven, the shepherds said to one another, "Let us go over to Bethlehem and see this thing that has happened, which the Lord has made known to us." ¹⁶And they went with haste, and found Mary and Joseph, and the babe lying in a manger. ¹⁷And when they saw it they made known the saying which had been told them concerning this child; ¹⁸and all who heard it wondered at what the shepherds told them. ¹⁹But Mary kept all these things, pondering them in her heart. ²⁰And the shepherds returned, glorifying and praising God for all they had heard and seen, as it had been told them.

Jesus is circumcised
and presented in the temple at Jerusalem
Lk 2, 21-40

²¹And at the end of eight days, when he was circumcised, he was called Jesus, the name given by the angel before he was conceived in the womb.

* The angelic message includes the titles which proclaim Jesus' greatness: Saviour, Messiah, Lord, the bringer of peace and all good gifts, and men's sign that God loves them.

Bethlehem. The Basilica of the Nativity, which encloses the cave in which Jesus was born. In the past, in order to prevent inroads and profanations, the façade was protected by iron bars, and of the three doors only a low, narrow passage remains.

* 22 And when the time came for their purification according to the law of Moses, they brought him up to Jerusalem to present him to the Lord 23 (as it is written in the law of the Lord, "Every male that opens the womb shall be called holy to the Lord") 24 and to offer a sacrifice according to what is said in the law of the Lord, "a pair of turtledoves, or two young pigeons." 25 Now there was a man in Jerusalem, whose name was Simeon, and this man

** was righteous and devout, looking for the consolation of Israel, and the Holy Spirit was upon him. 26 And it had been revealed to him by the Holy Spirit that he should not see death before he had seen the Lord's Christ. 27 And inspired by the Spirit he came into the temple; and when the parents brought in the child Jesus, to do for him according to the custom of the law, 28 he took him up in his arms and blessed God and said,

** 29 "Lord, now lettest thou thy servant
depart in peace,
according to thy word;
30 for mine eyes have seen thy salvation
31 which thou hast prepared
in the presence of all peoples,
32 a light for revelation to the Gentiles,
and for glory to thy people Israel."

33 And his father and his mother marvelled at what was said about him; 34 and Simeon blessed them and said to Mary his mother, "Behold, this child is set for the fall and rising of many in Israel, and for a sign that is spoken against 35 (and a sword will pierce through your

* The law of Moses prescribed the purification of the mother after every birth (Lev. 12, 3-6) and ordered the first-born son to be offered to the Lord and then redeemed (Ex. 13, 12-15). For the redemption Mary presented the offering of the poor (Lev. 12, 8).

** There was a very lively expectation of the Messiah at that time. Many good Jews, especially among the poor, were awaiting it, confident in God's promises.

*** The beautiful song of Simeon proclaims the fulfilment of the promises, and announces the mission of Jesus as saviour, not only of the Jews but of all peoples.

Nazareth. The so-called "Well of the Virgin". The spring used to feed the only fountain in the village. In that obscure hamlet Jesus spent the years of his childhood and youth (Lk. 2, 39-40, 52).

own soul also), that thoughts of many hearts may be revealed."

36 And there was a prophetess Anna, the daughter of Phanuel, of the tribe of Asher; she was of a great age, having lived with her husband seven years from her virginity, 37 and as a widow till she was eighty-four. She did not depart from the temple, worshipping with fasting and prayer night and day. 38 And coming up at that very hour she gave thanks to God, and spoke of him to all who were looking for the redemption of Jerusalem.

39 And when they had performed everything according to the law of the Lord, they returned into Galilee, to their own city, Nazareth. 40 And the child grew and became strong, filled with wisdom; and the favour of God was upon him.

Jesus shows himself in the temple
Lk 2, 41-50

* 41 Now his parents went to Jerusalem every year at the feast of the Passover. 42 And when he was twelve years old, they went up according to custom; 43 and when the feast was ended, as they were returning, the boy Jesus stayed behind in Jerusalem. His parents did not know it, 44 but supposing him to be in the company they went a day's journey, and they sought him among their kinsfolk and acquaintances; 45 and when they did not find him, they returned to Jerusalem, seeking him. 46 After three days they found him in the temple, sitting among the teachers, listening to them and asking them questions; 47 and all who heard

* Good Jews made their way to the Temple at Jerusalem at least once a year, especially at the time of the Passover; it was there that God's presence was worshipped and only there was sacrifice allowed.

57

him were amazed at his understanding and his answers. [48] And when they saw him they were astonished; and his mother said to him, "Son, why have you treated us so? Behold, your father and I have been looking for you anxiously." * [49] And he said to them, "How is it that you sought me? Did you not know that I must be in my Father's house?" [50] And they did not understand the saying which he spoke to them.

The "hidden life" of Jesus
Lk 2, 51-52

[51] And he went down with them and came to Nazareth, and was obedient to them; and his mother kept all these things in her heart. [52] And Jesus increased in wisdom and in stature, and in favour with God and man.

Other events, presented by Matthew

Jesus' descent from David
Mt 1, 1-17

[1] The book of the genealogy of Jesus Christ, the son of David, the son of Abraham.
[2] Abraham was the father of Isaac, and Isaac the father of Jacob, and Jacob the father of Judah and his brothers, [3] and Judah the father of Perez and Zerah by Tamar, and Perez the father of Hezron, and Hezron the father of Ram, [4] and Ram the father of Amminadab, and Amminadab the father of Nahson, and Nahson the father of Salmon, [5] and Salmon the father of Boaz by Rahab, and

* Jesus revealed himself for the first time in the house of God; he knew himself to be God's son and to be bound to fulfil the mission entrusted to him by the Father.

Boaz the father of Obed by Ruth, and Obed the father of Jesse, ⁶ and Jesse the father of David the king.

And David was the father of Solomon by the wife of Uriah, ⁷ and Solomon the father of Rehoboam, and Rehoboam the father of Abijah, and Abijah the father of Asa, ⁸ and Asa the father of Jehoshaphat, and Jehoshaphat the father of Joram, and Joram the father of Uzziah, ⁹ and Uzziah the father of Jotham, and Jotham the father of Ahaz, and Ahaz the father of Hezekiah, ¹⁰ and Hezekiah the father of Manasseh, and Manasseh the father of Amos, and Amos the father of Josiah, ¹¹ and Josiah the father of Jechoniah and his brothers, at the time of the deportation to Babylon.

¹² And after the deportation to Babylon: Jechoniah was the father of Shealtiel, and Shealtiel the father of Zerubbabel, ¹³ and Zerubbabel the father of Abiud, and Abiud the father of Eliakim, and Eliakim the father of Azor, ¹⁴ and Azor the father of Zadok, and Zadok the father of Achim, and Achim the father of Eliud, ¹⁵ and Eliud the father of Eleazar, and Eleazar the father of Matthan, and Matthan the father of Jacob, ¹⁶ and Jacob the father of Joseph the husband of Mary, of whom Jesus was born, who is called Christ.

¹⁷ So all the generations from Abraham to David were fourteen generations, and from David to the deportation to Babylon fourteen generations, and from the deportation to Babylon to the Christ fourteen generations.

* In this genealogical outline Matthew showed that Jesus was descended from Abraham and a legal scion of David. In him were to be realized the promises made to Abraham (Gen. 12, 3) and to David (2 Sam. 7).

Bethlehem. Cave of the Nativity. On the silver star beneath the altar these words were carved in Latin: "Here Jesus Christ was born of the Virgin Mary".

The announcement to Joseph
of the birth of Jesus
Mt 1, 18-25

¹⁸ Now the birth of Jesus Christ took place in this way. When his mother Mary had been betrothed to Joseph, before they came together she was found to be
* with child of the Holy Spirit; ¹⁹ and her husband Joseph, being a just man and unwilling to put her to shame, resolved to send her away quietly. ²⁰ But as he considered this, behold, an angel of the Lord appeared to him in a dream, saying, "Joseph, son of David, do not fear to take Mary your wife, for that which is conceived in her is of the Holy Spirit; ²¹ she will bear a son, and you shall call his name Jesus, for he will save his people from their sins." ²² All this took place to fulfil what the Lord had spoken
** by the prophet: ²³ "Behold, a virgin shall conceive and bear a son, and his name shall be called Emmanuel" (which means, God with us). ²⁴ When Joseph woke from sleep, he did as the angel of the Lord commanded him; he took his wife, ²⁵ but knew her not until she had borne a son; and he called his name Jesus.

Jesus is worshipped
by the Wise Men of the East
Mt 2, 1-12

¹ Now when Jesus was born in Bethlehem of Judea in the days of Herod the king, behold, wise men from the East came to Jerusalem, saying, ² "Where is he who has been born king of the Jews?

*   Perhaps Joseph was afraid that he would have no authority over Mary's son, since the latter was miraculously conceived, but the angel reassured him, telling him that it would be for him, Joseph to give the name and the legal title of "son of David" to the child who was about to be born. "Jesus" means "the Lord saves."

** The quotation is taken from the book of Isaiah (7, 14); the prophecy of Emmanuel, "God with us."

The pyramid of Gizeh in Egypt. In the nearby village of Matariyeh there lived a flourishing Jewish community. There, according to tradition, the Holy Family took refuge (Mt. 2, 13-14).

For we have seen his star in the East, and have come to worship him." ³ When Herod the king heard this, he was troubled, and all Jerusalem with him; ⁴ and assembling all the chief priests and scribes of the people, he inquired of them where the Christ was to be born. ⁵ They told him, "In Bethlehem of Judea;
∗ for so it is written by the prophet: ⁶'And you, O Bethlehem, in the land of Judah, are by no means least among the rulers of Judah; for from you shall come a ruler who will govern my people Israel'."

∗∗ ⁷ Then Herod summoned the wise men secretly and ascertained from them what time the star appeared; ⁸ and he sent them to Bethlehem, saying, "Go and search diligently for the child, and when you have found him bring me word, that I too may come and worship him." ⁹ When they had heard the king they went their way; and lo, the star which they had seen in the East went before them, till it came to rest over the place where the child was. ¹⁰ When they saw the star, they rejoiced exceedingly with great joy; ¹¹ and going into the house they saw the child with Mary his mother, and they fell down and worshiped him. Then, opening their treasures, they offered him gifts, gold and frankincense and myrrh. ¹² And being warned in a dream not to return to Herod, they departed to their own country by another way.

The Holy Family flees to Egypt
Mt 2, 13-15

¹³ Now when they had departed, behold,

∗ The quotation is from the book of the prophet Micah 5, 1.

∗∗ The Magi were probably Persian and/or Babylonian priests, experts in astrology and the natural sciences. The evangelist saw them as the first representatives of the Gentiles to recognize Jesus as Messiah whereas most of the Israelites showed themselves indifferent or even hostile.

Bethlehem. Rachel's Tomb. The poetic figure of Rachel weeping from her tomb expresses the grief of the mothers of Bethlehem when they were robbed of their children (Mt. 2, 17-18).

an angel of the Lord appeared to Joseph in a dream and said, "Rise, take the child and his mother, and flee to Egypt, and remain there till I tell you; for Herod is about to search for the child, to destroy him." ¹⁴ And he rose and took the child and his mother by night, and departed
* to Egypt, ¹⁵ and remained there until the death of Herod. This was to fulfil what the Lord had spoken by the prophet, "Out of Egypt have I called my son."

The slaughter of the children at Bethlehem
Mt 2, 16-18

¹⁶ Then Herod, when he saw that he had been tricked by the wise men, was in a furious rage, and he sent and killed all the male children in Bethlehem and in all that region who were two years old or under, according to the time which he had ascertained from the wise men. ¹⁷ Then was fulfilled what was spoken
** by the prophet Jeremiah: ¹⁸ "A voice was heard in Ramah, wailing and loud lamentation, Rachel weeping for her children; she refused to be consoled, because they were no more."

The Holy Family returns to Nazareth
Mt 2, 19-23

¹⁹ But when Herod died, behold, an angel of the Lord appeared in a dream to Joseph in Egypt, saying, ²⁰ "Rise, take the child and his mother, and go to the land of Israel, for those who sought the child's life are dead." ²¹ And he rose and

* Jesus had to flee from Herod. Then he was freed and recalled from Egypt, as happened to the Israelites at the Exodus: so says the quotation from Hosea 11, 1.

** Jeremiah, to express the grief of the exiled people, had pictured Rachel weeping from her tomb over her descendants, herded together in Ramah to be deported, killed or scattered (Jer. 31, 15).

65

took the child and his mother, and went to the land of Israel, ²² But when he heard that Archelaus reigned over Judea in place of his father Herod, he was afraid to go there, and being warned in a dream he withdrew to the district of Galilee. ²³ And he went and dwelt in a city called Nazareth, that what was spoken by the prophets might be fulfilled, "He shall be called a Nazarene."

Nazareth. The scratched Hail Mary. On the plaster of the very ancient pre-byzantine sanctuary built over the Virgin's home has been found this graffito in Greek: XE MAPIA (chàire Maria), i.e. Hail Mary.

II - JOHN THE BAPTIST
AND THE BEGINNING OF JESUS' ACTIVITY

A short time before Jesus began his public activity, John, surnamed the Baptizer or Baptist, appeared on the banks of the Jordan, preaching repentance in preparation for future events.

Then Jesus, having been baptized by John, made a start to his public messianic activity in full accord with the Father's will, conquering every adverse temptation. John the evangelist insists that John the Baptist was not only the Forerunner but above all the Witness to the Christ, drawing attention to his presence in the world. In addition, the fourth evangelist speaks of a short stay by Jesus in Jerusalem, perhaps for the Passover of 28 A.D., a stay which seems, as it were, framed by two miracles at Cana.

The preparation for the Messiah

John the Baptist begins his mission
Lk 3, 1-6 (Mt 3, 1-6   Mk 1, 1-6)

¹ In the fifteenth year of the reign of Tiberius Caesar, Pontius Pilate being governor of Judea, and Herod being
* tetrarch of Galilee, and his brother Philip tetrarch of the region of Ituraea and Trachonitis, and Lysanias tetrarch of Abilene, ² in the high-priesthood of Annas and Caiaphas, the word of God came to John the son of Zechariah in the
** wilderness; ³ and he went into all the region about the Jordan, preaching a baptism of repentance for the forgiveness of sins. ⁴ As it is written in the book of the words of Isaiah the prophet,
"The voice of one crying
   in the wilderness:
Prepare the way of the Lord,
   make his paths straight.
⁵ Every valley shall be filled,
   and every mountain and hill
   shall be brought low,
   and the crooked shall be made straight,
   and the rough ways
   shall be made smooth;
⁶ and all flesh shall see
   the salvation of God."

John preaches repentance
Lk 3, 7-9 (Mt 3, 7-10)

⁷ He said therefore to the multitudes that came out to be baptized by him, "You brood of vipers! Who warned you to flee from the wrath to come? ⁸ Bear

* The kingdom of Herod the Great had been divided into four parts; "tetrarch" means precisely "ruler of a quarter of the kingdom."

** God sent a "special messenger" to prepare for his coming. The prophecy of Isaiah (40, 3-5), which referred to the liberation and return from the Exile, is applied to the Baptist who prepared sympathetic souls for the Messiah when he was about to start his mission.

fruits that befit repentance, and do not begin to say to yourselves, 'We have Abraham as our father'; for I tell you. God is able from these stones to raise up children to Abraham. ⁹ Even now the axe is laid to the root of the trees; every tree therefore that does not bear good fruit is cut down and thrown into the fire."

John counsels charity and justice
Lk 3, 10-14

¹⁰ And the multitudes asked him, "What then shall we do?" ¹¹ And he answered them, "He who has two coats, let him share with him who has none; and he who has food, let him do likewise." * ¹² Tax collectors also came to be baptized, and said to him, "Teacher, what shall we do?" ¹³ And he said to them, "Collect no more than is appointed you." ¹⁴ Soldiers also asked him, "And we, what shall we do?" And he said to them, "Rob no one by violence or by false accusation, and be content with your wages."

John proclaims that the Messiah is near
Lk 3, 15-18 (Mt 3, 11-12 Mk 1, 7-8)

¹⁵ As the people were in expectation, and all men questioned in their hearts concerning John, whether perhaps he were the Christ, ¹⁶ John answered them all, "I baptize you with water; but he who is mightier than I is coming, the thong of whose sandals I am not worthy to untie; he will baptize you with the ** Holy Spirit and with fire. ¹⁷ His winnow-

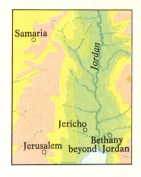

* The tax collectors were regarded as public sinners because they received payment of taxes on behalf of the oppressor and were often greedy to the point of injustice.

** The Baptist depicts the Messiah as the stern, unyielding judge who will radically purify his people.

69

The river Jordan. Here, according to tradition, Jesus was baptized by John, and hence he went to start his mission (Lk. 3, 21-23).

ing fork is in his hand, to clear his threshing floor, and to gather the wheat into his granary, but the chaff he will burn with unquenchable fire."

¹⁸ So, with many other exhortations, he preached good news to the people.

Jesus is proclaimed Son of God at his baptism
Lk 3, 21-22 (Mt 3, 13-17 Mk 1, 9-11)

* ²¹ Now when all the people were baptized, and when Jesus also had been baptized and was praying, the heaven was opened, ²² and the Holy Spirit descended upon him in bodily form, as a dove, and a voice came from heaven, "Thou art my beloved Son; with thee I am well pleased."

Genealogy of Jesus, the Saviour of all men
Lk 3, 23-38

²³ Jesus, when he began his ministry, was about thirty years of age, being the
**son (as was supposed) of Joseph, the son of Heli, ²⁴ the son of Matthat, the son of Levi, the son of Melchi, the son of Jannai, the son of Joseph, ²⁵ the son of Mattathias, the son of Amos, the son of Nahum, the son of Eli, the son of Naggai, ²⁶ the son of Maath, the son of Mattathias, the son of Semein, the son of Josech, the son of Joda, ²⁷ the son of Joannan, the son of Rhesa, the son of Zerubbabel, the son of Shealtiel, the son of Neri, ²⁸ the son of Melchi, the son of Addi, the son of Cosam, the son of

* Jesus, being guiltless, had no need of baptism. Matthew tries to deal with this difficulty: "John would have prevented him, saying: 'I need to be baptized by you, and do you come to me?' But Jesus answered him: 'Let it be so now, for thus it is fitting for us to fulfil all righteousness' " (Mt. 3, 14-15). Indeed it was the Father's will for Jesus thus to unite himself with sinners. The baptism represented for Jesus the entry upon his mission. It was for this that the Spirit descended upon him and the divine voice proclaimed him Messiah, Son of God, and Servant. It is worthy of note that Jesus prayed at this important moment.

** Luke gives a rather different genealogy

The Mount of the Temptation, not far from the ancient city of Jericho. Jesus probably retired here for prayer and fasting before starting to preach the gospel (Lk. 4, 1-2).

Elmadam, the son of Er, 29 the son of Joshua, the son of Eliezer, the son of Jorim, the son of Matthat, the son of Levi, 30 the son of Simeon, the son of Judah, the son of Joseph, the son of Jonam, the son of Eliakim, 31 the son of Melea, the son of Menna, the son of Mattatha, the son of Nathan, the son of David, 32 the son of Jesse, the son of Obed, the son of Boaz, the son of Sala, the son of Nahshon, 33 the son of Amminadab, the son of Admin, the son of Arni, the son of Hezron, the son of Perez, the son of Judah, 34 the son of Jacob, the son of Isaac, the son of Abraham, the son of Terah, the son of Nahor, 35 the son of Serug, the son of Reu, the son of Peleg, the son of Eber, the son of Shelah, 36 the son of Cainan, the son of Arphaxad, the son of Shem, the son of Noah, the son of Lamech, 37 the son of Methuselah, the son of Enoch, the son of Jared, the son of Mahalaleel, the son of Cainan, 38 the son of Enos, the son of Seth, the son of Adam, the son of God.

Mt of the Temptation▲ Jericho
Jerusalem Bethany
beyond Jordan
Jordan

from Matthew's. With names taken from the Bible he goes back to Adam so as to show that Jesus is the Saviour, not of the Jews only, but of all mankind.

* In the Bible the wilderness is the place of nearness to God and of trial. Before starting his public life Jesus was tempted; there came to him suggestions to oppose the Father's will and to choose an easier way, through domination and power. Later he met the same temptation from the crowd and even from the disciples. But he, full of the Holy Spirit and strong in the word of God, overcame it. In his replies Jesus quoted Deuteronomy (8, 3; 6, 13; 6, 16) which referred to the temptations of Israel during the forty years in the wilderness.

In the wilderness
Jesus conquers temptation
Lk 4, 1-13 (Mt 4, 1-11 Mk 1, 12-13)

1 And Jesus, full of the Holy Spirit, returned from the Jordan, and was led by the Spirit 2 for forty days in the wilderness, tempted by the devil. And he ate nothing in those days; and when they were ended, he was hungry. 3 The devil said to him, "If you are the Son of God, command this stone to become

bread." ⁴ And Jesus answered him, "It is written, 'Man shall not live by bread alone.'" ⁵ And the devil took him up, and showed him all the kingdoms of the world in a moment of time, ⁶ and said to him, "To you I will give all this authority and their glory; for it has been delivered to me, and I give it to whom I will. ⁷ If you, then, will worship me, it shall all be yours." ⁸ And Jesus answered him, "It is written,

'You shall worship the Lord your God,
and him only shall you serve.'"

⁹ And he took him to Jerusalem, and set him on the pinnacle of the temple, and said to him, "If you are the Son of God, throw yourself down from here; ¹⁰ for it is written,

'He will give his angels charge of you,
to guard you,'

¹¹ and

'On their hands they will bear you up,
lest you strike your foot
against a stone.'"

¹² And Jesus answered him, "It is said, 'You shall not tempt the Lord your God.'" ¹³ And when the devil had ended every temptation, he departed from him
* until an opportune time.

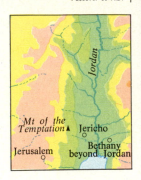

John the Baptist bears witness to the Word of God

Opening hymn of John the Evangelist Jn 1, 1-18

** ¹ In the beginning was the Word, and the Word was with God, and the Word

* The "opportune time" was the moment of the Passion, when the devil and the powers of darkness let loose their attack on Jesus.

** John begins his gospel with a hymn declaring that Jesus is the Son of God made man. As Son of God ("Logos" or "Word") he is eternal like the Father, and with him is God and Creator of the universe. Taking weak human nature ("flesh") he reveals the Father and brings into the world life and light, grace and truth. In view of his revelation, foretold by John Baptist, he cannot be gainsaid; who, then, accepts Christ can himself become a son of God, sharing in the gift of the divine life.

was God. ² He was in the beginning with God; ³ all things were made through him, and without him was not anything made that was made. ⁴ In him was life, and the life was the light of men. ⁵ The light shines in the darkness, and the darkness has not overcome it.

⁶ There was a man sent from God, whose name was John. ⁷ He came for testimony, to bear witness to the light, that all might believe through him. ⁸ He was not the light, but came to bear witness to the light.

⁹ The true light that enlightens every man was coming into the world. ¹⁰ He was in the world, and the world was made through him, yet the world knew him not. ¹¹ He came to his own home, and his own people received him not. ¹² But to all who received him, who believed in his name, he gave power to become children of God; ¹³ who were born, not of blood nor of the will of the flesh nor of the will of man, but of God.

* ¹⁴ And the Word became flesh and dwelt among us, full of grace and truth; we have beheld his glory, glory as of the only Son from the Father. ¹⁵ (John bore witness to him, and cried, "This was he of whom I said, 'He who comes after me ranks before me, for he was before me.'") ¹⁶ And from his fulness have we all received, grace upon grace. ¹⁷ For the law was given through Moses; grace and truth came through Jesus Christ. ¹⁸ No one has ever seen God; the only Son, ** who is in the bosom of the Father, he has made him known.

Capernaum

Nazareth

Jerusalem
Bethlehem

* This is the climax of the hymn: the mystery of the Incarnation, the union of God and man in Jesus. The believer recognizes in his person and his story the glory of the love of God. He is that Wisdom who has "tabernacled" among us.

** The phrase "in the bosom of the Father" expresses the essential union of the Son of God with the Father.

A view of the valley of the Jordan. While John was preaching and baptizing on the banks of this river messengers from Jerusalem came to him (Jn. 1, 19).

John the Baptist defines his mission
Jn 1, 19-28

¹⁹ And this is the testimony of John, when the Jews sent priests and Levites from Jerusalem to ask him, "Who are you?" ²⁰ He confessed, he did not deny, but confessed, "I am not the Christ." ²¹ And they asked him, "What then? Are you Elijah?" He said, "I am not." "Are you the prophet?" And he answered, "No." ²² They said to him then, "Who are you? Let us have an answer for those who sent us. What do you say about yourself?" ²³ He said, "I am the voice of one crying in the wilderness, 'Make straight the way of the Lord,' as the prophet Isaiah said."

²⁴ Now they had been sent from the Pharisees. ²⁵ They asked him, " Then why are you baptizing, if you are neither the Christ, nor Elijah, nor the prophet?" ²⁶ John answered them, "I baptize with water; but among you stands one whom you do not know, ²⁷ even he who comes after me, the thong of whose sandal I am not worthy to untie." ²⁸ This took place in Bethany beyond the Jordan, where John was baptizing.

John points to Jesus and says "Behold the Lamb of God"
Jn 1, 29-34

²⁹ The next day he saw Jesus coming toward him, and said, "Behold, the Lamb of God, who takes away the sin of the world! ³⁰ This is he of whom I said,

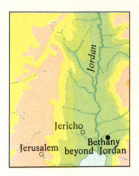

* Among the Jews there was eager expectation of the messenger sent by God, i.e. the "Messiah" or "Christ." Furthermore the Jews, interpreting Malachi 3, 23 literally, believed that Elijah would return to the earth immediately before the Messiah came. Another school of thought awaited the "Prophet", i.e. the new Moses foretold in Deut. 18, 15-18.

** The metaphor of the "Lamb of God" was suggested to John by the prophecy of Isaiah who compares the Servant of the Lord to the Lamb which suffers in silence (Isa. 53, 12). There was also an allusion to the paschal lamb whose blood, sprinkled on the door-posts, was a sign of liberation and salvation (Ex. 12, 27).

77

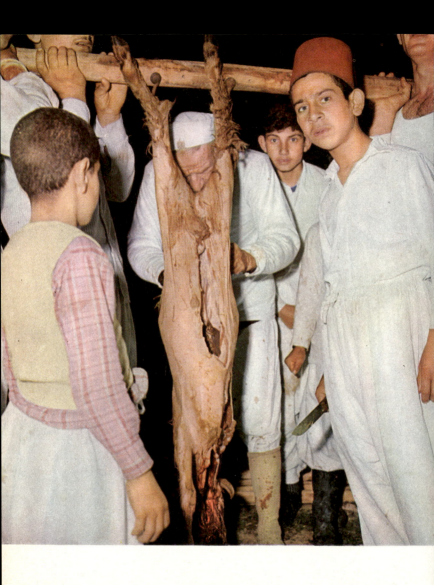

The Samaritan High Priest offers the sacrifice of the Paschal lamb. John presented Jesus to the crowd as the Lamb of God, sacrificed for our sins.

'After me comes a man who ranks before me, for he was before me.' [31] I myself did not know him; but for this I came baptizing with water, that he might be
* revealed to Israel." [32] And John bore witness, "I saw the Spirit descend as a dove from heaven, and it remained on him. [33] I myself did not know him; but he who sent me to baptize with water said to me, 'He on whom you see the Spirit descend and remain, this is he who baptizes with the Holy Spirit.' [34] And I have seen and have borne witness that this is the Son of God."

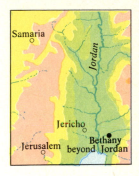

First meeting with Jesus of certain disciples
Jn 1, 35-51

[35] The next day again John was standing with two of his disciples; [36] and he looked at Jesus as he walked, and said, "Behold, the Lamb of God!" [37] The two disciples heard him say this, and they followed Jesus. [38] Jesus turned, and saw them following, and said to them, "What do you seek?" And they said to him, "Rabbi" (which means Teacher), "where are you staying?" [39] He said to them, "Come and see." They came and saw where he was staying; and they stayed with him that day, for it was about the tenth hour. [40] One of the two who heard John speak, and followed him, was Andrew, Simon Peter's brother. [41] He first found his brother Simon, and said to him, "We have found the Messiah" (which means Christ). [42] He brought him

* By direct revelation from God John understood that Jesus was the Messiah and publicly bore witness to that fact.

Cana in Galilee. The ancient way. Along this street stands a chapel which commemorates Nathanael's first meeting with Jesus (Jn. 1, 47-51).

to Jesus. Jesus looked at him, and said, "So you are Simon the son of John? You shall be called Cephas" (which means Peter).

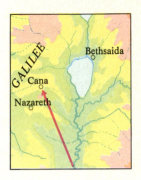

⁴³ The next day Jesus decided to go to Galilee. And he found Philip and said to him, "Follow me." ⁴⁴ Now Philip was from Bethsaida, the city of Andrew and Peter. ⁴⁵ Philip found Nathanael, and said to him, "We have found him of whom Moses in the law and also the prophets wrote, Jesus of Nazareth, the son of Joseph." ⁴⁶ Nathanael said to him, "Can anything good come out of Naza-

* reth?" Philip said to him, "Come and see." ⁴⁷ Jesus saw Nathanael coming to him, and said of him, "Behold, and Israelite indeed, in whom is no guile!" ⁴⁸ Nathanael said to him, "How do you know me?" Jesus answered him, "Before Philip called you, when you were under the fig tree, I saw you." ⁴⁹ Nathanael answered him, "Rabbi, you are the Son of God! You are the King of Israel!" ⁵⁰ Jesus answered him, "Because I said to you, I saw you under the fig tree, do you believe? You shall see greater things than these." ⁵¹ And he said to him, "Truly, truly, I say to you, you will see heaven opened, and the angels of God ascending and descending upon the Son of man."

Jesus work his first miracle, at Cana
Jn 2, 1-12

¹ On the third day there was a marriage at Cana in Galilee, and the mother of Jesus was there; ² Jesus also was invited

* The village of Nazareth had played no part at all in the history of the Jewish people. From Nathanael's remark it seems that it did not enjoy a good reputation even in Jesus' day.

Cana of Galilee. The Orthodox church has preserved this great stone jar, which is similar to those used for Jewish ritual ablutions in Jesus' time (cf. Jn. 2, 6).

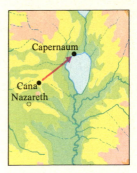

to the marriage, with his disciples. ³ When the wine failed, the mother of Jesus said to him, "They have no wine." * ⁴ And Jesus said to her, "O woman, what have you to do with me? My hour has not yet come." ⁵ His mother said to the servants, "Do whatever he tells you." ⁶ Now six stone jars were standing there, for the Jewish rites of purification, each holding twenty or thirty gallons. ⁷ Jesus said to them, "Fill the jars with water." And they filled them up to the brim. ⁸ He said to them, "Now draw some out, and take it to the steward of the feast." So they took it. ⁹ When the steward of the feast tasted the water now become wine, and did not know where it came from (though the servants who had drawn the water knew), the steward of the feast called the bridegroom ¹⁰ and said to him, "Every man serves the good wine first; and when men have drunk freely, then the poor wine; but you have ** kept the good wine until now." ¹¹ This, the first of his signs, Jesus did at Cana in Galilee, and manifested his glory; and his disciples believed in him.

¹² After this he went down to Capernaum, with his mother and his brethren and his disciples; and there they stayed for a few days.

Jesus drives the merchants from the temple at Jerusalem
Jn 2, 13-25

¹³ The Passover of the Jews was at hand, and Jesus went up to Jerusalem.

* Jesus worked his first miracle at the instance of his mother. But, though he consented to her wishes, he himself showed a certain indifference and seemed pre-occupied from the beginning with the thought of his final "hour," that of the Passion and Resurrection. There again Mary, the "Woman," would be present in her role of mother and pattern for believers (Jn. 19, 25-27).

** John saw in the miracles of Jesus "signs" which confirmed his words as Christ, the Son of God, and at the same time symbolically revealed something of his ministry. The wine — plentiful and of better quality — was for the evangelist a symbol of the new age inaugurated by Jesus. These signs are to lead to belief in him.

83

Jerusalem. This is what the Temple area looks like to-day. Here, in the so-called "courtyard of the Gentiles", Jesus drove out the merchants and money-changers (Jn. 2, 13-16).

¹⁴ In the temple he found those who were selling oxen and sheep and pigeons, and the money-changers at their business. ¹⁵ And making a whip of cords, he drove them all, with the sheep and oxen, out of the temple; and he poured out the coins of the money-changers and overturned their tables. ¹⁶ And he told those who sold the pigeons, "Take these things away; you shall not make my Father's house a house of trade." ¹⁷ His disciples remembered that it was written, "Zeal

* for thy house will consume me." ¹⁸ The Jews then said to him, "What sign have you to show us for doing this?" ¹⁹ Jesus answered them, "Destroy this temple, and in three ways I will raise it up." ²⁰ The Jews then said, "It has taken forty-six years to build this temple, and will you raise it up in three days?" ²¹ But

** he spoke of the temple of his body. ²² When therefore he was raised from the dead, his disciples remembered that he had said this; and they believed the scripture and the word which Jesus had spoken.

²³ Now when he was in Jerusalem at the Passover feast, many believed in his name when they saw the signs which he did; ²⁴ but Jesus did not trust himself to them, ²⁵ because he knew all men and needed no one to bear witness of man; for he himself knew what was in man.

Jesus talks with Nicodemus
Jn 3, 1-21

¹ Now there was a man of the Pharisees, named Nicodemus, a ruler of the

* The quotation is from Psalm 69, 10.

** Jesus' body is the true Temple, for it is the place where men meet the Father and discover their unity.

Jews. ² This man came to Jesus by night and said to him, "Rabbi, we know that you are a teacher come from God; for no one can do these signs that you do, unless God is with him." ³ Jesus answer-
* ed him, "Truly, truly, I say to you, unless one is born anew, he cannot see the kingdom of God." ⁴ Nicodemus said to him, "How can a man be born when he is old? Can he enter a second time into his mother's womb and be born?" ⁵ Jesus answered, "Truly, truly, I say to you, unless one is born of water and the Spirit, he cannot enter the kingdom of God. ⁶ That which is born of the flesh is flesh, and that which is born of the Spirit is spirit. ⁷ Do not marvel that I said to you, 'You must be born anew.' ⁸ The wind blows where it wills, and you hear the sound of it, but you do not know whence it comes or whither it goes; so it is with every one who is born of the Spirit." ⁹ Nicodemus said to him, "How can this be?" ¹⁰ Jesus answered him, "Are you a teacher of Israel, and yet you do not understand this? ¹¹ Truly, truly, I say to you, we speak of what we know, and bear witness to what we have seen; but you do not receive our testimony. ¹² If I have told you earthly things and you do not believe, how can you believe if I tell you heavenly things?

¹³ No one has ascended into heaven but he who descended from heaven, the Son
** of man. ¹⁴ And as Moses lifted up the serpent in the wilderness, so must the Son of man be lifted up, ¹⁵ that whoever believes in him may have eternal life."

*   Jesus told Nicodemus that it is not enough to be educated and religious men and to see miracles, but there is also need for a rebirth in the Spirit. He also spoke of the necessity of Christian baptism as a sign and agent of that rebirth.

**   Jesus refers to an Old Testament story (Num. 21, 4-9); the people, in rebellion against God, were perishing by reason of poisonous snakes. By God's command Moses put up a brazen serpent in the middle of the camp. If anyone bitten by a snake looked at Moses' serpent he was cured. So, said Jesus, anyone who would look with faith to him, crucified and risen, would be saved.

* ¹⁶ For God so loved the world that he gave his only Son, that whoever believes in him should not perish but have eternal life. ¹⁷ For God sent the Son into the world, not to condemn the world, but that the world might be saved through him. ¹⁸ He who believes in him is not condemned; he who does not believe is condemned already, because he has not believed in the name of the only Son of God. ¹⁹ And this is the judgment, that the light has come into the world, and men loved darkness rather than light, because their deeds were evil. ²⁰ For every one who does evil hates the light, and does not come to the light, lest his deeds should be exposed. ²¹ But he who does what is true comes to the light, that it may be clearly seen that his deeds have been wrought in God.

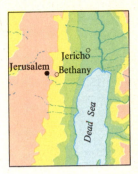

It is Jesus who reveals God
Jn 3, 31-36

** ³¹ He who comes from above is above all; he who is of the earth belongs to the earth, and of the earth he speaks; he who comes from heaven is above all. ³² He bears witness to what he has seen and heard, yet no one receives his testimony; ³³ he who receives his testimony sets his seal to this, that God is true. ³⁴ For he whom God has sent utters the words of God, for it is not by measure that he gives the Spirit; ³⁵ the Father loves the Son, and has given all things

* Jesus is the greatest proof of God's love. The decisive choice is made in his presence.

** The thoughts which conclude the conversation with Nicodemus were probably the evangelist's reflections. They were therefore anticipated here.

A picturesque view of the Jordan as it flows into the Lake of Gennesaret. At Aenon, near to the river, John gave his last testimony to Jesus (Jn. 3, 27-30).

into his hand. ³⁶ He who believes in the Son has eternal life; he who does not obey the Son shall not see life, but the wrath of God rests upon him.

John's last testimony: Jesus is the Messiah
Jn 3, 22-30

²² After this Jesus and his disciples went into the land of Judea; there he remained with them and baptized. ²³ John also was baptizing at Aenon near Salim, because there was much water there; and people came and were baptized. ²⁴ For John had not yet been put in prison.

²⁵ Now a discussion arose between John's disciples and a Jew over purifying. ²⁶ And they came to John, and said to him, "Rabbi, he who was with you beyond the Jordan, to whom you bore witness, here he is, baptizing, and all are going to him." ²⁷ John answered, "No one can receive anything except what is given him from heaven. ²⁸ You yourselves bear me witness, that I said,
* I am not the Christ, but I have been sent before him. ²⁹ He who has the bride is the bridegroom; the friend of the bridegroom, who stands and hears him, rejoices greatly at the bridegroom's voice; therefore this joy of mine is now full. ³⁰ He must increase, but I must decrease."

* All the greatness of John appears in this expression. He never worked for his own glory, but always for that of Another, the Messiah; he did not try to draw the people (the bride) to himself but gladly prepared them and presented them to Christ (the bridegroom).

The broad Vale of Sichem. In the background, Mounts Ebal (on the right) and Gerizim (on the left). The road between Samaria and Galilee lay across this valley midway between the two mountains (Jn. 4, 3-6). There stood the village of Sychar.

Jesus leaves Judea
Jn 4, 1-3

¹ Now when the Lord knew that the Pharisees had heard that Jesus was making and baptizing more disciples than John ² (although Jesus himself did not baptize, but only his disciples), ³ he left Judea and departed again to Galilee.

Jesus talks with the woman of Samaria
Jn 4, 4-42

⁴ He had to pass through Samaria. ⁵ So he came to a city of Samaria, called Sychar, near the field that Jacob gave to his son Joseph. ⁶ Jacob's well was * there, and so Jesus, wearied as he was with his journey, sat down beside the well. It was about the sixth hour.

⁷ There came a woman of Samaria to draw water. Jesus said to her, "Give me a drink." ⁸ For his disciples had gone away into the city to buy food. ⁹ The Samaritan woman said to him, "How is it that you, a Jew, ask a drink of me, ** a woman of Samaria?" For Jews have no dealings with Samaritans. ¹⁰ Jesus answered her, "If you knew the gift of God, and who it is that is saying to you, 'Give me a drink,' you would have asked him, and he would have given you living water." ¹¹ The woman said to him, "Sir, you have nothing to draw with, and the well is deep; where do you get that living water? ¹² Are you greater than our father

* The evangelist mentions a human characteristic of Jesus: after a long walk in the sun, he was tired.

** The Jews scorned the Samaritans and considered them unclean like the Gentiles. Further the rabbis thought it rather improper to talk with a woman in a public place. So Jesus' conduct aroused the Samaritan woman's surprise.

91

Typical well in Palestine. On its rim may be noticed the deep furrows made by the cords with which the water has been drawn through the centuries. Wells were the favourite halting-places on long journeys (cf. Jn. 4, 6).

Jacob, who gave us the well, and drank from it himself, and his sons, and his
* cattle?" 13 Jesus said to her, "Every one who drinks of this water will thirst again, 14 but whoever drinks of the water that I shall give him will never thirst; the water that I shall give him will become in him a spring of water welling up to eternal life." 15 The woman said to him, "Sir, give me this water, that I may not thirst, nor come here to draw."

** 16 Jesus said to her, "Go, call your husband, and come here." 17 The woman answered him, "I have no husband." Jesus said to her, "You are right in saying, 'I have no husband'; 18 for you have had five husbands and he whom you now have is not your husband; this you said truly." 19 The woman said to him, "Sir, I perceive that you are a prophet. 20 Our fathers worshipped on this mountain; and you say that in Jerusalem is the place where men ought to worship." 21 Jesus said to her, "Woman, believe me, the hour is coming when neither on this mountain nor in Jerusalem will you worship the Father. 22 You worship what you do not know; we worship what we know, for salvation is
*** from the Jews. 23 But the hour is coming, and now is, when the true worshippers will worship the Father in spirit and truth, for such the Father seeks to worship him. 24 God is spirit, and those who worship him must worship in spirit and truth." 25 The woman said to him, "I know that Messiah is coming (he who is called Christ); when he comes, he will

* Jesus used the symbol of fresh spring water to describe the gift which he had come to bring to men —truth, the life of God, the Spirit.

** Jesus was trying to bring the woman gradually to understand that he was the Messiah.

*** This is the solemn declaration of the new spirit in religion which Jesus brought. Believers will primarily recognize and worship God in their hearts as, moved by the Spirit, they welcome and appreciate the truth.

93

Mount Gerizim, seen from the neighbourhood of ancient Sichem, near which was Jacob's Well. This is how it appeared to Jesus and the Samaritan woman during their conversation (Jn. 4, 19-30).

show us all things." 26 Jesus said to her, "I who speak to you am he."

27 Just then his disciples came. They marvelled that he was talking with a woman, but none said, "What do you wish?" or, "Why are you talking with her?" 28 So the woman left her water jar and went away into the city, and said to the people, 29 "Come, see a man who told me all that I ever did. Can this be the Christ?" 30 They went out of the city and were coming to him.

31 Meanwhile the disciples besought him, saying, "Rabbi, eat." 32 But he said to them, "I have food to eat of which you do not know." 33 So the disciples said to one another, "Has any one brought him food?" 34 Jesus said to them, "My food is to do the will of him who sent me, and to accomplish his work. 35 Do you not say, 'There are yet four months, then comes the harvest'? I tell * you, lift up your eyes, and see how the fields are already white for harvest. 36 He who reaps receives wages, and gathers fruit for eternal life, so that sower and reaper may rejoice together. 37 For here the saying holds true, 'One sows and another reaps.' 38 I sent you to reap that for which you did not labour; others have laboured, and you have entered into their labour."

39 Many Samaritans from that city believed in him because of the woman's testimony, "He told me all that I ever did." 40 So when the Samaritans came to him, they asked him to stay with them; and he stayed there two days. 41 And

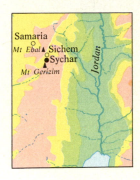

* In the woman who showed herself ready to accept his revelation and in the Samaritans who came to him, Jesus saw the firstfruits of an abundant harvest.

Cana. Panorama of the village in Galilee in which Jesus worked two great "signs": the changing of the water into wine and the cure of the official's son (Jn. 4, 46).

many more believed because of his word.
42 They said to the woman, "It is no
longer because of your words that we
believe, for we have heard for ourselves,
and we know that this is indeed the
Saviour of the world."

Jesus cures the son of an officer at Cana
Jn 4, 43-54

43 After the two days he departed to
Galilee. 44 For Jesus himself testified that
a prophet has no honour in his own
country. 45 So when he came to Galilee,
the Galileans welcomed him, having seen
all that he had done in Jerusalem at the
feast, for they too had gone to the feast.
46 So he came again to Cana in Galilee,
where he had made the water wine.
And at Capernaum there was an official
whose son was ill. 47 When he heard that
Jesus had come from Judea to Galilee,
he went and begged him to come down
and heal his son, for he was at the point
* of death. 48 Jesus therefore said to him,
"Unless you see signs and wonders you
will not believe." 49 The official said to
him, "Sir, come down before my child
dies." 50 Jesus said to him, "Go; your
son will live." The man believed the
word that Jesus spoke to him and went
his way. 51 As he was going down, his
servants met him and told him that his
son was living. 52 So he asked them the
hour when he began to mend, and they
said to him, "Yesterday at the seventh
hour the fever left him." 53 The father

* Jesus called the
centurion and the by-
standers to a more ma-
ture faith. They should
believe in him as a
result of the miracles
already seen, without
continually asking for
new ones. Nonethe-
less, he agreed to give
this new sign and the
officer really arrived at
an authentic act of
faith.

knew that was the hour when Jesus had said to him, "Your son will live"; and he himself believed, and all his household. ⁵⁴ This was now the second sign that Jesus did when he had come from Judea to Galilee.

III - EARLY ACTIVITY IN GALILEE

Galilee, and particularly the region around the lake, was the scene of Jesus' first public preaching. He made his proclamation: expectations are fulfilled, God is intervening in history so as to free and save mankind; you must repent at these good tidings. He confirmed his words with miracles, which were signs of the new world which was flooding in.

Some disciples whom he himself had called, followed him everywhere.

The presence of the new prophet was welcomed by the poor and by sinners, but aroused suspicion and hostility among the Pharisees and teachers of the Law. But the question, Who is Jesus? was asked ever more and more eagerly.

View of the Lake of Gennesaret. Jesus seated in a boat taught the people (Lk. 5, 3). His first disciples were lake fishermen.

The proclamation and the signs of the Kingdom of God

Jesus proclaims:
the Kingdom of God is at hand
Mk 1, 14-15 (Mt 4, 12-17   Lk 4, 14-15)

14 Now after John was arrested, Jesus came into Galilee, preaching the gospel of God, 15 and saying, "The time is ful-
* filled, and the kingdom of God is at hand; repent, and believe in the gospel."

The first disciples:
Jesus calls the fishermen
Lk 5, 1-11 (Mt 4, 18-22   Mk 1, 16-20)

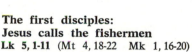

1 While the people pressed upon him to hear the word of God, he was standing by the lake of Gennesaret. 2 And he saw two boats by the lake; but the fishermen had gone out of them and were washing their nets. 3 Getting into one of the boats, which was Simon's, he asked him to put out a little from the land. And he sat down and taught the people from the boat. 4 And when he had ceased speaking, he said to Simon, "Put out into the deep and let down your nets for a catch." 5 And Simon answered, "Master, we toiled all night and took nothing! But at your word I will let down the nets." 6 And when they had done this, they enclosed a great shoal of fish; and as their nets were breaking, 7 they beckoned to their partners in the other boat to come and help them. And they came and filled both the

* The phrase "Kingdom of God" points to God's saving action foretold by the prophets. That decisive intervention was now imminent. Jesus' proclamation was thus both glad tidings ("evangel") and urgent challenge. Matthew saw it as a Light kindled in the darkness, and quoted the prophet Isaiah (Mt. 4, 15-16).

A peaceful glimpse of the Lake of Gennesaret seen from the south-west. This was the scene of Jesus' early activity in Galilee (Mk. 1, 21 ff.).

boats, so that they began to sink. ⁸ But when Simon Peter saw it, he fell down at Jesus' knees, saying, "Depart from me, for I am a sinful man, O Lord." ⁹ For he was astonished, and all that were with him, at the catch of fish which they had taken; ¹⁰ and so also were James and John, sons of Zebedee, who were partners with Simon. And Jesus said to Simon, "Do not be afraid; * henceforth you will be catching men." ¹¹ And when they had brought their boats ** to land, they left everything and followed him.

Jesus at work:
he teaches, and he defeats Satan
Mk 1, 21-28 (Lk 4, 31-37)

*** ²¹ And they went into Capernaum; and immediately on the sabbath he entered the synagogue and taught. ²² And they were astonished at his teaching, for he taught them as one who had authority, and not as the scribes. ²³ And immediately there was in their synagogue a man with an unclean spirit; ²⁴ and he cried out, "What have you to do with us, Jesus of Nazareth? Have you come to destroy us? I know who you are, the Holy One of God." ²⁵ But Jesus rebuked him saying, "Be silent, and come out of him!" ²⁶ And the unclean spirit, convulsing him and crying with a loud voice, came out of him. ²⁷ And they were all amazed, so that they questioned among themselves, saying, "What is this? A new teaching! With authority he commands even the unclean spirits, and they obey

* The miraculous draught of fishes was taken as a sign of the future apostolate of Peter and his companions.

** Following Jesus and leaving everything for his sake was the mark of a disciple.

*** It seems as though the evangelist Mark wished to portray a typical day of Jesus' work in Galilee. His teaching and his power over evil raised problems about his person.

103

him." 28 And at once his fame spread everywhere throughout all the surrounding region of Galilee.

Jesus cures Peter's mother-in-law
Mk 1, 29-31 (Mt 8, 14-15 Lk 4, 38-39)

29 And immediately he left the synagogue, and entered the house of Simon and Andrew, with James and John. 30 Now Simon's mother-in-law lay sick with a fever, and immediately they told him of her. 31 And he came and took her by the hand and lifted her up, and the fever left her; and she served them.

In the evening, Jesus cures other folk
Mk 1, 32-34 (Mt 8, 16-17 Lk 4, 40-41)

32 That evening, at sundown, they brought to him all who were sick or possessed with demons. 33 And the whole city was gathered together about the door. 34 And he healed many who were sick with various diseases, and cast out many demons; and he would not permit
* the demons to speak, because they knew him.

Jesus prays
and goes on with his mission
Mk 1, 35-39 (Mt 4, 23-25 Lk 4, 42-44)

35 And in the morning, a geat while before day, he rose and went out to a lonely place, and there he prayed. 36 And Simon and those who were with him followed him, 37 and they found him and said to him, "Every one is searching for

* Jesus, particularly in Mark's gospel, adopted a rather strange attitude; he worked in public but desired secrecy, wrought miracles as Messiah but forbade anyone to say so. He wanted to avoid the expectant multitude's misunderstanding him and welcoming him as a nationalist, earthly, Messiah in conformity with its own desires. Jesus was, by contrast, a different sort of Messiah and voluntarily followed the way of the cross.

you." ³⁸ And he said to them, "Let us go on to the next towns, that I may preach there also; for that is why I came out." ³⁹ And he went throughout all Galilee, preaching in their synagogues and casting out demons.

Jesus cures a leper
Mk 1, 40-45 (Mt 8, 1-4 Lk 5, 12-16)

⁴⁰ And a leper came to him beseeching him, and kneeling said to him, "If you will, you can make me clean." ⁴¹ Moved with pity, he stretched out his hand and touched him, and said to him, "I will; be clean." ⁴² And immediately the leprosy left him, and he was made clean. ⁴³ And he sternly charged him, and sent him away at once, ⁴⁴ and said to him, "See ∗ that you say nothing to any one; but go, show yourself to the priest, and offer for your cleansing what Moses commanded, for a proof to the people." ⁴⁵ But he went out and began to talk freely about it, and to spread the news, so that Jesus could no longer openly enter a town, but was out in the country; and people came to him from every quarter.

Jesus forgives sins and heals a paralytic
Mk 2, 1-12 (Mt 9, 1-8 Lk 5, 17-26)

∗∗ ¹ And when he returned to Capernaum after some days, it was reported that he was at home. ² And many were gathered together, so that there was no longer room for them, not even about the door; and he was preaching the word

∗ Lepers were obliged by the Mosaic Law to live at a distance from other people for reasons of hygiene, and their eventual cure had to be attested by a certificate from a priest. The general opinion was that they were suffering God's punishment. Jesus however touched an untouchable and re-admitted him to the community.

∗∗ Mark now groups together a series of five controversies between Jesus and the Pharisees. Around him the new idea of the Kingdom of God was blossoming, but there were already signs of its rejection and a growing opposition.

105

Another view of the Lake. from the north, from the hill called the Mount of the Beatitudes. The Lake of Gennesaret was also called the Sea of Galilee or simply "the sea" (Mk. 2, 13).

to them. ³ And they came, bringing to him a paralytic carried by four men. ⁴ And when they could not get near him because of the crowd, they removed the roof above him; and when they had made an opening, they let down the pallet on wich the paralytic lay. ⁵ And when Jesus saw their faith, he said to the paralytic, "My son, your sins are forgiven." ⁶ Now some of the scribes were sitting there, questioning in their hearts, ⁷ "Why does this man speak thus? It is blasphemy! Who can forgive sins but God alone?" ⁸ And immediately Jesus, perceiving in his spirit that they thus questioned within themselves, said to them, "Why do you question thus in your hearts? ⁹ Which is easier, to say to the paralytic, 'Your sins are forgiven,' or to say, 'Rise, take up your pallet and walk'? ¹⁰ But that you may know that * the Son of man has authority on earth to forgive sins" — he said to the paralytic — ¹¹ "I say to you, rise, take up your pallet and go home." ¹² And he rose, and immediately took up the pallet and went out before them all; so that they were all amazed and glorified God, saying, "We never saw anything like this!"

The call of Levi:
Jesus comes for the sake of sinners
Mk 2, 13-17 (Mt 9, 14-17 Lk 5, 27-32)

¹³ He went out again beside the sea; and all the crowd gathered about him, and he taught them. ¹⁴ And as he passed on, he saw Levi the son of Alphaeus sitting at the tax office, and he said

* For those who listened to Jesus, "Son of Man" might mean weak and persecuted "man" as in the book of Ezekiel: or it might recall the mysterious prophecy of Daniel (chapter 7), who speaks of "one like the son of man" who appears in heaven as judge, and takes possession of an eternal kingdom. Jesus made use of this title so as to reveal his own mystery little by little; i.e. the weakness of his human nature and the glory of his godhead. Here he proved by a miracle that he had the divine power of forgiving sins.

107

to him, "Follow me." And he rose and followed him.

¹⁵ And as he sat at table in his house, many tax collectors and sinners were sitting with Jesus and his disciples; for there were many who followed him. ¹⁶ And the scribes of the Pharisees, when they saw that he was eating with sinners and tax collectors, said to his disciples, "Why does he eat with tax collectors and sinners?" ¹⁷ And when Jesus heard it, he said to them, "Those who are well have no need of a physician, but those who are sick; I came not to call the righteous, but sinners."

The question of fasting
Mk 2, 18-22 (Mt 9, 14-17 Lk 5, 33-39)

¹⁸ Now John's disciples and the Pharisees were fasting; and people came and said to him, "Why do John's disciples and the disciples of the Pharisees fast, but your disciples do not fast?" ¹⁹ And
* Jesus said to them, "Can the wedding guests fast while the bridegroom is with them? As long as they have the bridegroom with them, they cannot fast. ²⁰ The days will come, when the bridegroom is taken away from them, and
** then they will fast in that day. ²¹ No one sews a piece of unshrunk cloth on an old garment; if he does, the patch tears away from it, the new from the old, and a worse tear is made. ²² And no one puts new wine into old wineskins; if he does, the wine will burst the skins, and the wine is lost, and so are the skins; but new wine is for fresh skins."

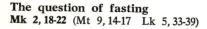

* The time of rejoicing in the presence of the "bridegroom" (the Messiah) had come. Then Jesus alluded to his death; the "bridegroom" was to be taken away from them.

** Ignoring excuses, Jesus revealed the real reason for his rejection; the new conception of the Kingdom of God was intolerable for the "old garments" and "old wineskins."

The incident of the ears of corn: "the sabbath is made for man"
Mk 2, 23-28 (Mt 12, 1-8   Lk 6, 1-5)

²³ One sabbath he was going through the grainfields; and as they made their way his disciples began to pluck ears of grain. ²⁴ And the Pharisees said to him, "Look, why are they doing what is not lawful on the sabbath?" ²⁵ And he said ∗to them, "Have you never read what David did, when he was in need and was hungry, he and those who were with him: ²⁶ how he entered the house of God, when Abiathar was high priest, and ate the bread of the Presence, which it is not lawful for any but the priests to eat, and also gave it to those who were with him?" ²⁷ And he said to them, "The sabbath was made for man, not ∗∗man for the sabbath; ²⁸ so the Son of man is lord even of the sabbath."

Jesus cures a man on the sabbath day
Mk 3, 1-6 (Mt 12, 9-14   Lk 6, 6-11)

¹ Again he entered the synagogue, and a man was there who had a withered hand. ² And they watched him, to see whether he would heal him on the sabbath, so that they might accuse him. ³ And he said to the man who had the withered hand, "Come here." ⁴ And he said to them, " Is it lawful on the sabbath to do good or to do harm, to save ∗∗∗life or to kill?" But they were silent. ⁵ And he looked around at them with anger, grieved at their hardness of heart, and said to the man, "Stretch out your

∗   This event is recorded in I Sam. 21.

∗∗   In Jesus' time the Sabbath Day was treated with very great respect, above all in so far as it concerned rest. Jesus stated that he was superior to the sabbath, and so revealed his own divinity. He wished also to combat the merely formal keeping of divine precepts.

∗∗∗ As it is never allowed to do wrong, so it is always allowed and even commended, to do right, and to save a life even on the sabbath.

109

Nazareth. The supposed synagogue in which Jesus avowed that the Messianic prophecy of Isaiah was fulfilled in him (Lk. 4, 16-18).

hand." He stretched it out, and his hand was restored. 6 The Pharisees went out, and immediately held counsel with the Herodians against him, how to destroy him.

All men seek for Jesus
Mk 3, 7-12.20-21 (Mt 12, 15-21)

7 Jesus withdrew with his disciples to the sea, and a great multitude from Galilee followed; also from Judea 8 and Jerusalem and Idumea and from beyond the Jordan and from about Tyre and Sidon a great multitude, hearing all that he did, came to him. 9 And he told his disciples to have a boat ready for him because of the crowd, lest they should crush him; 10 for he had healed many, so that all who had diseases pressed upon him to touch him. 11 And whenever the unclean spirits beheld him, they fell down before him and cried out, "You are the Son of God." 12 And he strictly
* ordered them not to make him known.

Then he went home; 20 and the crowd came together again, so that they could not even eat. 21 And when his friends heard it, they went out to seize him, for they said, "He is beside himself."

At Nazareth Jesus proclaims his programme, but is rejected
Lk 4, 16-30

16 And he came to Nazareth, where he had been brought up; and he went to the synagogue, as his custom was, on the sabbath day. And he stood up to

* At this point Matthew sees in Jesus the realization of the Servant of the Lord who is both gentle and strong, announced by Iasiah (42, 1 ff.): "Behold my servant, whom I uphold, my chosen, in whom my soul delights; I have put my Spirit upon him, he will bring forth justice to the nations. He will not cry nor lift up his voice, or make it heard in the street; a bruised reed he will not break, and a dimly burning wick he will not quench; he will faithfully bring forth justice... and the coastlands wait for his law."

The so-called Mount of the Precipice (cf. Lk. 4, 28-29). The ancient road in the valley descends to the south towards the fertile plain of Esdraelon.

read; 17 and there was given to him the
* book of the prophet Isaiah. He opened
the book and found the place where
it was written,

18 "The Spirit of the Lord is upon me,
because he has anointed me to preach
good news to the poor.
He has sent me to proclaim release
to the captives
and recovering of sight to the blind,
to set at liberty those
who are oppressed,
19 to proclaim the acceptable year
of the Lord."

20 And he closed the book, and gave it
back to the attendant, and sat down;
and the eyes of all in the synagogue
were fixed on him. 21 And he began to
say to them, "Today this scripture has
been fulfilled in your hearing." 22 And
all spoke well of him, and wondered at
the gracious words which proceeded out
of his mouth; and they said, "Is not
** this Joseph's son?" 23 And he said to
them, "Doubtless you will quote to me
this proverb, 'Physician, heal yourself;
what we have heard you did at Capernaum, do here also in your own country.' " 24 And he said, "Truly, I say to you,
no prophet is acceptable in his own
country. 25 But in truth, I tell you, there
were many widows in Israel in the days
*** of Elijah, when the heaven was shut up
three years and six months, when there
came a great famine over all the land;
26 and Elijah was sent to none of them
but only to Zarephath, in the land of
Sidon, to a woman who was a widow.

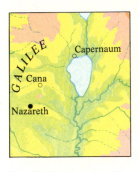

Capernaum
GALILEE
Cana
Nazareth

* In this passage Isa-
iah (61, 1-2) described
the Messiah as a pro-
phet sent for the be-
nefit of the poor. Jes-
us, having read the
text aloud, declared:
"Today this prophecy
is fulfilled in me."

** Unexpectedly the
mood of the people
changed; admiration
turned to disenchant-
ment, scepticism and,
finally, persecution.
This may have happen-
ed on some other oc-
casion at Nazareth but
Luke has combined the
two events to illustrate
the fate of the gospel:
welcome and then re-
jection.

*** Elijah, during a
long drought, sought
hospitality of a Gentile
woman, in whose fa-
vour he was able to
work a miracle (I
Kings 17). Elisha, his
disciple and successor,

113

The western shore of the Lake of Gennesaret, near which Jesus preached and worked so many miracles. It was also the district from which
most of the Twelve came.

²⁷ And there were many lepers in Israel in the time of the prophet Elisha; and none of them was cleansed, but only Naaman the Syrian." ²⁸ When they heard this, all in the synagogue were filled with wrath. ²⁹ And they rose up and put him out of the city, and led him to the brow of the hill on which their city was built, that they might throw him down headlong. ³⁰ But passing through the midst of them he went away.

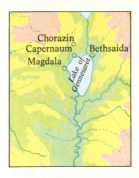

Jesus chooses the Twelve
Lk 6, 12-16 (Mt 10, 1-4   Mk 3, 13-19)

¹² In these days he went out into the hills to pray; and all night he continued
* in prayer to God. ¹³ And when it was day, he called his disciples, and chose from them twelve, whom he named apostles: ¹⁴ Simon, whom he named Peter, and Andrew his brother, and James and John, and Philip, and Bartholomew, ¹⁵ and Matthew, and Thomas, and James the son of Alphaeus, and Simon who was called the Zealot, ¹⁶ and Judas the son of James, and Judas Iscariot, who became a traitor.

Jesus reverses human judgments
Lk 6, 17-26

¹⁷ And he came down with them and stood on a level place, with a great crowd of his disciples and a great multitude of people from all Judea and Jerusalem and the sea coast of Tyre and Sidon, who came to hear him and to be healed of their diseases; ¹⁸ and those who were troubled with unclean spirits

in turn, by another miracle cured of leprosy another Gentile, Naaman, the commander of the Syrian army (II Kings 5). The two miracles were quoted by Jesus as showing that God makes no distinction of persons and, as he finds no response from his own people, turns instead to the Gentiles, who are better disposed.

* Luke emphasizes Jesus' long prayer before choosing the Twelve; Mark on the other hand stresses the freedom and scope of his choice: "...he called to him those he desired; and they came to him. And he appointed twelve, to be with him, and to be sent out to preach and have authority to cast out demons" (3, 13-15).

115

This shrine is built on the hill called the Mount of the Beatitudes to the north-west of Capernaum. It commemorates the Sermon on the Mount (Mt. 5, 1-2).

were cured. ¹⁹ And all the crowd sought to touch him, for power came forth from him and healed them all.

²⁰ And he lifted up his eyes on his disciples, and said:

* "Blessed are you poor, for yours is the kingdom of God.

²¹ "Blessed are you that hunger now, for you shall be satisfied.

"Blessed are you that weep now, for you shall laugh.

²² "Blessed are you when men hate you, and when they exclude you and revile you, and cast out your name as evil, on account of the Son of man! ²³ Rejoice in that day, and leap for joy, for behold, your reward is great in heaven; for so their fathers did to the prophets.

²⁴ "But woe to you that are rich, for you have received your consolation.

²⁵ "Woe to you that are full now, for you shall hunger.

"Woe to you that laugh now, for you shall mourn and weep.

²⁶ "Woe to you, when all men speak well of you, for so their fathers did to the false prophets."

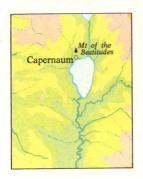

The Sermon on the Mount

The beatitudes of the Kingdom of God
Mt 5, 1-12

¹ Seeing the crowds, he went up on the mountain, and when he sat down his disciples came to him. ² And he open-

* Of Jesus' famous "Sermon" we have in Matthew and Luke two different presentations, each with its own meaning and teaching. Luke's four beatitudes declare to the poor, the oppressed and the unconsidered, freedom and the love of God. The four corresponding "woes" make the sermon sterner and more radical; they are a severe judgment and a threat to the rich and careless who are normally considered fortunate.

117

Safed, 20 km. north of Capernaum, a "city set on a hill" which can be seen from afar (cf. Mt. 5, 14).

* ed his mouth and taught them, saying:

** ³ "Blessed are the poor in spirit,
for theirs is the kingdom of heaven.

⁴ "Blessed are those who mourn,
for they shall be comforted.

⁵ "Blessed are the meek,
for they shall inherit the earth.

⁶ "Blessed are those who hunger
and thirst for righteousness,
for they shall be satisfied.

⁷ "Blessed are the merciful,
for they shall obtain mercy.

⁸ "Blessed are the pure in heart,
for they shall see God.

⁹ "Blessed are the peacemakers,
for they shall be called sons of God.

¹⁰ "Blessed are those who are
persecuted for righteousness' sake,
for theirs is the kingdom of heaven.

¹¹ "Blessed are you when men revile you
and persecute you and utter all kinds
of evil against you falsely on my account. ¹² Rejoice and be glad, for your
reward is great in heaven, for so men
persecuted the prophets who were before you."

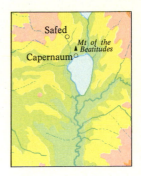

" You are the salt of the earth and the light of the world"
Mt 5, 13-16 (Lk 11,33)

¹³ "You are the salt of the earth; but
if salt has lost its taste, how shall its
saltness be restored? It is no longer
good for anything except to be thrown
out and trodden under foot by men.
¹⁴ "You are the light of the world. A
city set on a hill cannot be hid. ¹⁵ Nor

*   In his beatitudes Matthew brings out, not so much the social situation as the atti-tude of the soul, and its behaviour towards God and one's neigh-bour. E.g. the "poor in spirit" are humble and put their trust in God alone, like the typical poor man of the Bible. These beatitudes are modelled on the way Jesus himself behaved.

** The expression "kingdom of heaven" found in Matthew's gospel is the equivalent of "kingdom of God" and so means the reali-ty of God's saving act-ion for men.

119

do men light a lamp and put it under a bushel, but on a stand, and it gives light to all in the house. ¹⁶ Let your light so shine before men, that they may see your good works and give glory to your Father who is in heaven."

"I have not come to abolish but to fulfil"
Mt 5, 17-20

¹⁷ "Think not that I have come to abolish the law and the prophets; I have come not to abolish them but to fulfil them. ¹⁸ For truly, I say to you, till heaven and earth pass away, not an iota, not a dot, will pass from the law until all is accomplished. ¹⁹ Whoever then relaxes one of the least of these commandments and teaches men so, shall be called least in the kingdom of heaven; * ²⁰ but he who does them and teaches them shall be called great in the kingdom of heaven."

"Go; first be reconciled with your brother"
Mt 5, 21-26

²¹ "You have heard that it was said to the men of old, 'You shall not kill; and whoever kills shall be liable to ** judgment.' ²² But I say to you that every one who is angry with his brother shall be liable to judgment; whoever insults his brother shall be liable to the council, and whoever says, 'You fool!' shall be liable to the hell of fire. ²³ So if you are

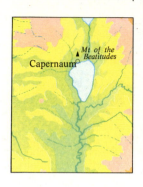

* The first part of the sermon was given up to a contrast between the righteousness of the scribes, which is the keeping of a Law, still imperfect, and the righteousness of the disciple of Jesus who sincerely seeks the will of God and lovingly fulfils it. This was illustrated by six examples: "You have heard... But I say to you..."

** While murder is condemned in the Mosaic law (5th commandment), Jesus also condemns lack of love for one's neighbour. Concord is a condition for offering worship acceptable to God.

offering your gift at the altar, and there remember that your brother has something against you, 24 leave your gift there before the altar and go; first be reconciled to your brother, and then come and offer your gift. 25 Make friends quickly with your accuser, while you are going with him to court, lest your accuser hand you over to the judge, and the judge to the guard, and you be put in prison; 26 truly, I say to you, you will never get out till you have paid the last penny."

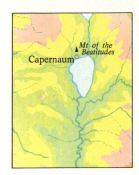

Jesus condemns evil thoughts
Mt 5, 27-30

27 "You have heard that it was said, * 'You shall not commit adultery.' 28 But I say to you that every one who looks at a woman lustfully has already committed adultery with her in his heart. 29 If your right eye causes you to sin, pluck it out and throw it away; it is better that you lose one of your members than that your whole body be thrown into hell. 30 And if your right hand causes you to sin, cut it off and throw it away; it is better that you lose one of your members than that your ** whole body go into hell."

Jesus condemns divorce
Mt 5, 31-32 (Lk 16, 18)

31 "It was also said, 'Whoever divorces his wife, let him give her a certificate of divorce.' 32 But I say to you that every

* Whereas the Mosaic law condemned the outward act of adultery (the sixth commandment), Jesus taught that the sin is primarily in the inner will of the person.

** Gehenna lies to the south west of Jerusalem. It had a sad reputation as having been the site of human sacrifices, and was later used for burning rubbish. So, in the gospels it was a symbol of hell.

121

A glimpse of the Lake of Gennesaret from the Mount of the Beatitudes. It was in this setting that Jesus gave his important "sermon".

* one who divorces his wife, except on the ground of unchastity, makes her an adulteress; and whoever marries a divorced woman commits adultery."

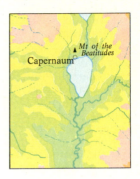

"Let what you say be simply 'Yes' or 'No'"
Mt 5, 33-37

³³ "Again you have heard that it was said to the men of old, 'You shall not swear falsely, but shall perform to the Lord what you have sworn.' ³⁴ But I say ** to you, Do not swear at all, either by heaven, for it is the throne of God, ³⁵ or by the earth, for it is his footstool, or by Jerusalem, for it is the city of the great King. ³⁶ And do not swear by your head, for you cannot make one hair white or black. ³⁷ Let what you say be simply 'Yes' or 'No'; anything more than this comes from evil."

"Love your enemies"
Mt 5, 38-48 (Lk 6, 27-36)

³⁸ "You have heard that it was said, ** 'An eye for an eye and a tooth for a tooth.' ³⁹ But I say to you, Do not resist one who is evil. But if any one strikes you on the right cheek, turn to him the other also; ⁴⁰ and if any one would sue you and take your coat, let him have your cloak as well; ⁴¹ and if any one forces you to go one mile, go with him two miles. ⁴² Give to him who begs from

* Jesus not only completed but also corrected the Mosaic law which allowed divorce (Deut. 24, 1). He declared: "It is God's will for marriage to be indissoluble."

** Swearing is calling God to witness to the truth of what is being affirmed (Lev. 19, 12). But Jesus desired of his disciples such trustworthiness that they would always be believed without having recourse to futile oaths.

*** The Mosaic law did not seek with this saying (Ex. 21, 24) to encourage private vendettas but rather to prevent their abuse. To this law of equivalence Jesus opposed forgiveness and complete charity.

123

you, and do not refuse him who would borrow from you.

43 "You have heard that it was said,
* 'You shall love your neighbour and hate your enemy.' 44 But I say to you, Love your enemies and pray for those who persecute you, 45 so that you may be sons of your Father who is in heaven; for he makes his sun rise on the evil and on the good, and sends rain on the just and on the unjust. 46 For if you love those who love you, what reward have you? Do not even the tax collectors do the same? 47 And if you salute only your brethren, what more are you doing than others? Do not even the Gentiles do the same? 48 You, therefore, must be perfect, as your heavenly Father is perfect."

Do not seek the admiration of men
Mt 6, 1-4

** 1 "Beware of practising your piety before men in order to be seen by them; for then you will have no reward from your Father who is in heaven.

2 Thus, when you give alms, sound no trumpet before you, as the hypocrites do in the synagogues and in the streets, that they may be praised by men. Truly, I say to you, they have their reward. 3 But when you give alms, do not let your left hand know what your right hand is doing, 4 so that your alms may be in secret; and your Father who sees in secret will reward you."

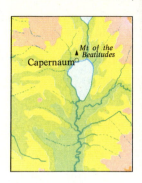

Capernaum

Mt of the Beatitudes

* In fact the law of Moses (Lev. 19, 18) did say only "Love your neighbour" but its usual interpretation had added to this, "Hate your enemy." Jesus said that his disciples were to love even their enemies and to pray for them. The model to aim for was the perfection of their havenly Father.

** The second part of the discourse is concerned with good works — almsgiving, prayer and fasting — which Jesus' disciples were to practise in a manner different from that of the Pharisees: i.e. with genuine intention, as in the sight of the Father, and without calculation or boasting before God.

"Pray to your Father in secret"
Mt 6, 5-6

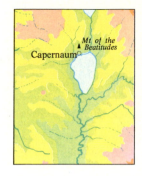

Capernaum

Mt of the Beatitudes

5 "And when you pray, you must not be like the hypocrites; for they love to stand and pray in the synagogues and at the street corners, that they may be seen by men. Truly, I say to you, they have their reward. 6 But when you pray, go into your room and shut the door and pray to your Father who is in secret; and your Father who sees in secret will reward you."

"Our Father"
Mt 6, 7-15

* 7 "And in praying do not heap up empty phrases as the Gentiles do; for they think that they will be heard for their many words. 8 Do not be like them, for your Father knows what you need before you ask him. 9 Pray then like this:

Our Father who art in heaven,
Hallowed be thy name.
10 Thy kingdom come,
Thy will be done,
On earth as it is in heaven.
11 Give us this day our daily bread;
12 And forgive us our debts,
As we also have forgiven our debtors;
13 And lead us not into temptation,
But deliver us from evil.

14 For if you forgive men their trespasses, your heavenly Father also will forgive you; 15 but if you do not forgive men their trespasses, neither will your Father forgive your trespasses."

* At this point Matthew inserted other connected sayings of Jesus and in particular the prayer which he himself taught. The "Our Father" is the finest summary and model of authentic Christian prayer to the Father.

125

"Your Father who sees in secret will reward you"
Mt 6, 16-18

¹⁶ "And when you fast, do not look dismal, like the hypocrites, for they disfigure their faces that their fasting may be seen by men. Truly, I say to you, they have their reward. ¹⁷ But when you fast, anoint your head and wash your face, ¹⁸ that your fasting may not be seen by men but by your Father who is in secret; and your Father who sees in secret will reward you."

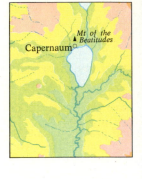

Mt of the Beatitudes

Capernaum

"Lay up for yourselves treasures in heaven"
Mt 6, 19-21

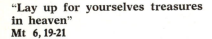

*   ¹⁹ "Do not lay up for yourselves treasures on earth, where moth and rust consume and where thieves break in and steal, ²⁰ but lay up for yourselves treasures in heaven, where neither moth nor rust consumes and where thieves do not break in and steal. ²¹ For where your treasure is, there will your heart be also."

Inner light
Mt 6, 22-23 (Lk 11, 34-36)

²² "The eye is the lamp of the body. So, if your eye is sound, your whole body will be full of light; ²³ but if your eye is not sound, your whole body will be full of darkness. If then the light in you is darkness, how great is the darkness!"

*   In the third part of the sermon Matthew collected various sayings and exhortations of Jesus which deal with the character of a disciple; indifference to possessions, clarity of mind, trust in the Father, charity in judgment, prudence and integrity.

"Seek first his kingdom"
Mt 6, 24-34 (Lk 12, 22-31)

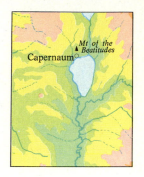

24 "No one can serve two masters; for either he will hate the one and love the other, or he will be devoted to the one and despise the other. You cannot * serve God and mammon.

25 "Therefore I tell you, do not be anxious about your life, what you shall eat or what you shall drink, nor about your body, what you shall put on. Is not life more than food, and the body more than clothing? 26 Look at the birds of the air; they neither sow nor reap nor gather into barns, and yet your heavenly Father feeds them. Are you not of more value than they? 27 And which of you by being anxious can add one cubit to his span of life? 28 And why are you anxious about clothing? Consider the lilies of the field, how they grow; they neither toil nor spin; 29 yet I tell you, even Solomon in all his glory was not arrayed like one of these. 30 But if God so clothes the grass of the field, which today is alive and tomorrow is thrown into the oven, will he not much more clothe you, O men of little faith? 31 Therefore do not be anxious, saying, 'What shall we eat?' or 'What shall we drink?' or 'What shall we wear?' 32 For the Gentiles seek all these things; and your heavenly Father knows that you need them all. 33 But seek first his kingdom and his righteousness, and all these things shall be yours as well.

34 "Therefore do not be anxious about

* The word "mammon" is of Arabic origin and means money. Here it suggests a personification of the money-god in contradistinction to God the Father.

127

A poetic view of the Lake of Gennesaret. Such places, untouched for centuries, lend a sort of enchantment to the background of the gospel.

tomorrow, for tomorrow will be anxious for itself. Let the day's own trouble be sufficient for the day."

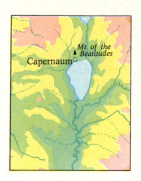

Capernaum
Mt of the Beatitudes

"Judge not"
Mt 7, 1-6 (Lk 6, 37-42)

1 "Judge not, that you be not judged. 2 For with the judgment you pronounce you will be judged, and the measure you give will be the measure you get. 3 Why do you see the speck that is in your brother's eye, but do not notice the log that is in your own eye? 4 Or how can you say to your brother, 'Let me take the speck out of your eye,' when there is the log in your own eye? 5 You hypocrite, first take the log out of your own eye, and then you will see clearly to take the speck out of your brother's eye.

* 6 "Do not give dogs what is holy; and do not throw your pearls before swine, lest they trample them under foot and turn to attack you."

"Ask and it shall be given you"
Mt 7, 7-11

7 "Ask, and it will be given you; seek, and you will find; knock, and it will be opened to you. 8 For every one who asks receives, and he who seeks finds, and to him who knocks it will be opened. 9 Or what man of you, if his son asks him for bread, will give him a stone? 10 Or if he asks for a fish, will give him a serpent? 11 If you then, who are evil,

* This saying seems to have been taken out of its original context. It urges discretion in not displaying the finest and holiest things to people who are hostile and may well merely mock and profane them.

129

know how to give good gifts to your children, how much more will your Father who is in heaven give good things to those who ask him!"

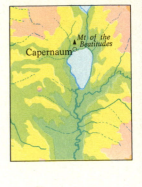

Jesus gives the rule of loving one's neighbour
Mt 7, 12

12 "So whatever you wish that men would do to you, do so to them; for * this is the law and the prophets."

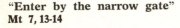

"Enter by the narrow gate"
Mt 7, 13-14

13 "Enter by the narrow gate; for the gate is wide and the way is easy, that leads to destruction, and those who enter by it are many. 14 For the gate is narrow and the way is hard, that leads to life, and those who find it are few."

"Beware of false prophets"
Mt 7, 15-20 (Lk 6, 43-45)

15 "Beware of false prophets, who come to you in sheep's clothing but inwardly are ravenous wolves. 16 You will know them by their fruits. Are grapes gathered from thorns, or figs from thistles? 17 So, every sound tree bears good fruit, but the bad tree bears evil fruit. 18 A sound tree cannot bear evil fruit, nor can a bad tree bear good fruit. 19 Every tree that does not bear good fruit is cut down and thrown into the fire. 20 Thus you will know them by their fruits."

* This is a sort of resumé of the sermon. Jesus summarizes all the laws, focussing them in a true and solid love of one's neighbour. To the negative precepts already known to the Jews ("Do to no one what you would not like done to you," Tobit 4, 15) Jesus substitutes more binding and demanding forms.

It is not enough to say: Lord, Lord!
Mt 7, 21-23 (Lk 6, 46)

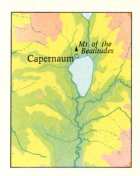

21 "Not every one who says to me, 'Lord, Lord,' shall enter the kingdom of heaven, but he who does the will of my
* Father who is in heaven. 22 On that day many will say to me, 'Lord, Lord, did we not prophesy in your name, and cast out demons in your name, and do many mighty works in your name?' 23 And then will I declare to them, 'I never knew you; depart from me, you evildoers.' "

Conclusion:
hear and put into practice
Mt 7, 24-29 (Lk 6, 47-49)

24 "Every one then who hears these words of mine and does them will be like a wise man who built his house upon the rock; 25 and the rain fell, and the floods came, and the winds blew and beat upon that house, but it did not fall, because it had been founded on the rock. 26 And every one who hears these words of mine and does not do them will be like a foolish man who built his house upon the sand; 27 and the rain fell, and the floods came, and the winds blew and beat against that house, and it fell; and great was the fall of it."

28 And when Jesus finished these sayings, the crowds were astonished at his teaching, 29 for he taught them as one who had authority, and not as their scribes.

* The mark of the true disciple is not liturgical entreaty, preaching or miracles, but true obedience to the Father's will. "That day" is the day of the last judgment.

131

View of Capernaum as it appears today. Among trees one descries the remains of the synagogue and various excavations. Capernaum was the centre of Jesus' activity in Galilee.

Various encounters

Jesus is astonished by the faith of the centurion
Lk 7,1-10 (Mt 8,5-13)

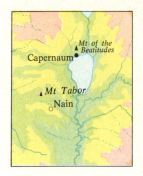

¹ After he had ended all his sayings in the hearing of the people he entered *Capernaum. ² Now a centurion had a slave who was dear to him, who was sick and at the point of death. ³ When he heard of Jesus, he sent to him elders of the Jews, asking him to come and heal his slave. ⁴ And when they came to Jesus, they besought him earnestly, saying, "He is worthy to have you do this for him, ⁵ for he loves our nation, and he built us our synagogue." ⁶ And Jesus went with them. When he was not far from the house, the centurion sent friends to him, saying to him, "Lord, do not trouble yourself, for I am not worthy to have you come under my roof; ⁷ therefore I did not presume to come to you. But say the word, and let ** my servant be healed. ⁸ For I am a man set under authority, with soldiers under me: and I say to one, 'Go,' and he goes; and to another, 'Come,' and he comes; and to my slave, 'Do this,' and he does it." ⁹ When Jesus heard this he marvelled at him, and turned and said to the multitude that followed him, "I tell you, not even in Israel have I found such faith." ¹⁰ And when those who had been

* This centurion was probably an officer in the service of the te-trarch, Herod Antipas.

** The centurion re-cognizes that, as he gives orders to his sol-diers, so Jesus has the divine power of com-manding diseases, and that without any need of a magic "touch." Here is an example of humility and faith in a Gentile.

133

Panorama of Nain in Galilee. In the present Arab village there is a chapel commemorating the miracle which happened there (Lk. 7, 11-15).

sent returned to the house, they found the slave well.

Jesus restores to life the widow's son
Lk 7, 11-17

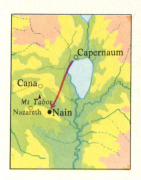

11 Soon afterward he went to a city called Nain, and his disciples and a great crowd went with him. 12 As he drew near to the gate of the city, behold, a man who had died was being carried out, the only son of his mother, and she was a widow; and a large crowd from the city was with her. 13 And when the Lord saw her, he had compassion on her and said to her, "Do not weep." 14 And he came and touched the bier, and the bearers stood still. And he said, "Young man, I say to you, arise." 15 And the dead man sat up, and began to speak. And he gave him to his mother. 16 Fear
* seized them all; and they glorified God, saying, "A great prophet has arisen among us!" and "God has visited his people!" 17 And this report concerning him spread through the whole of Judea and all the surrounding country.

Jesus and the messengers of John the Baptist
Lk 7, 18-23 (Mt 11, 2-6)

18 The disciples of John told him of
** all these things. 19 And John, calling to him two of his disciples, sent them to the Lord, saying, "Are you he who is to come, or shall we look for another?" 20 And when the men had come to him,

* This deed brings back to mind two similar miracles granted to the prophets Elijah (I Kg. 17) and Elisha (II Kg. 4). Because of it the crowd acclaimed Jesus as a new and extraordinary prophet through whom the power of God the Saviour worked.

** Perhaps the Baptist, who had proclaimed severe judgment, was puzzled by Jesus' gentle patience. Therefore he sent from prison to ask explanations for himself and for his disciples.

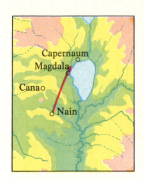

they said, "John the Baptist has sent us to you, saying, 'Are you he who is to come, or shall we look for another?' " ²¹ In that hour he cured many of diseases and plagues and evil spirits, and on many that were blind he bestowed sight. ²² And he answered them, "Go and tell
* John what you have seen and heard: the blind receive their sight, the lame walk, lepers are cleansed, and the deaf hear, the dead are raised up, the poor have good news preached to them. ²³ And blessed is he who takes no offence at me."

Jesus commends John
Lk 7, 24-28 (Mt 11, 7-11)

²⁴ When the messengers of John had gone, he began to speak to the crowds concerning John: "What did you go out into the wilderness to behold? A reed shaken by the wind? ²⁵ What then did you go out to see? A man clothed in soft raiment? Behold, those who are gorgeously apparelled and live in luxury are in kings' courts. ²⁶ What then did you go out to see? A prophet? Yes, I tell you, and more than a prophet. ²⁷ This is he of whom it is written,
** 'Behold, I send my messenger
before thy face,
who shall prepare
thy way before thee.'
²⁸ I tell you, among those born of women none is greater than John; yet he who
*** is least in the kingdom of God is greater than he."

* Jesus replied that what Isaiah had predicted about the Messianic age (35, 5-6; 61, 1) was being fulfilled in his liberating action and his message to the poor. Jesus was a Messiah-Saviour before being a Messiah-Judge. John, whom otherwise Jesus valued highly (as was to appear immediately afterwards) had to learn to accept God's timing.

** The quotation is from Mal. 3, 1.

*** The reason was that John had not been able to enter into the spiritual riches of the New Covenant; he was in fact the last of the Old Testament prophets.

136

Jesus and John, both rejected
Lk 7, 29-35 (Mt 11, 16-19)

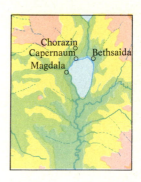

Chorazin
Capernaum   Bethsaida
Magdala

29 (When they heard this all the people and the tax collectors justified God, having been baptized with the baptism of John; 30 but the Pharisees and the * lawyers rejected the purpose of God for themselves, not having been baptized by him.)

31 "To what then shall I compare the men of this generation, and what are they like? 32 They are like children sitting in the market place and calling to one another,

'We piped to you,
and you did not dance;
we wailed, and you did not weep.'

33 For John the Baptist has come eating no bread and drinking no wine; and you say, 'He has a demon.' 34 The Son of man has come eating and drinking; and you say, 'Behold, a glutton and a drunkard, a friend of tax collectors and sinners!' 35 Yet wisdom is justified by all her children."

Jesus pardons the sinful woman
Lk 7, 36-50

36 One of the Pharisees asked him to eat with him, and he went into the Pharisee's house, and sat at table. 37 And ** behold, a woman of the city, who was a sinner, when she learned that he was sitting at table in the Pharisee's house, brought an alabaster flask of ointment, 38 and standing behind him at his feet, weeping, she began to wet his feet with

*   The poor and sinners had recognized the wisdom of God either in the Baptist's austerity or in Jesus' obvious goodness. On the other hand, those who were unwilling to repent always found an excuse for refusing to do so. With the vivid simile of children playing and being wayward, Jesus expressed God's disappointment with some people who did not respond either to John or to him.

**   This woman is not to be identified with Mary the sister of Lazarus nor with Mary Magdalene. It must be the case of a third person.

137

The Plain of Gennesaret by the lake-side. In the background on the left are the "Horns of Hattin", between which passed the direct road from Nazareth to the lake.

her tears, and wiped them with the hair of her head, and kissed his feet, and anointed them with the ointment. 39 Now when the Pharisee who had invited him saw it, he said to himself, "If this man were a prophet, he would have known who and what sort of woman this is who is touching him, for she is a sinner." 40 And Jesus answering said to him, "Simon, I have something to say to you." And he answered, "What is it, Teacher?" 41 "A certain creditor had two debtors; one owed five hundred denarii, and the other fifty. 42 When they could not pay, he forgave them both. Now * which of them will love him more?" 43 Simon answered, "The one, I suppose, to whom he forgave more." And he said to him, "You have judged rightly." 44 Then turning toward the woman he said to Simon, "Do you see this woman? I entered your house, you gave me no ** water for my feet, but she has wet my feet with her tears and wiped them with her hair. 45 You gave me no kiss, but from the time I came in she has not ceased to kiss my feet. 46 You did not anoint my head with oil, but she has anointed my feet with ointment. 47 Therefore I tell you, her sins, which are many, are forgiven, for she loved much; but he who is forgiven little, loves little." 48 And he said to her, "Your sins are forgiven." 49 Then those who were at table with him began to say among themselves, "Who is this, who even forgives sins?" 50 And he said to the woman, "Your faith has saved you; go in peace."

*   The parable shows that the initiative comes from God's goodness. God forgives anyone who turns to him in humility and needing salvation Then, after being forgiven, that person grows in more generous love and gratitude.

** This refers to customs of courteous behaviour towards a guest which were current at that time.

Certain women attend to Jesus' needs
Lk 8, 1-3

¹ Soon afterward he went on through cities and villages, preaching and bringing the good news of the kingdom of God. And the twelve were with him, ² and also some women who had been healed of evil spirits and infirmities: Mary, called Magdalene, from whom seven demons had gone out, ³ and Joanna, the wife of Chuza, Herod's steward, and Susanna, and many others, who provided for them out of their means.

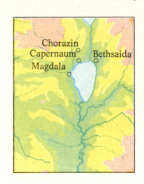

The great argument: Jesus or Beelzebul?

"The Kingdom of God is come upon you: He that is not with me is against me"
Mt 12, 22-30 (Mk 3, 22-27 Lk 11, 14-23)

²² Then a blind and dumb demoniac was brought to him, and he healed him, so that the dumb man spoke and saw. ²³ And all the people were amazed, and said, "Can this be the Son of David?" ²⁴ But when the Pharisees heard it they * said, "It is only by Beelzebul, the prince of demons, that this man casts out demons." ²⁵ Knowing their thoughts, he ** said to them, "Every kingdom divided against itself is laid waste, and no city or house divided against itself will stand; ²⁶ and if Satan casts out Satan, he is divided against himself; how then will his kingdom stand? ²⁷ And if I cast out

* Beelzebul was an idol of Ekron, a Philistine city. The Jews contemptuously named him Belzebub ("god of flies") and identified him with the devil.

** Jesus could not allow the whole meaning of his work to be maliciously turned upside down, so he defended himself with precise care. Victory over Satan is a sign that the Kingdom of God has arrived. Satan was the "strong man" who ruled the world, but now Jesus, a stronger than he, has come to fetter and conquer him.

demons by Beelzebul, by whom do your sons cast them out? Therefore they shall be your judges. 28 But if it is by the Spirit of God that I cast out demons, then the kingdom of God has come upon you. 29 Or how can one enter a strong man's house and plunder his goods, unless he first binds the strong man? Then indeed he may plunder his house. 30 He who is not with me is against me, and he who does not gather with me scatters."

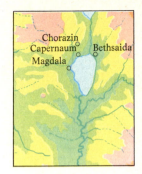

The sin for which there is no forgiveness
Mt 12, 31-37 (Mk 3, 28-30 Lk 12, 10)

31 Therefore I tell you, every sin and blasphemy will be forgiven men, but the * blasphemy against the Spirit will not be forgiven. 32 And whoever says a word against the Son of man will be forgiven; but whoever speaks against the Holy Spirit will not be forgiven, either in this age or in the age to come.

33 "Either make the tree good, and its fruit good; or make the tree bad, and its fruit bad; for the tree is known by its fruit. 34 You brood of vipers! how can you speak good, when you are evil? For out of the abundance of the heart the mouth speaks. 35 The good man out of his good treasure brings forth good, and the evil man out of his evil treasure brings forth evil. 36 I tell you, on the day of judgment men will render account for every careless word they utter; 37 for by your words you will be justified, and by your words you will be condemned."

* Jesus proclaims that shutting the eyes to the truth is blasphemy against the Holy Spirit. To be unwilling to look, so as to be able not to believe, excludes the sinner from the possibility of repentance and therefore of forgiveness.

141

An aerial photograph of Capernaum. On the left may be seen the octagon of tne Byzantine church built on the "house of St. Peter", in the centre, the ruins of dwelling-houses, and on the right the remains of the synagogue.

The sign of Jonah
Mt 12, 38-42 (Lk 11, 29-32)

³⁸ Then some of the scribes and Pharisees said to him, "Teacher, we wish to see a sign from you." ³⁹ But he answered them, "An evil and adulterous generation seeks for a sign; but no sign shall be given to it except the sign of the
* prophet Jonah. ⁴⁰ For as Jonah was three days and three nights in the belly of the whale, so will the Son of man be three days and three nights in the heart of the earth. ⁴¹ The men of Nineveh will arise at the judgment with this generation and condemn it; for they repented at the preaching of Jonah, and behold, something greater than Jonah is here. ⁴² The queen of the South will arise at the judgment with this generation and condemn it; for she came from the ends of the earth to hear the wisdom of Solomon, and behold, something greater than Solomon is here."

Falling back into sin
Mt 12, 43-45 (Lk 11, 24-26)

⁴³ "When the unclean spirit has gone out of a man, he passes through waterless places seeking rest, but he finds none. ⁴⁴ Then he says, 'I will return to my house from which I came.' And when he comes he finds it empty, swept, and put in order. ⁴⁵ Then he goes and brings with him seven other spirits more evil than himself, and they enter and dwell there; and the last state of that

* Henceforth the only sign that Jesus would give was that of Jonah, and it was in his own person. As Jonah was swallowed by waves and then brought back to shore, so Jesus would be swallowed by death and then would rise again. And as Jonah was a call to repentance to the Ninevites, so was Jesus to his contemporaries.

143

A stretch of country in Palestine which recalls the parable of the sower. Here we see a pathway, a patch of stony ground, a thicket of prickly thistles and, higher up, a strip of good soil (cf. Mt. 13, 4-8).

man becomes worse than the first. So shall it be also with this evil generation."

Jesus' true family
Mt 12, 46-50 (Mk 3, 31-35   Lk 8, 19-21)

46 While he was still speaking to the people, behold, his mother and his brethren stood outside, asking to speak to him. 48 But he replied to the man who told him, "Who is my mother, and who are my brethren?" 49 And stretching out his hand toward his disciples, he said,
* "Here are my mother and my brethren! 50 For whoever does the will of my Father in heaven is my brother, and sister, and mother."

Parables of the Kingdom

The parable of the sower
Mt 13, 1-9 (Mk 4, 1-9   Lk 8, 4-8)

1 That same day Jesus went out of the house and sat beside the sea. 2 And great crowds gathered about him, so that he got into a boat and sat there; and the whole crowd stood on the beach. 3 And
** he told them many things in parables, saying: "A sower went out to sow. 4 And as he sowed, some seeds fell along the path, and the birds came and devoured them. 5 Other seeds fell on rocky ground, where they had not much soil, and immediately they sprang up, since they had no depth of soil, 6 but when the sun rose they were scorched; and since they

* Jesus wishes it to be understood that the greatness of his Mother was due first of all to her loyalty to God. Luke refers to a similar incident (11, 27-28): "As he said this, a woman in the crowd raised her voice and said to him; 'Blessed is the womb that bore you and the breasts that you sucked!' But he said: 'Blessed are those who hear the word of God and keep it!' ".

** A parable is the story of a happening taken from real life and seen as a picture of another and higher reality, that is the Kingdom of God. Such symbolic language is suitable for giving people an idea of the Kingdom; greater understanding is then reserved for those who show themselves sympathetic.

145

had no root they withered away. ⁷ Other seeds fell upon thorns, and the thorns grew up and choked them. ⁸ Other seeds fell on good soil and brought forth grain, some a hundredfold, some sixty, some * thirty. ⁹ He who has ears, let him hear."

Chorazin
Capernaum   Bethsaida
Magdala
Lake of Gennesaret

Why Jesus speaks in parables
Mt 13, 10-17 (Mk 4, 10-12 Lk 8, 9-10)

¹⁰ Then the disciples came and said to him, "Why do you speak to them in parables?" ¹¹ And he answered them, "To you it has been given to know the secrets of the kingdom of heaven, but to them it has not been given. ¹² For to him who has will more be given, and he will have abundance; but from him who has not, even what he has will be taken away. ¹³ This is why I speak to ** them in parables, because seeing they do not see, and hearing they do not hear, nor do they understand. ¹⁴ With them indeed is fulfilled the prophecy of Isaiah which says:

*** 'You shall indeed hear but never understand,
and you shall indeed see
but never perceive.
¹⁵ For this people's heart has grown dull,
and their ears are heavy of hearing,
and their eyes they have closed,
lest they should perceive
with their eyes,
and hear with their ears,
and understand with their heart,
and turn for me to heal them.'
¹⁶ But blessed are your eyes, for they

* The seed, even if in some cases it seems to have been scattered fruitlessly, will in reality find the good soil and bear abundant fruit.

** The believer in Christ alone will understand better and better the profound meaning of his parables and, having heard them, will find his faith richer, while those who reject the initial gift of faith will find Jesus' words incomprehensible and will in the end lose all faith in him.

*** Isa. 6, 9-10, as if to say: You who have been unwilling to listen to the Lord will end by understanding his words less and less. Your sin will itself become your punishment.

see, and your ears, for they hear. ¹⁷ Truly, I say to you, many prophets and righteous men longed to see what you see, and did not see it, and to hear what you hear, and did not hear it."

Jesus explains the parable of the sower
Mt 13, 18-23 (Mk 4, 13-20   Lk 8, 11-15)

Chorazin
Capernaum   Bethsaida
Magdala
Lake of Gennesaret

* ¹⁸ "Hear then the parable of the sower. ¹⁹ When any one hears the word of the kingdom and does not understand it, the evil one comes and snatches away what is sown in his heart; this is what was sown along the path. ²⁰ As for what was sown on rocky ground, this is he who hears the word and immediately receives it with joy; ²¹ yet he has no root in himself, but endures for a while, and when tribulation or persecution arises on account of the word, immediately he falls away. ²² As for what was sown among thorns, this is he who hears the word, but the cares of the world and the delight in riches choke the word, and it proves unfruitful. ²³ As for what was sown on good soil, this is he who hears the word and understands it; he indeed bears fruit, and yields, in one case a hundredfold, in another sixty,
** and in another thirty."

The parable of the good seed and the weeds
Mt 13, 24-30

²⁴ Another parable he put before them, saying, "The kingdom of heaven may be

*   In the explanation of the parable the tone becomes more hortatory, and the attention is turned primarily to the different dispositions with which the seed, i.e. the Word of God, is received.

**   At this point Mark adds a little parable on the inner strength of the growth of the Kingdom: "He said: 'The Kingdom of God is as if a man should scatter seed upon the ground, and should sleep and rise night and day, and the seed should sprout and grow, he knows not how. The earth produces of itself, first the blade, then the ear, then the full grain in the ear. But when the grain is ripe, at once he puts in the sickle, because the harvest has come'" (Mk. 4, 26-29).

147

Grains of mustard, "the smallest of all the seeds" (Mk. 13, 32). Even in small details the gospel shows itself extraordinarily true to reality.

compared to a man who sowed good seed in his field; ²⁵ but while men were sleeping, his enemy came and sowed weeds among the wheat, and went away. ²⁶ So when the plants came up and bore grain, then the weeds appeared also. ²⁷ And the servants of the householder came and said to him, 'Sir, did you not sow good seed in your field? How then has it weeds?' ²⁸ He said to them, 'An enemy has done this.' The servants said to him, 'Then do you want us to go and gather them?' ²⁹ But he said, 'No; lest in gathering the weeds you root up the ∗ wheat along with them. ³⁰ Let both grow together until the harvest; and at harvest time I will tell the reapers, Gather the weeds first and bind them in bundles to be burned, but gather the wheat into my barn.' "

Chorazin
Capernaum   Bethsaida
Magdala
Lake of Gennesaret

The parables of the mustard seed and of the leaven
Mt 13, 31-33 (Mk 4, 30-32 Lk 13, 18-21)

∗∗ ³¹ Another parable he put before them, saying, "The kingdom of heaven is like a grain of mustard seed which a man took and sowed in his field; ³² it is the smallest of all seeds, but when it has grown it is the greatest of shrubs and becomes a tree, so that the birds of the air come and make nests in its branches."

³³ He told them another parable. "The kingdom of heaven is like leaven which a woman took and hid in three measures of meal, till it was all leavened."

∗   Another disconcerting aspect of the Kingdom is the co-existence of good and evil people, and the long-suffering of God.

∗∗   The two little parables emphasize the contrast between the humble, insignificant beginnings of the Kingdom and its ability to grow up to a final tremendous result.

Jesus speaks to the crowd in parables
Mt 13, 34-35 (Mk 4, 33-34)

³⁴ All this Jesus said to the crowds in parables; indeed he said nothing to them without a parable. ³⁵ This was to fulfil what was spoken by the prophet:

*   "I will open my mouth in parables,
I will utter what has been hidden
since the foundation of the world."

Jesus explains the parable of the weeds to the disciples
Mt 13, 36-43

³⁶ Then he left the crowds and went into the house. And his disciples came to him, saying, "Explain to us the parable of the weeds of the field." ³⁷ He answered, "He who sows the good seed is the Son of man; ³⁸ the field is the world, and the good seed means the sons of the kingdom; the weeds are the sons of the evil one, ³⁹ and the enemy who sowed them is the devil; the harvest is the close of the age, and the reapers are angels. ⁴⁰ Just as the weeds are gathered and burned with fire, so will it be at the close of the age. ⁴¹ The Son of man will send his angels, and they will gather out of his kingdom all causes of sin and all evildoers, ⁴² and throw them into the furnace of fire; there men will weep and gnash their teeth. ⁴³ Then the righteous will shine like the sun in the kingdom of their Father. He who has ears, let him hear."

*   The prophet is the author of Psalm 78, who claims that he wants to reveal God's mysteries in images and parables.

**   The catechetical tone typical of the evangelist Matthew is obvious in this explanation of the parable.

150

The parables of the treasure and of the pearl of great value
Mt 13, 44-46

* ⁴⁴ "The kingdom of heaven is like treasure hidden in a field, which a man found and covered up; then in his joy he goes and sells all that he has and buys that field.

⁴⁵ "Again, the kingdom of heaven is like a merchant in search of fine pearls, ⁴⁶ who, on finding one pearl of great value, went and sold all that he had and bought it."

The parable of the fishing net
Mt 13, 47-50

** ⁴⁷ "Again, the kingdom of heaven is like a net which was thrown into the sea and gathered fish of every kind; ⁴⁸ when it was full, men drew it ashore and sat down and sorted the good into vessels but threw away the bad. ⁴⁹ So it will be at the close of the age. The angels will come out and separate the evil from the righteous, ⁵⁰ and throw them into the furnace of fire; there men will weep and gnash their teeth."

Jesus ends his speaking in parables
Mt 13, 51-52

⁵¹ "Have you understood all this?" They said to him, "Yes." ⁵² And he said to them, "Therefore every scribe who has been trained for the kingdom of heaven is like a householder who brings out of his treasure what is new and *** what is old."

*   These two little parables have the same lesson: the Kingdom of God is worth so much that everything is not too high a price to pay for it.

**   This repeats the argument of the parable of the weeds.

***Jesus' disciples were the true teachers of the Word of God, being very familiar with both the Ancient Law and its fulfilment in the New Covenant.

151

The region of the Decapolis seen from Magdala. In the crossing of the lake, which reaches its greatest width here, unexpected storms of wind arise from time to time.

Great miracles

Jesus stills the storm
Mk 4, 35-41 (Mt 8, 23-27 Lk 8, 22-25)

* ³⁵ On that day, when evening had come, he said to them, "Let us go across to the other side." ³⁶ And leaving the crowd, they took him with them just as he was, in the boat. And other boats were with him. ³⁷ And a great storm of wind arose, and the waves beat into the boat, so that the boat was already filling. ³⁸ But he was in the stern, asleep on the cushion; and they woke him and said to him, "Teacher, do you not care if we perish?" ³⁹ And he awoke and rebuked the wind, and said to the sea, "Peace! Be still!" And the wind ceased, and there was a great calm. ⁴⁰ He said to them, "Why are you afraid? Have you no faith?" ⁴¹ And they were filled with awe, and said to one another, "Who then is this, that even wind and sea obey him?"

Jesus tames the evil spirit
Mk 5, 1-20 (Mt 8, 23-24 Lk 8, 26-39)

¹ They came to the other side of the sea, to the country of the Gerasenes. ² And when he had come out of the boat, there met him out of the tombs a man with an unclean spirit, ³ who lived among the tombs; and no one could bind him any more, even with a chain; ⁴ for he had often been bound with fetters and chains, but the chains he wrenched apart, and the fetters he broke in pieces; and no one had the strength to subdue him.

* Mark next puts together a series of four miracles, narrated in a lively and lifelike way (one seems to hear Peter's reminiscences), but primarily united by the theme which appears: Jesus conquers evil in all its manifestations — in nature, in demons. in sickness and in death — and so invites belief in himself even in situations where humanly speaking there is no way out.

153

Kursi, in the country of the Gerasenes on the eastern shore of the lake. Here are the remains of a Byzantine church built as a memorial of the release of the man possessed by devils (Mk. 5, 1-20).

⁵ Night and day among the tombs and on the mountains he was always crying out, and bruising himself with stones. ⁶ And when he saw Jesus from afar, he ran and worshipped him; ⁷ and crying out with a loud voice, he said, "What have you to do with me, Jesus, Son of the Most High God? I adjure you by God, do not torment me." ⁸ For he had said to him, "Come out of the man, you unclean spirit!" ⁹ And Jesus asked him, "What is your name?" He replied, "My name is Legion; for we are many." ¹⁰ And he begged him eagerly not to send them out of the country. ¹¹ Now a great herd of swine was feeding there on the hillside; ¹² and they begged him, "Send us to the swine, let us enter them." ¹³ So he gave them leave. And the unclean spirits came out, and entered the swine; and the herd, numbering about two thousand, rushed down the steep bank into the sea, and were drowned in the sea.

¹⁴ The herdsmen fled, and told it in the city and in the country. And people came to see what it was that had happened. ¹⁵ And they came to Jesus, and saw the demoniac sitting there, clothed and in his right mind, the man who had had the legion; and they were afraid. ¹⁶ And those who had seen it told what had happened to the demoniac and to the swine. ¹⁷ And they began to beg Jesus to depart from their neighbourhood. ¹⁸ And as he was getting into the boat, the man who had been possessed with demons begged him that he might

Capernaum   Bethsaida
      Kursi

DECAPOLIS

*   The incident of the swine points out with amusing irony the complete discomfiture of the devils; the unclean spirits find their true home in the swine, which were thought unclean animals; they in turn become a trap for the demons and drag them down to the depths of the sea, a sign of utter destruction.

**   For the moment they reject the Liberator who seems a danger to their livelihood. Meanwhile the liberated sufferer has already become a missionary, and later the inhabitants of the Decapolis will be among the first Gentile converts.

155

be with him. ¹⁹ But he refused, and said to him, "Go home to your friends, and tell them how much the Lord has done for you, and how he has had mercy on you." ²⁰ And he went away and began to proclaim in the Decapolis how much Jesus had done for him; and all men marvelled.

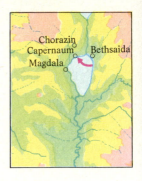

Faith in Jesus overcomes sickness
Mk 5, 21-34 (Mt 9, 18-22 Lk 8, 40-48)

²¹ And when Jesus had crossed again in the boat to the other side, a great crowd gathered about him; and he was beside the sea. ²² Then came one of the rulers of the synagogue, Jairus by name, and seeing him, he fell at his feet, ²³ and besought him, saying, "My little daughter is at the point of death. Come and lay your hands on her, so that she may be made well, and live." ²⁴ And he went with him.

And a great crowd followed him and
* thronged about him. ²⁵ And there was a woman who had had a flow of blood for twelve years, ²⁶ and who had suffered much under many physicians, and had spent all that she had, and was no better but rather grew worse. ²⁷ She had heard the reports about Jesus, and came up behind him in the crowd and touched his garment. ²⁸ For she said, "If I touch even his garments, I shall be made well." ²⁹ And immediately the hemorrhage ceased; and she felt in her body that she was healed of her disease. ³⁰ And Jesus, perceiving in himself that power had gone forth from him, immediately turned

* These are two intertwined stories united in their theme of the strength of Jesus and of the faith of anyone who turns to him. Here is a climax of both ideas. The vivid, life-like narrative also illustrates the human characteristics of Jesus.

about in the crowd, and said, "Who touched my garments?" ³¹ And his disciples said to him, "You see the crowd pressing around you, and yet you say, 'Who touched me?' ³² And he looked around to see who had done it. ³³ But the woman, knowing what had been done to her, came in fear and trembling and fell down before him, and told him the whole truth. ³⁴ And he said to her, "Daughter, your faith has made you
* well; go in peace, and be healed of your disease."

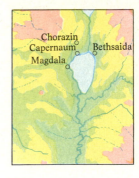

Faith in Jesus overcomes death
Mk 5, 35-43 (Mt 9, 23-26   Lk 8, 49-56)

³⁵ While he was still speaking, there came from the ruler's house some who said, "Your daughter is dead. Why trouble the Teacher any further?" ³⁶ But ignoring what they said, Jesus said to
** the ruler of the synagogue, "Do not fear, only believe." ³⁷ And he allowed no one to follow him except Peter and James and John the brother of James. ³⁸ When they came to the house of the ruler of the synagogue, he saw a tumult, and people weeping and wailing loudly. ³⁹ And when he had entered, he said to them, "Why do you make a tumult and weep? The child is not dead but sleeping." ⁴⁰ And they laughed at him. But he put them all outside, and took the child's father and mother and those who were with him, and went in where the child was. ⁴¹ Taking her by the hand he said to her, "Talitha cumi"; which means, "Little girl, I say to you, arise." ⁴² And

* The woman's faith has matured as she passes from an almost superstitious belief to a personal meeting with Jesus. Before this last step, the woman was merely "healed," now she is "made well"; the healing is the pledge of the more important being made well.

** Faith in Jesus must persist even when there is no hope and all is over, humanly speaking; then it is no longer enough to trust in a miracle-working healer, but in One who has the divine power of overcoming death.

157

A panorama of Nazareth from the east. To this village, where he had spent his childhood and adolescence, Jesus returned several times during his public life (Mk. 6, 1-6).

immediately the girl got up and walked; for she was twelve years old. And immediately they were overcome with amazement. ⁴³ And he strictly charged them that no one should know this, and told them to give her something to eat.

Jesus is not accepted in his own district
Mk 6, 1-6 (Mt 13, 53-58)

¹ He went away from there and came to his own country; and his disciples followed him. ² And on the sabbath he began to teach in the synagogue; and many who heard him were astonished, saying, "Where did this man get all this? What is the wisdom given to him? What mighty works are wrought by his hands! *³ Is not this the carpenter, the son of Mary and brother of James and Joses and Judas and Simon, and are not his sisters here with us?" And they took offence at him. ⁴ And Jesus said to them, "A prophet is not without honour, except in his own country, and among his own kin, and in his own house." ⁵ And he could do no mighty work there, except that he laid his hands upon a few sick people and healed them. ⁶ And he marvelled because of their unbelief.

Sayings about the Mission

Jesus sends the Twelve on a mission
Mt 9, 35-38; 10, 1 & 5-16 (Mk 6, 7-11 Lk 9, 1-5)

³⁵ And Jesus went about all the cities and villages, teaching in their synago-

*   Jesus' fellow countrymen would not accept the fact that the wisdom and authority of God was to be found in an humble artisan, living among them, and whose cousins and whole family they knew well. This "taking offence" is unbelief.

159

gues and preaching the gospel of the kingdom, and healing every disease and every infirmity. ³⁶ When he saw the
* crowds, he had compassion for them, because they were harassed and helpless, like sheep without a shepherd. ³⁷ Then he said to his disciples, "The harvest is plentiful, but the labourers are few; ³⁸ pray therefore the Lord of the harvest to send out labourers into his harvest."

¹ And he called to him his twelve disciples and gave them authority over unclean spirits, to cast them out, and to heal every disease and every infirmity.

⁵ These twelve Jesus sent out, charging them, "Go nowhere among the Gentiles, and enter no town of the Samaritans, ⁶ but go rather to the lost sheep of the house of Israel. ⁷ And preach as you go, saying, 'The kingdom of heaven is at hand. ⁸ Heal the sick, raise the dead, cleanse lepers, cast out demons. You received without pay, give
** without pay. ⁹ Take no gold, nor silver, nor copper in your belts, ¹⁰ no bag for your journey, nor two tunics, nor sandals, nor a staff; for the labourer deserves his food. ¹¹ And whatever town or village you enter, find out who is worthy in it, and stay with him until you depart. ¹² As you enter the house, salute it. ¹³ And if the house is worthy, let your peace come upon it; but if it is not worthy, let your peace return to you. ¹⁴ And if any one will not receive you or listen to your words, shake off the dust from your feet as you leave that house or town. ¹⁵ Truly, I say to you,

* Jesus takes pity on the weary, leaderless people and sends his disciples on their first experience of a mission, limited for the time to Galilee. The mission of the disciples is an extension of that of the Master.

** When Jesus sent his disciples on this first mission, he advised them not to put their trust in human methods but solely in God. They were to proclaim the approach of the Kingdom of God, even though they themselves were often not welcomed.

it shall be more tolerable on the day of judgment for the land of Sodom and Gomorrah than for that town.

¹⁶ Behold, I send you out as sheep in the midst of wolves; so be wise as serpents and innocent as doves."

Jesus gives instructions for the time of persecution
Mt 10, 17-42 (Lk 12, 2-12)

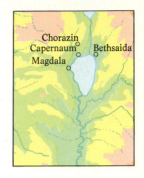

* ¹⁷ "Beware of men; for they will deliver you up to councils, and flog you in their synagogues, ¹⁸ and you will be dragged before governors and kings for my sake, to bear testimony before them and the Gentiles. ¹⁹ When they deliver you up, do not be anxious how you are to speak or what you are to say; for what you are to say will be given to you in that hour; ²⁰ for it is not you who speak, but the Spirit of your Father speaking through you. ²¹ Brother will deliver up brother to death, and the father his child, and children will rise against parents and have them put to death; ²² and you will be hated by all for my name's sake. But he who endures to the end will be saved. ²³ When they persecute you in one town, flee to the next; for truly, I say to you, you will not have gone through all the towns of Israel, before the Son of man comes.

²⁴ A disciple is not above his teacher, nor a servant above his master; ²⁵ it is enough for the disciple to be like his teacher, and the servant like his master.

* Once more, in this discourse, Matthew collects other sayings of Jesus concerned with the discourse is broadened and already envisages the mission of the Church: it was just in times of persecution that the disciples were to give witness to Christ with courage and calm fortitude.

Two sparrows on the shore of the Lake of Gennesaret. Even creatures as small as these are objects of God's paternal care; from them Jesus takes a cue for arousing faith in the Father (Mt. 10, 29-31).

If they have called the master of the house Beelzebul, how much more will they malign those of his household.

26 So have no fear of them; for nothing is covered that will not be revealed, or hidden that will not be known. 27 What I tell you in the dark, utter in the light; and what you hear whispered, proclaim upon the housetops. 28 And do not fear those who kill the body but cannot kill the soul; rather fear him who can destroy both soul and body in hell. 29 Are not two sparrows sold for a penny? And not one of them will fall to the ground without your Father's will. 30 But even the hairs of your head are all numbered. 31 Fear not, therefore; you are of more value than many sparrows. 32 So every one who acknowledges me before men, I also will acknowledge before my Father who is in heaven; 33 but whoever denies me before men, I also will deny before my Father who is in heaven.

34 Do not think that I have come to bring peace on earth; I have not come to bring peace, but a sword. 35 For I have come to set a man against his father, and a daughter against her mother, and a daughter-in-law against her mother-in-law; 36 and a man's foes will be those of his own household. 37 He who loves father or mother more than me is not worthy of me; and he who loves son or daughter more than me is not worthy of me; 38 and he who does not take his cross and follow me is not worthy of me. 39 He who finds his life will lose it, and

* The missionary must speak publicly and be heard by all. The "house-tops" of Palestinian houses were, and are, always made up of terraces reached by external flights of steps.

** Jesus does not desire the sort of disagreements which often divide families (Micah 7, 6), but it is inevitable that anyone who sincerely chooses Jesus will be faced with misunderstanding and hostility, often from his nearest and dearest.

163

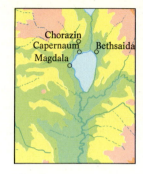

he who loses his life for my sake will find it.

⁴⁰ He who receives you receives me, and he who receives me receives him who sent me. ⁴¹ He who receives a prophet because he is a prophet shall receive a prophet's reward, and he who receives a righteous man because he is a righteous man shall receive a righteous man's reward. ⁴² And whoever gives to one of these little ones even a cup of cold water because he is a disciple, truly, I say to you, he shall not lose his reward."

Jesus and the Twelve preach in Galilee
Mt 11, 1 (Mk 6, 12-13 Lk 9, 6)

¹ And when Jesus had finished instructing his twelve disciples, he went on from there to teach and preach in their cities.

IV - THE "CRISIS" IN GALILEE

Now began a series of happenings which were signs for a change in Jesus' life. This was probably about the Passover of 29 A.D. The remarkable multiplication of the loaves brought the enthusiasm of the crowds to a head; they saw in Jesus the political and nationalistic Messiah of so many dreams.

But Jesus refused that path: the way marked out for him by the Father led through the cross. The crowds, greatly disappointed, left him, and even some disciples went away. Jesus gradually withdrew to the borders of Galilee and gave himself up to the training of his disciples. These, torn between admiration and incomprehension, at last recognized him, through the agency of Peter, as the promised Messiah; from that moment Jesus began to speak clearly of his passion, death and resurrection.

The site of the palace-fortress of Machaerus, on the eastern shore of the Dead Sea. There, John the Baptist was imprisoned and killed by order of Herod Antipas (Mk. 6, 17-28).

The miracles of the loaves: Misunderstanding

King Herod is troubled by doubts
Mk 6, 14-16 (Mt 14, 1-2 Lk 9, 7-9)

14 King Herod heard of it; for Jesus' name had become known. Some said, "John the baptizer has been raised from the dead; that is why these powers are at work in him." 15 But others said, "It is Elijah." And others said, "It is a prophet, like one of the prophets of old." 16 But when Herod heard of it, he
* said, "John, whom I beheaded, has been raised."

How the martyrdom of John the Baptist came about
Mk 6, 17-29 (Mt 14, 3-12 Lk 3, 19-20)

17 For Herod had sent and seized John, and bound him in prison for the sake of Herodias, his brother Philip's wife; because he had married her. 18 For John said to Herod, "It is not lawful for you to have your brother's wife." 19 And Herodias had a grudge against him, and wanted to kill him. But she could not, 20 for Herod feared John, knowing that he was a righteous and holy man, and kept him safe. When he heard him, he was much perplexed; and yet he heard him gladly. 21 But an opportunity came when Herod on his birthday gave a banquet for his courtiers and officers and the leading men of Galilee. 22 For

*   At this point Mark includes the story of the martyrdom of the Baptist. A similar fate was to be faced by Jesus and many of the disciples whom he sent to the mission.

167

Samaria. Here, according to tradition, John the Baptist was buried. His tomb was later turned into a mosque.

when Herodias' daughter came in and danced, she pleased Herod and his guests; and the king said to the girl, "Ask me for whatever you wish, and I will grant it." ²³ And he vowed to her, "Whatever you ask me, I will give you, even half of my kingdom." ²⁴ And she went out, and said to her mother, "What shall I ask?" And she said, "The head of John the baptizer." ²⁵ And she came in immediately with haste to the king, and asked, saying, "I want you to give me at once the head of John the Baptist on a platter." ²⁶ And the king was exceedingly sorry; but because of his oaths and his guests he did not want to break his word to her. ²⁷ And immediately the king sent a soldier of the guard and gave orders to bring his head. He went and beheaded him in the prison, ²⁸ and brought his head on a platter, and gave it to the girl; and the girl gave it to her mother. ²⁹ When his disciples heard of it, they came and took his body, and laid it in a tomb.

Jesus multiplies the loaves
Mk 6, 30-34 (Mt 14, 13-21 Lk 9, 10-17 Jn 6, 1-13)

³⁰ The apostles returned to Jesus, and told him all that they had done and taught. ³¹ And he said to them, "Come away by yourselves to a lonely place, and rest a while." For many were coming and going, and they had no leisure even to eat. ³² And they went away in the boat ＊ to a lonely place by themselves. ³³ Now many saw them going, and knew them,

＊ The manner of telling the story of the miracle emphasizes its significance: Jesus, with his word and with the gift of his bread, is the food of his people on their journey through the desert. There are numerous references to the Biblical account of the manna (Ex. 16) and also to the eucharistic meal of Christians.

169

and they ran there on foot from all the towns, and got there ahead of them. ³⁴ As he landed he saw a great throng, and he had compassion on them, because they were like sheep without a shepherd; and he began to teach them many things. ³⁵ And when it grew late, his disciples came to him and said, "This is a lonely place, and the hour is now late; ³⁶ send them away, to go into the country and villages round about and buy themselves something to eat." ³⁷ But he answered them, "You give them something to eat." And they said to him, "Shall we go and buy two hundred denarii worth of bread, and give it to them to eat?" ³⁸ And he said to them, "How many loaves have you? Go and see." And when they had found out, they said, "Five, and two fish." ³⁹ Then he commanded them all to sit down by companies upon the green grass. ⁴⁰ So they sat down in groups, by hundreds and by fifties. ⁴¹ And taking the five loaves and the two fish he looked up to heaven, and blessed, and broke the loaves, and gave them to the disciples to set before the people; and he divided the two fish among them all. ⁴² And they all ate and were satisfied. ⁴³ And they took up twelve baskets full of broken pieces and of the fish. ⁴⁴ And those who ate the loaves were five thousand men.

Capernaum Bethsaida

Hippos

*   The evangelist John adds: "When the people saw the sign which he had done, they said, 'This is indeed the prophet who is to come into the world!' Perceiving then that they were about to come and take him by force to make him king, Jesus withdrew again to the hills by himself" (Jn. 6, 14-15). Mark also lets it be understood that this was a critical moment: Jesus sent the disciples away, tried to escape from the crowd, and then prayed.

Jesus walks on the water of the lake
Mk 6, 45-52 (Mt 14, 22-23 Jn 6, 14-21)

*   ⁴⁵ Immediately he made his disciples get into the boat and go before him to the other side, to Bethsaida, while he dis-

170

Plain of Gennesaret

Bethsaida

missed the crowd. ⁴⁶ And after he had taken leave of them, he went into the hills to pray. ⁴⁷ And when evening came, the boat was out on the sea, and he was alone on the land. ⁴⁸ And he saw that they were distressed in rowing, for the wind was against them. And about the fourth watch of the night he came to them, walking on the sea. He meant to pass by them, ⁴⁹ but when they saw him walking on the sea they thought it was a ghost, and cried out; ⁵⁰ for they all saw him, and were terrified. But immediately he spoke to them and said, * "Take heart, it is I; have no fear." ⁵¹ And he got into the boat with them and the wind ceased. And they were utterly astounded, ⁵² for they did not understand about the loaves, but their hearts were hardened.

Jesus and the disciples return to the west bank of the lake
Mk 6, 53-56 (Mt 14, 34-36)

⁵³ And when they had crossed over, they came to land at Gennesaret, and moored to the shore. ⁵⁴ And when they got out of the boat, immediately the people recognized him, ⁵⁵ and ran about the whole neighbourhood and began to bring sick people on their pallets to any place where they heard he was. ⁵⁶ And wherever he came, in villages, cities, or country, they laid the sick in the market places, and besought him that they might touch even the fringe of his garment; and as many as touched it were made well.

* Mark stresses the contrast between the sovereign power of Jesus and the fear of the disciples, who had not realised that it was Jesus. Matthew adds the following incident: "Peter answered him: 'Lord, if it is you, bid me come to you on the water.' He said 'Come.' So Peter got out of the boat and walked on the water and came to Jesus; but when he saw the wind he was afraid, and beginning to sink he cried out: 'Lord, save me.' Jesus immediately reached out his hand and caught him, saying to him: 'O man of little faith, why did you doubt?' " (Mt. 14, 28-31).

171

Capernaum. Remains of the synagogue. Even though this building is probably later, it was built on the foundations of the earlier synagogue, where Jesus gave the celebrated discourse on the "Bread of life".

Discourse on the Bread of Life

"I am the bread which came down from heaven"
Jn 6, 22-47

22 On the next day the people who remained on the other side of the sea saw that there had been only one boat there, and that Jesus had not entered the boat with his disciples, but that his disciples had gone away alone. 23 However, boats from Tiberias came near the place where they ate the bread after the Lord had given thanks. 24 So when the people saw that Jesus was not there, nor his disciples, they themselves got into the boats and went to Capernaum, seeking Jesus.

25 When they found him on the other side of the sea, they said to him, "Rabbi,
* when did you come here?" 26 Jesus answered them, "Truly, truly, I say to you, you seek me, not because you saw signs, but because you ate your fill of the loaves. 27 Do not labour for the food which perishes, but for the food which endures to eternal life, which the Son of man will give to you; for on him has God the Father set his seal." 28 Then they said to him, "What must we do, to be doing the works of God?" 29 Jesus answered them, "This is the work of God, that you believe in him whom he has sent." 30 So they said to him, "Then what sign do you do, that we may see, and believe you? What work do you

* After the multiplication of the loaves, the evangelist John gives the important discourse on the bread of life, which makes us understand the meaning of that "sign." The first part develops the theme of the mystery of Jesus: Christ is the bread which comes from heaven to give life, he is the gift of salvation for men: they must believe in him.

173

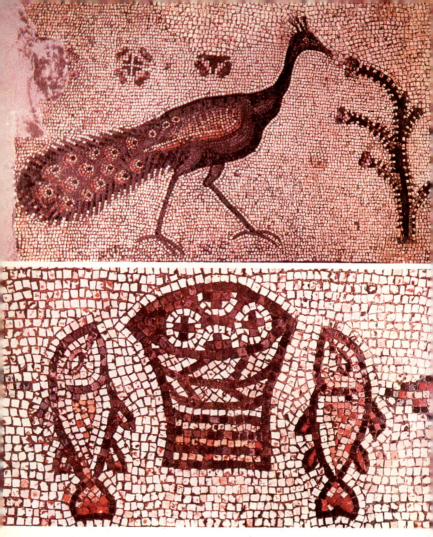

Tabgah, a place in the outskirts of Capernaum. Byzantine mosaics picture the loaves and fishes, and also the peacock, the symbol of immortality. The allusion to the miracle of the loaves and the discourse on the bread of "eternal life" (Jn. 6) is clear.

perform? ³¹ Our fathers ate the manna in the wilderness; as it is written, 'He gave them bread from heaven to eat'." ³² Jesus then said to them, "Truly, truly, I say to you, it was not Moses who gave you the bread from heaven; my Father gives you the true bread from heaven. ³³ For the bread of God is that which comes down from heaven, and gives life to the world." ³⁴ They said to him, "Lord, give us this bread always."

³⁵ Jesus said to them, "I am the bread of life; he who comes to me shall not hunger, and he who believes in me shall never thirst. ³⁶ But I said to you that you have seen me and yet do not believe. ³⁷ All that the Father gives me will come to me; and him who comes to me I will not cast out. ³⁸ For I have come down from heaven, not to do my own will, but the will of him who sent me; ³⁹ and this is the will of him who sent me, that I should lose nothing of all that he has given me, but raise it up at the last day. ⁴⁰ For this is the will of my Father, that every one who sees the Son and believes in him should have eternal life; and I will raise him up at the last day."

⁴¹ The Jews then murmured at him, because he said, "I am the bread which came down from heaven." ⁴² They said, "Is not this Jesus, the son of Joseph, whose father and mother we know? How does he now say, 'I have come down from heaven'?" ⁴³ Jesus answered them, "Do not murmur among yourselves. ⁴⁴ No one can come to me unless

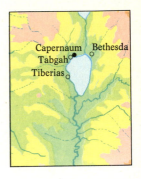

Capernaum Bethesda
Tabgah
Tiberias

* The analogy of manna is apparent throughout the discourse. Here Psalm 78, 24 is quoted. But manna was prophetic; the new gift surpasses the old, for it gives an eternal life which overcomes death and is therefore offered to the whole world.

* the Father who sent me draws him; and I will raise him up at the last day. ⁴⁵ It is written in the prophets, 'And they shall all be taught by God.' Every one who has heard and learned from the Father comes to me. ⁴⁶ Not that any one has seen the Father except him who is from God; he has seen the Father. ⁴⁷ Truly, truly, I say to you, he who believes has eternal life."

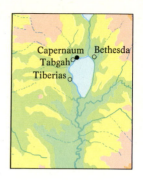

Capernaum   Bethesda
Tabgah
Tiberias

"The bread which I shall give for the life of the world is my flesh"
Jn 6, 48-59

⁴⁸ "I am the bread of life. ⁴⁹ Your fathers ate the manna in the wilderness, and they died. ⁵⁰ This is the bread which comes down from heaven, that a man may eat of it and not die. ⁵¹ I am the living bread which came down from heaven; if any one eats of this bread, he will live for ever; and the bread
** which I shall give for the life of the world is my flesh."

⁵² The Jews then disputed among themselves, saying. "How can this man give us his flesh to eat?" ⁵³ So Jesus said to them, "Truly, truly, I say to you, unless you eat the flesh of the Son of man and drink his blood, you have no life in you; ⁵⁴ he who eats my flesh and drinks my blood has eternal life, and I will raise him up at the last day. ⁵⁵ For my flesh is food indeed, and my blood is drink indeed. ⁵⁶ He who eats my flesh and drinks my blood abides in me, and I in him. ⁵⁷ As the living Father sent me,

*   It is God who brings about the movement of faith which draws man to him; and it is he who inwardly teaches those who do not resist him. The prophecy quoted (Isa. 54, 13) came true by the work of Jesus, the Father's messenger.

**   In the second part of the discourse Jesus speaks more directly of the sacrament of the Eucharist; he will give his Body to be eaten and his Blood to be drunk to nourish the divine life which he came to bring to men. He who eats of this bread will be fundamentally united with Christ, will live through him and like him will make a gift of his own life.

176

and I live because of the Father, so he who eats me will live because of me. ⁵⁸ This is the bread which came down from heaven, not such as the fathers ate and died; he who eats this bread will live for ever." ⁵⁹ This he said in the synagogue, as he taught at Capernaum.

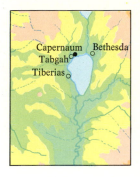

Disbelief of the disciples and faith of the Twelve
Jn 6, 60-71

* ⁶⁰ Many of his disciples, when they heard it, said, "This is a hard saying; who can listen to it?" ⁶¹ But Jesus, knowing in himself that his disciples murmured at it, said to them, "Do you take offence at this? ⁶² Then what if you were to see the Son of man ascending where he was before? ⁶³ It is the spirit that gives life, the flesh is of no avail; the words that I have spoken to you are spirit and life. ⁶⁴ But there are some of you that do not believe." For Jesus knew from the first who those were that did not believe, and who it was that should betray him. ⁶⁵ And he said, "This is why I told you that no one can come to me unless it is granted him by the Father."

⁶⁶ After this many of his disciples drew back and no longer went about with him. ⁶⁷ Jesus said to the twelve, "Will you also go away?" ⁶⁸ Simon Peter answered him, "Lord, to whom shall we go? You have the words of eternal life; ⁶⁹ and we have believed, and have come

** to know, that you are the Holy One of

* Here is misunderstanding and disbelief, even among the disciples, in the face of Jesus' revelation. He replies to it as he did to Nicodemus: a man is powerless by himself; he needs the Spirit to give him new birth and true understanding of the things of God.

** If many disciples withdrew, the Twelve nonetheless stayed and their faith grew and ripened. Peter was their spokesman and expressed their personal attachment to and trust in Christ. Jesus encouraged the Twelve and at the same time warned them, mindful of the possibility of his being betrayed.

177

Jerusalem. A view of the excavations of the pool of the "Sheep Gate", or Bethesda "with five porticoes" (Jn. 5, 2): four on the perimeter and one across the diameter. The excavations have confirmed the accuracy of the description in the fourth gospel.

God." ⁷⁰ Jesus answered them, "Did I not choose you, the twelve, and one of you is a devil?" ⁷¹ He spoke of Judas the son of Simon Iscariot, for he, one of the twelve, was to betray him.

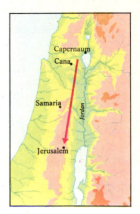

The Passover at Jerusalem

At Jerusalem, Jesus cures a paralytic on the sabbath day
Jn 5, 1-18

¹ After this there was a feast of the Jews, and Jesus went up to Jerusalem. ² Now there is in Jerusalem by the Sheep Gate a pool, in Hebrew called Bethzatha, which has five porticoes. ³ In these lay a multitude of invalids, blind,
* lame, paralyzed. ⁵ One man was there,
** who had been ill for thirty-eight years. ⁶ When Jesus saw him and knew that he had been lying there a long time, he said to him, "Do you want to be healed?" ⁷ The sick man answered him, "Sir, I have no man to put me into the pool when the water is troubled, and while I am going another steps down before me." ⁸ Jesus said to him, "Rise, take up your pallet, and walk." ⁹ And at once the man was healed, and he took up his pallet and walked.

Now that day was the sabbath. ¹⁰ So

* Verse 4 is omitted by several important codices.

** In the face of popular devotion which sought bodily healing in a rather superstitious way, Jesus shows himself as the real saviour who has come to heal the whole man.

the Jews said to the man who was cured, "It is the sabbath, it is not lawful for you to carry your pallet." [11] But he answered them, "The man who healed me said to me, 'Take up your pallet, and walk.'" [12] They asked him, "Who is the man who said to you, 'Take up your pallet, and walk'?" [13] Now the man who had been healed did not know who it was, for Jesus had withdrawn, as there was a crowd in the place. [14] Afterward, Jesus found him in the temple, and said to him, "See, you are well! Sin no more, that nothing worse befall you." [15] The man went away and told the Jews that it was Jesus who had healed him. [16] And this was why the Jews persecuted Jesus, because he did this on the sabbath. [17] But Jesus answered them, "My Father is working still, and I am working." [18] This

* was why the Jews sought all the more to kill him, because he not only broke the sabbath but also called God his Father, making himself equal with God.

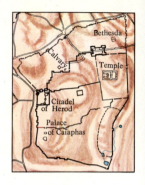

Jesus speaks in his own defence
Jn 5, 19-47; 7, 1

** [19] Jesus said to them, "Truly, truly, I say to you, the Son can do nothing of his own accord, but only what he sees the Father doing; for whatever he does, that the Son does likewise. [20] For the Father loves the Son, and shows him all that he himself is doing; and greater works than these will he show him, that you may marvel. [21] For as the Father

* By this time the Jews have realized that Jesus is claiming to be the Son of God. Henceforward they accuse him of blasphemy and begin the persecution which is to lead to his condemnation to death.

** Jesus defends himself first of all by affirming that in his works he is imitating the Father and fulfilling the mission that the latter has entrusted to him, viz: to bring salvation, life and resurrection.

180

raises the dead and gives them life, so also the Son gives life to whom he will. 22 The Father judges no one, but has given all judgment to the Son, 23 that all may honour the Son, even as they honour the Father. He who does not honour the Son does not honour the Father who sent him. 24 Truly, truly, I say to you, he who hears my word and believes him who sent me, has eternal life; he does not come into judgment, but has passed from death to life.

25 "Truly, truly, I say to you, the hour is coming, and now is, when the dead will hear the voice of the Son of God, and those who hear will live. 26 For as the Father has life in himself, so he has granted the Son also to have life in himself, 27 and has given him authority to execute judgment, because he is the Son of man. 28 Do not marvel at this; for the hour is coming when all who are in the tombs will hear his voice 29 and come forth, those who have done good, to the resurrection of life, and those who have done evil, to the resurrection of judgment.

30 "I can do nothing on my own authority; as I hear, I judge; and my judgment is just, because I seek not my own will but the will of him who sent me. 31 If I * bear witness to myself, my testimony is not true; 32 there is another who bears witness to me, and I know that the testimony which he bears to me is true. 33 You sent to John, and he has borne witness to the truth. 34 Not that the testimony which I receive is from man;

*   In the second part of the discourse Jesus puts forward witnesses to his defence: the Father has borne witness by means of John the Baptist, of the miracles and of Holy Scripture. Finally Jesus exposes the root of disbelief, personal pride and mutual adulation.

Another view of the excavations of the pool of Bethesda. The construction in the centre of the photograph is the crumbling apse of a mediaeval church built on the site.

but I say this that you may be saved. [35] He was a burning and shining lamp, and you were willing to rejoice for a while in his light. [36] But the testimony which I have is greater than that of John; for the works which the Father has granted me to accomplish, these very works which I am doing, bear me witness that the Father has sent me. [37] And the Father who sent me has himself borne witness to me. His voice you have never heard, his form you have never seen; [38] and you do not have his word abiding in you, for you do not believe him whom he has sent. [39] You search the scriptures, because you think that in them you have eternal life; and it is they that bear witness to me; [40] yet you refuse to come to me that you may have life. [41] I do not receive glory from men. [42] But I know that you have not the love of God within you. [43] I have come in my Father's name, and you do not receive me; if another comes in his own name, him you will receive. [44] How can you believe, who receive glory from one another and do not seek the glory that comes from the only God? [45] Do not think that I shall accuse you to the Father; it is Moses who accuses you, on whom you set your hope. [46] If you believed Moses, you would believe

* me, for he wrote of me. [47] But if you do not believe his writings, how will you believe my words?"

[1] After this Jesus went about in Galilee; he would not go about in Judea, because the Jews sought to kill him.

* Jesus states that he is the central light which illuminates all the Scriptures, and the goal to which they point.

A typical oriental "souk" (market) of our time. The Pharisees thought that the market might pollute them, and therefore washed scrupulously when they returned home (Mk. 7, 3-4).

The training of the disciples on the borders of Galilee

What God wills, and what defiles a man
Mk 7, 1-23 (Mt 15, 1-20)

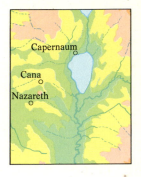

¹ Now when the Pharisees gathered together to him, with some of the scribes, who had come from Jerusalem, ² they saw that some of his disciples ate with hands defiled, that is, unwashed. ³ (For the Pharisees, and all the Jews, do not eat unless they wash their hands, observing the tradition of the elders; ⁴ and when they come from the market place, they do not eat unless they purify themselves; and there are many other traditions which they observe, the washing of cups and pots and vessels of bronze.) ⁵ And the Pharisees and the scribes asked him, "Why do your disciples not live according to the tradition of the elders, but eat with hands defiled? ⁶ And he said to them, "Well did Isaiah prophesy of you hypocrites, as it is written,

'This people honours me
with their lips,
but their heart is far from me;
⁷ in vain do they worship me,
teaching as doctrines
the precepts of men.'
⁸ You leave the commandment of God, and hold fast the tradition of men."
⁹ And he said to them, "You have a fine way of rejecting the commandment of God, in order to keep your tradition!

* Jesus made his own the lament of the prophet Isaiah (29, 13) when he accused the people of honouring God on the surface only, while in their hearts they paid no attention to him.

185

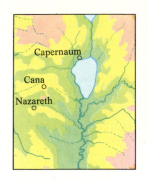

10 For Moses said, 'Honour your father and your mother'; and, 'He who speaks evil of father or mother, let him surely * die'; 11 but you say, 'If a man tells his father or his mother, What you would have gained from me is Corban' (that is, given to God)—12 then you no longer permit him to do anything for his father or mother, 13 thus making void the word of God through your tradition which you hand on. And many such things you do."

14 And he called the people to him again, and said to them, "Hear me, all of you, and understand: 15 there is nothing outside a man which by going into him can defile him; but the things which come out of a man are what defile him." 17 And when he had entered the house, and left the people, his disciples asked him about the parable. 18 And he said to them, "Then are you also without understanding? Do you not see that whatever goes into a man from outside cannot defile him, 19 since it enters, not his heart but his stomach, and so passes ** on?" (Thus he declared all foods clean.) 20 And he said, "What comes out of a man is what defiles a man. 21 For from within, out of the heart of man, come evil thoughts, fornication, theft, murder, adultery, 22 coveting, wickedness, deceit, licentiousness, envy, slander, pride, foolishness. 23 All these evil things come from within, and they defile a man."

The faith of a Gentile woman
Mk 7, 24-30 (Mt 15, 21-28)

24 And from there he arose and went

* God's obvious will was in practice brought to nothing by sophisticated interpretations and traditions. For example, the fourth commandment was clear (Exod. 20, 19 & 21, 17) but a legal means of avoiding the duty of helping one's parents with money had been found: it was enough to declare that what they might expect was "Corban," that is a sacred offering and the property of the Temple.

** In the Old Testament there was a clear distinction between clean and unclean foods. Jesus asserted that cleanliness and uncleanness were not inherent in things, but in a person's heart. Indirectly Jesus declared

away to the region of Tyre and Sidon. And he entered a house, and would not have any one know it; yet he could not be hid. ²⁵ But immediately a woman, whose little daughter was possessed by an unclean spirit, heard of him, and came and fell down at his feet. ²⁶ Now the woman was a Greek, a Syrophoenician by birth. And she begged him to cast the demon out of her daughter. ²⁷ And he said to her, "Let the children first be fed, for it is not right to take the children's bread and throw it to the dogs." ²⁸ But she answered him, "Yes, Lord; yet even the dogs under the table eat the children's crumbs." ²⁹ And he said to her, "For this saying you may go your way; the demon has left your daughter." ³⁰ And she went home, and found the child lying in bed, and the demon gone.

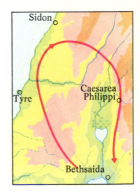

Jesus cures a deaf mute
Mk 7, 31-37

³¹ Then he returned from the region of Tyre, and went through Sidon to the Sea of Galilee, through the region of the Decapolis. ³² And they brought to him a man who was deaf and had an impediment in his speech; and they besought him to lay his hand upon him. ³³ And taking him aside from the multitude privately, he put his fingers into his *ears, and he spat and touched his tongue; ³⁴ and looking up to heaven, he sighed, and said to him, "Ephphatha," that is, "Be opened." ³⁵ And his ears were opened, his tongue was released, and he

that such rules were quite abrogated, having been provisional and made for a particular period in history.

* In Gentile countries it was usual to make gestures like this, and Jesus conformed to the custom. But in Mark's account these gestures have a symbolical value. Jesus effects as it were a new and difficult creation, and makes the man capable of speaking with God. It is with this meaning that the gesture has been repeated in the present day rite of baptism.

The ruins of Tyre, an important Phoenician city. Jesus withdrew to the borders of Galilee in the neighbourhood of Tyre (Mk. 7, 24), alone with his disciples.

spoke plainly. ³⁶ And he charged them
to tell no one; but the more he charged
them, the more zealously they proclaim-
ed it. ³⁷ And they were astonished beyond
measure, saying, "He has done all things
well; he even makes the deaf hear and
the dumb speak."

Jesus works the second miracle of the loaves
Mk 8, 1-10 (Mt 15, 32-39)

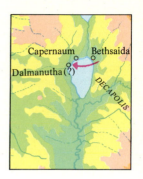

* ¹ In those days, when again a great
crowd had gathered, and they had nothing to eat, he called his disciples to
him, and said to them, ² "I have compassion on the crowd, because they have
been with me now three days, and have
nothing to eat; ³ and if I send them
away hungry to their homes, they will
faint on the way; and some of them
have come a long way." ⁴ And his disciples answered him, "How can one
feed these men with bread here in the
desert?" ⁵ And he asked them, "How
many loaves have you?" They said,
"Seven." ⁶ And he commanded the crowd
to sit down on the ground; and he took
the seven loaves, and having given thanks
he broke them and gave them to his
disciples to set before the people; and
they set them before the crowd. ⁷ And
they had a few small fish; and having
blessed them, he commanded that these
also should be set before them. ⁸ And
they ate, and were satisfied; and they
took up the broken pieces left over,
seven baskets full. ⁹ And there were about
four thousand people. ¹⁰ And he sent

* Mark and Matthew
give an account of a
second multiplication
of loaves. It is possible
that they may have
used two versions of
the same miracle.

189

them away; and immediately he got into the boat with his disciples, and went to the district of Dalmanutha.

Jesus refuses the obstinate Pharisees a sign from heaven
Mk 8, 11-13 (Mt 16, 1-4)

¹¹ The Pharisees came and began to argue with him, seeking from him a sign from heaven, to test him. ¹² And he sighed deeply in his spirit, and said,

* "Why does this generation seek a sign? Truly, I say to you, no sign shall be given to this generation." ¹³ And he left them, and getting into the boat again he departed to the other side.

"Beware of the leaven of the Pharisees"
Mk 8, 14-21 (Mt 16, 5-12)

¹⁴ Now they had forgotten to bring bread; and they had only one loaf with them in the boat. ¹⁵ And he cautioned them, saying, "Take heed, beware of the

** leaven of the Pharisees and the leaven of Herod." ¹⁶ And they discussed it with one another, saying, "We have no bread." ¹⁷ And being aware of it, Jesus said to them, "Why do you discuss the fact that you have no bread? Do you not yet perceive or understand? Are your hearts hardened? ¹⁸ Having eyes do you not see, and having ears do you not hear? And do you not remember? ¹⁹ When I broke the five loaves for the five thousand, how many baskets full of broken pieces did you take up?" They said to him, "Twelve." ²⁰ "And the seven for the four thousand, how many baskets full of

* Jesus had already worked many great miracles, enough signs for anyone willing to believe. The claim of the scribes and Pharisees had no justification.

** Fermenting yeast was for the Jews a sign of corruption.

190

broken pieces did you take up?" And they said to him, "Seven." 21 And he said to them, "Do you not yet understand?"

Jesus cures the blind man of Bethsaida
Mk 8, 22-26

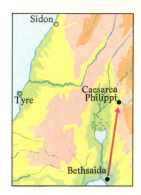

22 And they came to Bethsaida. And some people brought to him a blind man, and begged him to touch him. 23 And he took the blind man by the hand, and led him out of the village; and when he had spit on his eyes and laid his hands upon him, he asked him, "Do you see anything?" 24 And he looked up and said, "I see men; but they look like trees, walking." 25 Then again he laid his hands upon his eyes; and he looked intently and was restored, and saw everything clearly. 26 And he sent him away to his home, saying. " Do not even enter the village."

The profession of faith by Peter and the prophecy of the passion

Peter confesses Jesus' divinity;
Jesus promises him the primacy
Mt 16, 13-20 (Mk 8, 27-30   Lk 9, 18-21)

13 Now when Jesus came into the district of Cesarea Philippi, he asked his disciples, "Who do men say that the Son of man is?" 14 And they said, "Some say John the Baptist, others say Elijah, and others Jeremiah or one of the prophets." 15 He said to them, "But who do

* Jesus was trying to arouse his disciples who were enslaved by their own preconceived ideas, and incapable of understanding his words and signs.

Banyas, the site of the ancient Caesarea Philippi. There rises one of the sources of the river Jordan, and nearby is a famous cave, sacred to Pan, the god of nature. In this neighbourhood Jesus was recognized as Messiah by Peter (Mt. 16, 13-19).

you say that I am?" ¹⁶ Simon Peter replied, "You are the Christ, the Son of
* the living God." ¹⁷ And Jesus answered him, "Blessed are you, Simon Bar-Jona! For flesh and blood has not revealed this to you, but my Father who is in heaven. ¹⁸ And I tell you, you are Peter, and on this rock I will build my church, and the powers of death shall not prevail against it. ¹⁹ I will give you the keys of the kingdom of heaven, and whatever you bind on earth shall be bound in heaven, and whatever you loose on earth shall be loosed in heaven." ²⁰ Then he strictly charged the disciples to tell no one that he was the Christ.

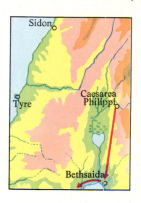

Jesus begins to speak of his passion, death and resurrection
Mt 16, 21-23 (Mk 8, 31-33 Lk 9, 22)

** ²¹ From that time Jesus began to show his disciples that he must go to Jerusalem and suffer many things from the elders and chief priests and scribes, and be killed, and on the third day be raised. ²² And Peter took him and began to rebuke him, saying, "God forbid, Lord! This shall never happen to you." ²³ But he turned and said to Peter, "Get behind me, Satan! You are a hindrance to me; for you are not on the side of God, but of men."

"If anyone would come after me..."
Mt 16, 24-28 (Mk 8, 34-38; 9, 1 Lk 9, 23-27)

²⁴ Then Jesus told his disciples, "If any man would come after me, let him

* For the first time Jesus was explicitly recognized as Messiah and Son of God. It was Peter who, inspired by God, professed faith in Jesus. Christ then spoke of his Church, firm as a house on a rock, a community which overcomes all difficulties external and internal and of which Peter was to be the pivot of unity, with Christ's authority.

** Now that the disciples know clearly that he is the Messiah, Jesus begins explicitly to reveal to them the painful side of his mission also. The entirely human protest of Peter is rejected as a temptation of Satan.

193

The summit of Tabor, the "high mountain" where, according to tradition, Jesus was transfigured (Mt. 17, 1-2). Near to the basilica stand the ruins of an ancient monastery; in the background is the plain.

deny himself and take up his cross and
*follow me. ²⁵ For whoever would save
his life will lose it, and whoever loses
his life for my sake will find it. ²⁶ For
what will it profit a man, if he gains
the whole world and forfeits his life?
Or what shall a man give in return for
his life? ²⁷ For the Son of man is to
come with his angels in the glory of his
Father, and then he will repay every
man for what he has done. ²⁸ Truly, I
say to you, there are some standing
here who will not taste death before
they see the Son of man coming in his
kingdom."

Jesus is transfigured on a hill and thus anticipates his Passover
Mt 17, 1-8 (Mk 9, 2-8 Lk 9, 28-36)

**** ¹ And after six days Jesus took with
him Peter and James and John his
brother, and led them up a high mountain apart. ² And he was transfigured
before them, and his face shone like
the sun, and his garments became white
as light. ³ And behold, there appeared to
them Moses and Elijah, talking with
him. ⁴ And Peter said to Jesus, "Lord,
it is well that we are here; if you wish,
I will make three booths here, one for
you and one for Moses and one for
Elijah." ⁵ He was still speaking, when lo,
a bright cloud overshadowed them, and
a voice from the cloud said, "This is my
beloved Son, with whom I am well
pleased; listen to him." ⁶ When the disciples heard this, they fell on their
faces, and were filled with awe. ⁷ But

*   A disciple is some-
one who follows Jesus
by his own path.

** Jesus was on his
way to the cross, but
it was just by way of
the cross that God's
glory and victory were
to appear. For a mo-
ment Jesus allowed the
irresolute disciples to
catch a glimpse of his
glory. That experience
meant to them that
God confirmed Jesus'
status, approved of the
way that he had cho-
sen, and invited and
encouraged the disci-
ples to follow him.

Jesus came and touched them, saying, "Rise, and have no fear." ⁸ And when they lifted up their eyes, they saw no one but Jesus only.

Queries about the resurrection and the coming of Elijah
Mk 9, 9-13 (Mt 17, 9-13)

⁹ And as they were coming down the mountain, he charged them to tell no one what they had seen, until the Son of man should have risen from the dead. ¹⁰ So they kept the matter to themselves, questioning what the rising from the dead meant. ¹¹ And they asked him, "Why do the scribes say that first Elijah must come?" ¹² And he said to them, "Elijah does come first to restore all things; and how is it written of the Son of man, that he should suffer many things and be treated with contempt? ¹³ But I tell you that Elijah has come, and they did to him whatever they pleased, as it is written of him."

Jesus cures an epileptic boy
Mk 9, 14-29 (Mt 17, 14-21   Lk 9, 37-43)

¹⁴ And when they came to the disciples, they saw a great crowd about them, and scribes arguing with them. ¹⁵ And immediately all the crowd, when they saw him, were greatly amazed, and ran up to him and greeted him. ¹⁶ And he asked them, "What are you discussing with them?" ¹⁷ And one of the crowd answered him, "Teacher, I brought my son to you, for he has a dumb spirit;

* Elijah had already come, said Jesus, in the person of John the Baptist, but he had not been recognized and, indeed, had been murdered. That would also happen to Jesus.

[18] and wherever it seizes him, it dashes him down; and he foams and grinds his teeth and becomes rigid; and I asked your disciples to cast it out, and they

* were not able." [19] And he answered them, "O faithless generation, how long am I to be with you? How long am I to bear with you? Bring him to me." [20] And they brought the boy to him; and when the spirit saw him, immediately it convulsed the boy, and he fell on the ground and rolled about, foaming at the mouth. [21] And Jesus asked his father, "How long has he had this?" And he said, "From childhood. [22] And it has often cast him into the fire and into the water, to destroy him; but if you can do anything, have pity on us and help us." [23] And Jesus said to him, "If you can! All things are possible to him who believes." [24] Immediately the father of the child cried out and said, "I believe; help my unbelief!" [25] And when Jesus saw that a crowd came running together, he rebuked the unclean spirit, saying to it, "You dumb and deaf spirit, I command you, come out of him, and never enter him again. [26] And after crying out and convulsing him terribly, it came out, and the boy was like a corpse; so that most of them said, "He is dead." [27] But Jesus took him by the hand and lifted him up, and he arose. [28] And when he had entered the house, his disciples asked him privately, "Why could we not cast it out?" [29] And he said to them, "This kind cannot be driven out by anything but prayer and fasting."

* This vivid account shows Jesus' power in the struggle against Satan. Further, it stresses man's weakness and therefore his need of faith and prayer.

The Lake of Gennesaret provides masses of fish. These are popularly called "Peter's fish", in memory of the fisherman apostle (cf. Mt. 17, 27).

Jesus again predicts his death
Mk 9, 30-32 (Mt 17, 22-23 Lk 9, 43-45)

30 They went on from there and passed through Galilee. And he would not have any one know it; 31 for he was teaching
* his disciples, saying to them, "The Son of man will be delivered into the hands of men, and they will kill him; and when he is killed, after three days he will rise." 32 But they did not understand the saying, and they were afraid to ask him.

Jesus counsels tolerance
Mk 9, 38-40 (Lk 9, 49-50)

38 John said to him, "Teacher, we saw a man casting out demons in your name, and we forbade him, because he was not following us." 39 But Jesus said, "Do not forbid him; for no one who does a mighty work in my name will be able
** soon after to speak evil of me. 40 For he that is not against us is for us."

The Temple tax
Mt 17, 24-27

24 When they came to Capernaum, the collectors of the half-shekel tax went up to Peter and said, "Does not your teacher pay the tax?" 25 He said, "Yes." And when he came home, Jesus spoke to him first, saying, "What do you think, Simon? From whom do kings of the earth take toll or tribute? From their sons or from others?" 26 And when he said, "From others," Jesus said to him,

* This is the second explicit prediction of the death and resurrection. But this talk always came up against the incomprehension of the disciples who were still involved in their own schemes and ambitions.

** No group has a monopoly of the name of Jesus; so not jealousy but collaboration and an open mind are required.

199

A heavy mill-stone of Jesus' day (cf. Mt. 18, 6). On the lower part, shaped like a cone, rested the upper, a double funnel, which was turned by a donkey.

"Then the sons are free. 27However, not to give offence to them, go to the sea and cast a hook, and take the first fish that comes up, and when you open its mouth you will find a shekel; take that and give it to them for me and for
* yourself."

Teaching about the community

Who is the greatest in the Kingdom of heaven?
Mt 18,1-5 (Mk 9, 33-37 Lk 9, 46-48)

** 1At that time the disciples came to Jesus, saying, "Who is the greatest in the kingdom of heaven?" 2And calling to him a child, he put him in the midst of them, 3and said, "Truly, I say to you, unless you turn and become like children, you will never enter the kingdom of heaven. 4Whoever humbles himself like this child, he is the greatest in the kingdom of heaven.

5Whoever receives one such child in my name receives me."

Woe to anyone who interferes with the faith of little ones
Mt 18, 6-9 (Mk 9, 41-50 Lk 17, 1-3)

6"But whoever causes one of these little ones who believe in me to sin, it would be better for him to have a great millstone fastened round his neck and to be drowned in the depth of the sea.

7Woe to the world for temptations to sin! For it is necessary that temptations

* The annual tax was the equivalent of the average pay for two days' work, and was paid for the temple at Jerusalem, i.e. for the "house of God." Jesus, being the Son of God, claimed to be exempt from such a duty.

** Here begins the fourth discourse of Matthew's gospel, that about the community. Various sayings of Jesus are collected, exhortations and rules for the life of the Church. The chief stress is laid on humility and simplicity, care for the most neglected, unity and forgiveness.

come, but woe to the man by whom the temptation comes! 8 And if your hand or your foot causes you to sin, cut it off and throw it from you; it is better for you to enter life maimed or lame than with two hands or two feet to be thrown into the eternal fire. 9 And if your eye causes you to sin, pluck it out and throw it from you; it is better for you to enter life with one eye than with two eyes to be thrown into the hell of fire."

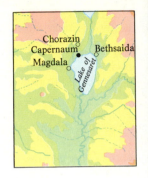

The will of the Father: not even one of these little ones shall be lost
Mt 18, 10-14

10 "See that you do not despise one of these little ones; 11 for I tell you that in heaven their angels always behold the face of my Father who is in heaven. 12 What do you think? If a man has a hundred sheep, and one of them has gone astray, does he not leave the ninety-nine on the hills and go in search of the one that went astray? 13 And if he finds it, truly, I say to you, he rejoices over it more than over the ninety-nine that never went astray? 14 So it is not the will of my Father who is in heaven that one of these little ones should
* perish."

Jesus teaches brotherly correction
Mt 18, 15-17

15 "If your brother sins against you, go and tell him his fault, between you
** and him alone. If he listens to you, you

* The term "little ones" is the key-word of this first part of the discourse and has various meanings; one must become little in mind like children, and welcome little ones in the name of Jesus; the neglected are little, and so are those of no account, the weak in faith, sinners and those who go astray.

** It is humble and sincere love which drives us to correct a brother and which suggests the method of doing so: the purpose is always a change of mind, to "win" the brother for Christ.

have gained your brother. ¹⁶ But if he does not listen, take one or two others along with you, that every word may be confirmed by the evidence of two or three witnesses. ¹⁷ If he refuses to listen to them, tell it to the church; and if he refuses to listen even to the church, let him be to you as a Gentile and a tax collector."

Jesus confers on the apostles the task of forgiveness
Mt 18,18

* ¹⁸ "Truly, I say to you, whatever you bind on earth shall be bound in heaven, and whatever you loose on earth shall be loosed in heaven."

Jesus is present in the community gathered in his name
Mt 18, 19-20

¹⁹ "Again I say to you, if two of you agree on earth about anything they ask, it will be done for them by my Father in heaven. ²⁰ For where two or three are gathered in my name, there am I in the ** midst of them."

Forgive your brother from your heart
Mt 18, 21-35 (Lk 17, 3-4)

²¹ Then Peter came up and said to him, "Lord, how often shall my brother sin against me, and I forgive him? As many as seven times?" ²² Jesus said to him, "I do not say to you seven times, but *** seventy times seven.

* The authority already conferred on Peter, is given to the apostles also.

** To be gathered together in Jesus' name means to be united in the search for unity in him. Then Jesus is present and makes prayer effective.

*** Seven is for the Jews the number of completeness. "Seventy times seven" therefore means "completeness of completeness" i.e. one must always forgive.

203

23 Therefore the kingdom of heaven may be compared to a king who wished to settle accounts with his servants. 24 When he began the reckoning, one was brought to him who owed him ten * thousand talents; 25 and as he could not pay, his lord ordered him to be sold, with his wife and children and all that he had, and payment to be made. 26 So the servant fell on his knees, imploring him, 'Lord, have patience with me, and I will pay you everything.' 27 And out of pity for him the lord of that servant released him and forgave him the debt. 28 But that same servant, as he went out, came upon one of his fellow servants who owed him a hundred denarii; and seizing him by the throat he said, 'Pay what you owe.' 29 So his fellow servant fell down and besought him, 'Have patience with me, and I will pay you.' 30 He refused and went and put him in prison till he should pay the debt. 31 When his fellow servants saw what had taken place, they were greatly distressed, and they went and reported to their lord all that had taken place. 32 Then his lord summoned him and said to him, 'You wicked servant! I forgave you all that debt because you besought me; 33 and should not you have had mercy on your fellow servant, as I had mercy on you?' 34 And in anger his lord delivered him to the jailers, till he should pay all his debt. 35 So also my heavenly Father will do to every one of you, if you do not forgive your brother from your heart."

* It was about sixty million pence that he owed his master, compared with the hundred pence owed to him by his fellow servant. The enormous difference is emphasized on purpose; we cannot be mean and severe on others because God has already forgiven us very much more without stint.

204

V - THE JOURNEY TO JERUSALEM AND JESUS' TEACHINGS

After the Galilee "crisis" Jesus sets out on his journey to Jerusalem and his passion. It is Luke who brings into special prominence that momentous journey, so much so, indeed, as to make it the most characteristic section of his gospel. In fact he there puts together the greater part of the material which he diligently collected and which is not to be found in the other gospels.

The common theme of the section is the journey and Jesus' impulsion towards Jerusalem where his death, resurrection and ascension will be accomplished. From Jerusalem the Church will set out on its journey. In this setting and in the light of these facts are found various teachings of Jesus, which deal with the manner of following him with the death and resurrection in mind.

A Samaritan village on the borders of Galilee and on the road which leads to Jerusalem (cf. Lk. 9, 52-53).

Jesus and the disciples

Jesus sets out for Jerusalem
Lk 9,51 (Mt 19, 1-2 Mk 10, 1)

51 When the days drew near for him to be received up, he set his face to go to Jerusalem.

Jesus is not welcome in Samaria
Lk 9, 52-56

52 And he sent messengers ahead of him, who went and entered a village of the Samaritans, to make ready for him; 53 but the people would not receive him, because his face was set toward Jerusalem. 54 And when his disciples James and John saw it, they said, "Lord, do you want us to bid fire come down from heaven and consume them?" 55 But he turned and rebuked them. 56 And they went on to another village.

*

Conditions for following Jesus
Lk 9, 57-62 (Mt 8, 18-22)

57 As they were going along the road, a man said to him, "I will follow you wherever you go." 58 And Jesus said to him, "Foxes have holes, and birds of the air have nests; but the Son of man has nowhere to lay his head." 59 To another he said, "Follow me." But he said, "Lord, let me first go and bury my father." 60 But he said to him, "Leave the dead to bury their own dead; but as for you, go and proclaim the kingdom

**

* There was a cordial mutual contempt between the inhabitants of Samaria and those of Jerusalem and Judaea.

** Jesus goes to the roots, and wants no compromise: he is to be followed in poverty, immediately, and without looking back.

207

A field of grain which is already whitening for an abundant harvest. Jesus often made use of this image to illustrate the greatness and urgency of his work (cf. Lk. 10, 2).

of God." ⁶¹ Another said, "I will follow you, Lord; but let me first say farewell to those at my home." ⁶² Jesus said to him, "No one who puts his hand to the plough and looks back is fit for the kingdom of God."

The mission of the disciples: "He who hears you hears me"
Lk 10, 1-16 (Mt 11, 20-24)

* ¹ After this the Lord appointed seventy others, and sent them on ahead of him, two by two, into every town and place where he himself was about to come. ² And he said to them, "The harvest is plentiful, but the labourers are few; pray therefore the Lord of the harvest to send out labourers into his harvest. ³ Go your way; behold, I send you out as lambs in the midst of wolves. ⁴ Carry no purse, no bag, no sandals; and salute ** no one on the road. ⁵ Whatever house you enter, first say, 'Peace be to this house!' ⁶ And if a son of peace is there, your peace shall rest upon him; but if not, it shall return to you. ⁷ And remain in the same house, eating and drinking what they provide, for the labourer deserves his wages; do not go from house to house. ⁸ Whenever you enter a town and they receive you, eat what is set before you; ⁹ heal the sick in it and say to them, 'The kingdom of God has come near to you.' ¹⁰ But whenever you enter a town and they do not receive you, go into its streets and say, ¹¹ 'Even the dust of your town that clings to our feet, we wipe off against you; never-

* In addition to the mission of the Twelve in Galilee, Luke mentions this one of 72 disciples, a foretelling of the mission to the Gentiles. Many of Jesus' words are the same as those reported in Mt. 10.

** "Greet no man by the way" means simply "do not lose precious time on the road in the long compliments normal among orientals."

209

The ruins of the synagogue at Chorazin, one of the towns in Galilee where Jesus worked so many miracles and which were not converted.

theless know this, that the kingdom of God has come near.' ¹² I tell you, it shall be more tolerable on that day for Sodom than for that town.

* ¹³ Woe to you, Chorazin! woe to you, Bethsaida! for if the mighty works done in you had been done in Tyre and Sidon, they would have repented long ago, sitting in sackcloth and ashes. ¹⁴ But it shall be more tolerable in the judgment for Tyre and Sidon than for you. ¹⁵ And you, Capernaum, will you be exalted to heaven? You shall be brought down to Hades.

¹⁶ He who hears you hears me, and he who rejects you rejects me, and he who rejects me rejects him who sent me."

The return of the disciples
Lk 10, 17-20

¹⁷ The seventy returned with joy, saying, "Lord, even the demons are subject to us in your name!" ¹⁸ And he said to them, "I saw Satan fall like lightning from heaven. ¹⁹ Behold, I have given you authority to tread upon serpents and scorpions, and over all the power of the enemy; and nothing shall hurt you. ²⁰ Nevertheless do not rejoice in this, that the spirits are subject to you; but rejoice that your names are written in heaven."

Revelation to 'babes'
Lk 10, 21-24 (Mt 11, 25-30)

²¹ In that same hour he rejoiced in the Holy Spirit and said, "I thank thee,

* Jesus himself experienced rejection. But woe to those who reject their own salvation.

211

A "Khan" on the desert road from Jerusalem to Jericho. It was a sort of inn, which provided a halt for travellers. Here Jesus set the scene of the parable of the good Samaritan (Lk. 10, 25-35).

Father, Lord of heaven and earth, that thou hast hidden these things from the wise and understanding and revealed them to babes; yea, Father, for such was thy gracious will. 22 All things have been delivered to me by my Father; and no one knows who the Son is except the Father, or who the Father is except the Son and any one to whom the Son
* chooses to reveal him."

23 Then turning to the disciples he said privately, "Blessed are the eyes which see what you see! 24 For I tell you that many prophets and kings desired to see what you see, and did not see it, and to hear what you hear, and did not hear it."

Love of one's neighbour, prayer, honesty

Loving one's neighbour: the good Samaritan
Lk 10, 25-37

25 And behold, a lawyer stood up to put him to the test, saying, "Teacher, what shall I do to inherit eternal life?" 26 He said to him, "What is written in the law? How do you read?" 27 And he
** answered, "You shall love the Lord your God with all your heart, and with all your soul, and with all your strength, and with all your mind: and your neighbour as yourself." 28 And he said to him, "You have answered right; do this, and you will live."

29 But he, desiring to justify himself, said to Jesus, "And who is my neigh-

* Jesus' very beautiful prayer about the revelation given by his Father to simple people ended, according to Matthew, with the invitation: "Come to me, all who labour and are heavy laden, and I will give you rest. Take my yoke upon you, and learn from me; for I am gentle and lowly in heart, and you will find rest for your souls. For my yoke is easy, and my burden is light" (Mt. 11, 28-30).

** One of these two commandments is found in Deut. 6, 5, the other in Lev. 19, 18.

Bethany, 3 km. east of Jerusalem. Here Jesus was often a guest of Lazarus and the latter's sisters, Martha and Mary. One of those visits was the occasion of the teaching reported by Lk. 10, 38-42.

bour?" [30] Jesus replied, "A man was going down from Jerusalem to Jericho, and he fell among robbers, who stripped him and beat him, and departed, leaving him half dead. [31] Now by chance a priest was going down that road; and when he saw him he passed by on the other side. [32] So likewise a Levite, when he came to the place and saw him, passed by on the other side. [33] But a Samaritan, as he journeyed, came to where he was; and when he saw him, he had compassion, [34] and went to him and bound up his wounds, pouring on oil and wine; then he set him on his own beast and brought him to an inn, and took care of him. [35] And the next day he took out two denarii and gave them to the innkeeper, saying, 'Take care of him; and whatever more you spend, I will repay you when I come back.' [36] Which of these three, * do you think, proved neighbour to the man who fell among the robbers?" [37] He said, "The one who showed mercy on him." And Jesus said to him, "Go and do likewise."

Jesus in the house of Martha and Mary
Lk 10, 38-42

[38] Now as they went on their way, he entered a village; and a woman named Martha received him into her house. [39] And she had a sister called Mary, who sat at the Lord's feet and listened to his teaching. [40] But Martha was distracted with much serving; and she went to him and said, "Lord, do you not care that my sister has left me to

* A neighbour is also a stranger, an enemy, anyone in need. The Samaritan made himself a neighbour by going to the injured man and giving him practical help.

215

serve alone? Tell her then to help me."
41 But the Lord answered her, "Martha,
Martha, you are anxious and troubled
about many things; 42 one thing is need-
ful. Mary has chosen the good portion,
which shall not be taken away from
her."

Jesus teaches to pray
Lk 11, 1-4

1 He was praying in a certain place,
and when he ceased, one of his disciples
said to him, "Lord, teach us to pray, as
John taught his disciples." 2 And he said
to them, "When you pray, say: 'Father,
hallowed be thy name. Thy kingdom
come. 3 Give us each day our daily bread;
4 and forgive us our sins, for we ourselves forgive every one who is indebted
to us; and lead us not into temptation."

Pray constantly and trustfully
Lk 11, 5-13

5 And he said to them, "Which of you
who has a friend will go to him at midnight and say to him, 'Friend, lend me
three loaves; 6 for a friend of mine has
arrived on a journey, and I have nothing
to set before him'; 7 and he will answer
from within, 'Do not bother me; the
door is now shut, and my children are
with me in bed; I cannot get up and
give you anything'? 8 I tell you, though
he will not get up and give him anything
because he is his friend, yet because
of his importunity he will rise and give
him whatever he needs. 9 And I tell you,

*   Jesus does not wish
to condemn the activi-
ty of Martha, but to
record that for a disci-
ple the only One who
gives value to anything
is God. Therefore the
Christian sets aside a
time entirely for the
Lord and for listening
to his word.

**   Luke here presents
a shorter version, re-
duced to its essentials,
of the prayer Jesus
taught, which was re-
ported by Matthew in
the Sermon on the
Mount.

* Ask, and it will be given you; seek, and you will find; knock, and it will be opened to you. ¹⁰ For every one who asks receives, and he who seeks finds, and to him who knocks it will be opened. ¹¹ What father among you, if his son asks for a fish, will instead of a fish give him a serpent; ¹² or if he asks for an egg, will give him a scorpion? ¹³ If you then, who are evil, know how to give good gifts to your children, how much more will the heavenly Father give the Holy Spirit to those who ask him!"

Indictment of the Pharisees and doctors of the Law
Lk 11, 37-48; 52-54; 12, 1

³⁷ While he was speaking, a Pharisee asked him to dine with him; so he went in and sat at table. ³⁸ The Pharisee was astonished to see that he did not first
** wash before dinner. ³⁹ And the Lord said to him, "Now you Pharisees cleanse the outside of the cup and of the dish, but inside you are full of extortion and wickedness. ⁴⁰ You fools! Did not he who made the outside make the inside also? ⁴¹ But give for alms those things which are within; and behold, everything is clean for you.
⁴² But woe to you Pharisees! for you tithe the mint and rue and every herb, and neglect justice and the love of God; these you ought to have done, without neglecting the others. ⁴³ Woe to you Pharisees! for you love the best seat in the synagogues and salutations in the market

* The disciple turns to God with the assurance with which he turns to a friend, persisting even when the latter seems to refuse, and with the trust with which someone turns to his own father. The heavenly Father always wants the true good of his children and above all desires to give them the Spirit.

** Jesus omits the washings so as to protest against the formalism of the Pharisees. Thus he is able to explain how the purely outward observance of the law is blameworthy in God's sight and shows insincerity of mind. The approach to God must be above all heartfelt.

217

Jerusalem. The tombs in the valley of the Kedron. Jesus rebuked the Pharisees for building the tombs of the prophets who had died instead of listening to those who were alive (Lk. 11, 47-48).

places. ⁴⁴Woe to you! for you are like graves which are not seen, and men walk over them without knowing it."

⁴⁵One of the lawyers answered him, "Teacher, in saying this you reproach us also." ⁴⁶And he said. "Woe to you lawyers also! for you load men with burdens hard to bear, and you yourselves do not touch the burdens with one of your fingers. ⁴⁷Woe to you! for you build the tombs of the prophets whom your fathers killed. ⁴⁸So you are witnesses and consent to the deeds of your fathers; for they killed them, and you build their tombs.

⁵²Woe to you lawyers! for you have taken away the key of knowledge; you did not enter yourselves, and you hindered those who were entering."

⁵³As he went away from there, the scribes and the Pharisees began to press him hard, and to provoke him to speak of many things, ⁵⁴lying in wait for him, to catch at something he might say.

¹In the meantime, when so many thousands of the multitude had gathered together that they trod upon one another, he began to say to his disciples first, "Beware of the leaven of the Pharisees, which is hypocrisy."

Poverty, watchfulness, conversion

"Beware of all covetousness"
Lk 12, 13-15

¹³One of the multitude said to him, "Teacher, bid my brother divide the in-

* The scribes considered that they held a monopoly of knowledge of the Scriptures. In reality, they oppressed men's consciences, and prevented both themselves and others from accepting the news of freedom and salvation brought by Jesus.

heritance with me." ¹⁴ But he said to him, "Man, who made me a judge or divider over you?" ¹⁵ And he said to them, "Take heed, and beware of all covetousness; for a man's life does not consist in the abundance of his possessions."

Parable of the rich fool
Lk 12, 16-21

¹⁶ And he told them a parable, saying, "The land of a rich man brought forth plentifully; ¹⁷ and he thought to himself, 'What shall I do, for I have nowhere to store my crops?' ¹⁸ And he said, 'I will do this: I will pull down my barns, and build larger ones; and there I will store all my grain and my goods. ¹⁹ And I will say to my soul, Soul, you have ample goods laid up for many years; take your ease, eat, drink, be merry.' ²⁰ But God said to him, 'Fool! This night your soul is required of you; and the things you have prepared, whose will they be?' ²¹ So is he who lays up treasure for himself, and is not rich toward God."

"Where your treasure is, there will your heart be also"
Lk 12, 32-34

³² "Fear not, little flock, for it is your Father's good pleasure to give you the kingdom. ³³ Sell your possessions, and give alms; provide yourselves with purses that do not grow old, with a treasure in the heavens that does not fail, where no thief approaches and no moth des-

*   It is not Jesus' task to decide on the division of material goods among men. He always aims at the inner conversion of a man. From a converted heart, detached from unreal and deceptive material riches, will spring the solid virtues of justice and charity.

220

troys. ³⁴ For where your treasure is, there will your heart be also."

Jesus urges watchfulness
Lk 12, 35-40 (Mt 24, 42-44 Mk 13, 33-37)

* ³⁵ "Let your loins be girded and your lamps burning, ³⁶ and be like men who are waiting for their master to come home from the marriage feast, so that they may open to him at once when he comes and knocks. ³⁷ Blessed are those servants whom the master finds awake when he comes; truly, I say to you, he will gird himself and have them sit at table, and he will come and serve them. ³⁸ If he comes in the second watch, or in the third, and finds them so, blessed are those servants! ³⁹ But know this, that if the householder had known at what hour the thief was coming, he would have been awake and would not have left his house to be broken into. ⁴⁰ You also must be ready; for the Son of man is coming at an hour you do not expect."

Parable of the watchful and trustworthy servant
Lk 12, 41-48 (Mt 24, 45-51)

⁴¹ Peter said, "Lord, are you telling this parable for us or for all?" ⁴² And the Lord said, "Who then is the faithful and wise steward, whom his master will set over his household, to give them their portion of food at the proper time? ⁴³ Blessed is that servant whom his master when he comes will find so doing.

* Waiting for the Lord is a mark of the disciple, who will not go to sleep in everyday routine, but is always active and ready; vigilance is a sign of faith, hope and adherence to him. These three little parables show different aspects of this theme; being wide awake, the unexpected coming, the conscientious fulfilling of one's duty, especially if one is in a position of responsibility.

221

⁴⁴ Truly I tell you, he will set him over all his possessions. ⁴⁵ But if that servant says to himself, 'My master is delayed in coming, and begins to beat the menservants and the maidservants, and to eat and drink and get drunk, ⁴⁶ the master of that servant will come on a day when he does not expect him and at an hour he does not know, and will punish him, and put him with the unfaithful. ⁴⁷ And that servant who knew his master's will, but did not make ready or act according to his will, shall receive a severe beating. ⁴⁸ But he who did not know, and did what deserved a beating, shall receive a light beating. Every one to whom much is given, of him will much be required; and of him to whom men commit much they will demand the more."

Jesus asks for enthusiasm and heroism
Lk 12, 49-53

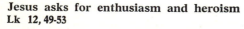

* ⁴⁹ "I came to cast fire upon the earth; and would that it were already kindled! ⁵⁰ I have a baptism to be baptized with; and how I am constrained until it is accomplished! ⁵¹ Do you think that I have come to give peace on earth? No, I tell you, but rather division; ⁵² for henceforth in one house there will be five divided, three against two and two against three; ⁵³ they will be divided, father against son and son against father, mother against daughter and daughter against her mother, mother-in-law against her daughter-in-law and daughter-in-law against her mother-in-law."

* Jesus wishes to speak of the renewal which he has come to bring to earth; it is like a spark which must set the world on fire, a fire which does not admit neutrality or compromise. The "baptism" to which Jesus refers is his passion.

222

Jesus urges men to conversion while there is time
Lk 12, 54-59

⁵⁴ He also said to the multitudes, "When you see a cloud rising in the west, you say at once, 'A shower is coming'; and so it happens. ⁵⁵ And when you see the south wind blowing you say, 'There will be scorching heat'; and it happens. ⁵⁶ You hypocrites! You know how to interpret the appearance of earth and sky; but why do you not know how to interpret the present time? *

⁵⁷ And why do you not judge for yourselves what is right? ⁵⁸ As you go with your accuser before the magistrate, make an effort to settle with him on the way, lest he drag you to the judge, and the judge hand you over to the officer, and the officer put you in prison. ⁵⁹ I tell you, you will never get out till you have paid the very last copper."

The need for a change in life
Lk 13, 1-5

¹ There were some present at that very time who told him of the Galileans whose blood Pilate had mingled with ** their sacrifices. ² And he answered them, "Do you think that these Galileans were worse sinners than all the other Galileans, because they suffered thus? ³ I tell you, No; but unless you repent you will all likewise perish. ⁴ Or those eighteen upon whom the tower in Siloam fell and killed them, do you think that they were worse offenders than all the

* As it is possible to foretell the weather from certain signs, so one must pay attention to, and then be really ready to recognize, God's signs, and to repent before coming into the presence of the Judge.

** It seems that during a Jewish feast in the Temple, Pilate suspected a revolt and intervened, causing the death of some Galileans. Public opinion was that if disaster strikes anyone, it is a sign that he has sinned and that God is punishing him at once. Jesus challenges this kind of thought and instead seriously warns every one to change his life.

223

Siloam (Jerusalem): the round base of a tower. Jesus spoke about the collapse of a tower at Siloam which caused the death of eighteen people (Lk. 13, 4).

others who dwelt in Jerusalem? ⁵ I tell you, No; but unless you repent you will all likewise perish."

The urgency of a change in life
Lk 13, 6-9

⁶ And he told this parable: "A man had a fig tree planted in his vineyard; and he came seeking fruit on it and found none. ⁷ And he said to the vinedresser, 'Lo, these three years I have come seeking fruit on this fig tree, and I find none. Cut it down; why should it use up the ground?" ⁸ And he answered him, 'Let it alone, sir, this year also, * till I dig about it and put on manure. ⁹ And if it bears fruit next year, well and good; but if not, you can cut it down.' "

Jesus heals a woman on the sabbath
Lk 13, 10-17

Tiberias •

Samaria •

Jerusalem •

¹⁰ Now he was teaching in one of the synagogues on the sabbath. ¹¹ And there was a woman who had had a spirit of infirmity for eighteen years; she was bent over and could not fully straighten herself. ¹² And when Jesus saw her, he called her and said to her, "Woman, you are freed from your infirmity." ¹³ And he laid his hands upon her, and immediately she was made straight, and she praised God. ¹⁴ But the ruler of the synagogue, indignant because Jesus had healed on the sabbath, said to the people, "There are six days on which work ought to be done; come on those

*   God is patient and still allows the possibility of repentance.

225

days and be healed, and not on the
* sabbath day." ¹⁵ Then the Lord answered
him, "You hypocrites! Does not each
of you on the sabbath untie his ox or
his ass from the manger, and lead it
away to water it? ¹⁶ And ought not this
woman, a daughter of Abraham whom
Satan bound for eighteen years, be loosed from this bond on the sabbath day?"
¹⁷ As he said this, all his adversaries
were put to shame; and all the people
rejoiced at all the glorious things that
were done by him.

The door to salvation is narrow
Lk 13, 22-30

²² He went on his way through towns
and villages, teaching, and journeying
toward Jerusalem. ²³ And some one said
to him, "Lord, will those who are saved
be few?" And he said to them, ²⁴ "Strive
to enter by the narrow door; for many,
I tell you, will seek to enter and will
not be able. ²⁵ When once the householder has risen up and shut the door, you
will begin to stand outside and to knock
at the door, saying, 'Lord, open to us.'
He will answer you, 'I do not know
where you come from.' ²⁶ Then you will
begin to say, 'We ate and drank in your
presence, and you taught in our streets.'
²⁷ But he will say, 'I tell you, I do not
know where you come from; depart
from me, all you workers of iniquity!'
²⁸ There you will weep and gnash your
teeth, when you see Abraham and Isaac
and Jacob and all the prophets in the

*   In this incident, as
in others of a similar
kind, Jesus wished to
protest against an ob-
servance of the sabbath
rest which had become
entirely external, with-
out any spirit of cha-
rity.

kingdom of God and you yourselves thrust out. ²⁹ And men will come from east and west, and from north and south, and sit at table in the kingdom of God. ³⁰ And behold, some are last who will be first, and some are first who will be last."

Jesus replies to Herod's threats
Lk 13, 31-33

³¹ At that very hour some Pharisees came, and said to him, "Get away from here, for Herod wants to kill you." ³² And he said to them, "Go and tell that fox, 'Behold, I cast out demons and perform cures today and tomorrow, and the third day I finish my course. ³³ Nevertheless I must go on my way today and tomorrow and the day following; for it cannot be that a prophet should perish away from Jerusalem.' "

A free gift and a generous reply

Another healing on the sabbath day
Lk 14, 1-6

¹ One sabbath when he went to dine at the house of a ruler who belonged to the Pharisees, they were watching him. ² And behold, there was a man before him who had dropsy. ³ And Jesus spoke to the lawyers and Pharisees, saying, "It is lawful to heal on the sabbath, or not?" ⁴ But they were silent. Then he took him and healed him, and

*   The Jewish people is the people chosen by God ("the first") but if it does not accept Jesus it will be rejected, and, in its place other peoples ("the last") will be called from all parts of the earth into the Kingdom of God.

**   The activity of Jesus appeared dangerous to the policies of Herod, who therefore feared and threatened him. But Jesus replied without any sort of fear that his time had not yet come and his life would end at Jerusalem. The "third day" refers to the passion which by then was not far away.

227

The Lake of Gennesaret at the level of Tiberias, the town which Herod
Antipas had founded in honour of Tiberius. "That fox" Herod wanted
to seize Jesus in the midst of his work.

let him go. ⁵ And he said to them, "Which of you, having an ass or an ox that has fallen into a well, will not immediately pull him out on a sabbath day?" ⁶ And they could not reply to this.

The criterion of choice: the lowest place and the poor
Lk 14, 7-14

⁷ Now he told a parable to those who were invited, when he marked how they chose the places of honour, saying to them, ⁸ "When you are invited by any one to a marriage feast, do not sit down in a place of honour, lest a more eminent man than you be invited by him; ⁹ and he who invited you both will come, and say to you, 'Give place to this man', and then you will begin with shame to take the lowest place. ¹⁰ But when you are invited, go and sit in the lowest place, so that when your host comes he may say to you, 'Friend, go up higher'; then you will be honoured in the presence of all who sit at table with you. ¹¹ For every one who exalts himself will be humbled, and he who humbles himself will be exalted."

* ¹² He said also to the man who had invited him, "When you give a dinner or a banquet, do not invite your friends or your brothers or your kinsmen or rich neighbours, lest they also invite you in return, and you be repaid. ¹³ But when you give a feast, invite the poor, the maimed, the lame, the blind, ¹⁴ and you will be blessed, because they cannot

* The banquet was the occasion for a series of lessons about the Kingdom of God as a feast. Humility, unselfishness and gratitude are the characteristics of those who have received God's invitation and gift. This is the law of grace: he who has received freely shall give freely and receive a blessing.

229

repay you. You will be repaid at the resurrection of the just."

The parable of the great supper and the invited guests
Lk 14, 15-24

15 When one of those who sat at table with him heard this, he said to him, "Blessed is he who shall eat bread in the kingdom of God!" 16 But he said to him, "A man once gave a great banquet, and invited many; 17 and at the time for the banquet he sent his servant to say to those who had been invited, 'Come; for all is now ready.' 18 But they all alike began to make excuses. The first said to him, 'I have bought a field, and I must go out and see it; I pray you, have me excused.' 19 And another said, 'I have bought five yoke of oxen, and I go to examine them; I pray you, have me excused.' 20 And another said, 'I have married a wife, and therefore I cannot come.' 21 So the servant came and reported this to his master. Then the householder in anger said to his servant, 'Go out quickly to the streets and lanes of the city, and bring in the poor and

* maimed and blind and lame.' 22 And the servant said, 'Sir, what you commanded has been done, and still there is room.' 23 And the master said to the servant, 'Go out to the highways and hedges, and compel people to come in, that my house may be filled. 24 For I tell you, none of those men who were invited shall taste my banquet.' "

* As those first invited, the leaders of the Jewish people, did not wish to respond, there were others, the poor, sinners, and even Gentiles who would share in the feast offered by God.

Following Jesus
involves a complete and radical change
Lk 14, 25-35

25 Now great multitudes accompanied him; and he turned and said to them, 26 "If any one comes to me and does not hate his own father and mother and wife and children and brothers and sisters, yes, and even his own life, he cannot be my disciple. 27 Whoever does not bear his own cross and come after me, cannot be my disciple. 28 For which of you, desiring to build a tower, does not first sit down and count the cost, whether he has enough to complete it? 29 Otherwise, when he has laid a foundation, and is not able to finish, all who see it begin to mock him, 30 saying. 'This man began to build, and was not able to finish.' 31 Or what king, going to encounter another king in war, will not sit down first and take counsel whether he is able with ten thousand to meet him who comes against him with twenty thousand? 32 And if not, while the other is yet a great way off, he sends an embassy and ask terms of peace. 33 So therefore, whoever of you does not renounce all that he has cannot be my disciple.

34 "Salt is good; but if salt has lost its taste, how shall its saltness be restored? 35 It is fit neither for the land nor for the dunghill; men throw it away. He who has ears to hear, let him hear."

* For easterns a comparison becomes a confrontation. Preferring one thing to another becomes "loving" the former and "hating" the latter. Jesus means that anyone who wants to follow him must be able to choose him in preference to any other person, even the dearest. This requirement by Jesus requires careful consideration and firm will-power.

A flock on the Palestinian hills. From the life of a shepherd Jesus drew ideas and illustrations for speaking of the Father's love for men, which shows itself in his own kindness towards sinners (cf. Lk. 15, 4-7).

Parables of mercy

The parable of the lost and found sheep
Lk 15, 1-7

Tiberias •

Samaria •

Jerusalem •

¹ Now the tax collectors and sinners were all drawing near to hear him. ² And the Pharisees and the scribes murmured, saying, "This man receives sin-
* ners and eats with them."

³ So he told them this parable: ⁴ "What man of you, having a hundred sheep, if he has lost one of them, does not leave the ninety-nine in the wilderness, and go after the one which is lost, until he finds it? ⁵ And when he has found it, he lays it on his shoulders, rejoicing. ⁶ And when he comes home, he calls together his friends and his neighbours, saying to them, 'Rejoice with me, for I have found my sheep which was lost.' ⁷ Just so, I tell you, there will be more joy in heaven over one sinner who repents than over ninety-nine righteous persons who need no repentance."

The parable of the lost and found coin
Lk 15, 8-10

** ⁸ "Or what woman, having ten silver coins, if she loses one coin, does not light a lamp and sweep the house and seek diligently until she finds it? ⁹ And when she has found it, she calls together her friends and neighbours, saying, 'Rejoice with me, for I have found the coin which I had lost.' ¹⁰ Just so, I tell you, there is joy before the angels of God over one sinner who repents."

* Jesus' kindness to sinners aroused grumbling among the Pharisees and Doctors of the Law. Jesus vindicated himself with three very lovely parables, contrasting with their meanness the love of God for sinners, his desire to recover them and his joy when even one returns to him.

** The drachma was a Greek coin also used in Palestine. It was the equivalent of a Roman denarius and was a day's pay.

The love of the father welcoming the prodigal son on his return
Lk 15, 11-32

* ¹¹ And he said, "There was a man who had two sons; ¹² and the younger of them said to his father, 'Father, give me the share of property that falls to me.' And he divided his living between them. ¹³ Not many days later, the younger son gathered all he had and took his journey into a far country, and there he squandered his property in loose living. ¹⁴ And when he had spent everything, a great famine arose in that country, and he began to be in want. ¹⁵ So he went and joined himself to one of the citizens of that country, who sent him into his ** fields to feed swine. ¹⁶ And he would gladly have fed on the pods that the swine ate; and no one gave him anything. ¹⁷ But when he came to himself he said, 'How many of my father's hired servants have bread enough and to spare, but I perish here with hunger! ¹⁸ I will arise and go to my father, and I will say to him, "Father, I have sinned against heaven and before you; ¹⁹ I am no longer worthy to be called your son; treat me as one of your hired servants."' ²⁰ And he arose and came to his father. But while he was yet at a distance, his father saw him and had compassion, and ran and embraced him and kissed him. ²¹ And the son said to him, 'Father, I have sinned against heaven and before you; I am no longer worthy to be called your son.' ²² But the father said to his servants, 'Bring quickly the best robe,

Tiberias •

Samaria •

Jordan

Jerusalem •

* This is the most interesting and touching parable of the merciful love of God the Father for sinners.

** The Jews loathed these animals which they held to be unclean. The young man, far from his father, has reached the limit of wretchedness.

234

and put it on him; and put a ring on his hand, and shoes on his feet; 23 and bring the fatted calf and kill it, and let us eat and make merry; 24 for this my son was dead, and is alive again; he was lost, and is found.' And they began to make merry.

* 25 "Now his elder son was in the field; and as he came and drew near to the house, he heard music and dancing. 26 And he called one of the servants and asked what this meant. 27 And he said to him, 'Your brother has come, and your father has killed the fatted calf, because he has received him safe and sound.' 28 But he was angry and refused to go in. His father came out and entreated him, 29 but he answered his father, 'Lo, these many years I have served you, and I never disobeyed your command; yet you never gave me a kid, that I might make merry with my friends. 30 But when this son of yours came, who has devoured your living with harlots, you killed for him the fatted calf!' 31 And he said to him, 'Son, you are always with me, and all that is mine is yours. 32 It was fitting to make merry and be glad, for this your brother was dead, and is alive; he was lost, and is found.' "

The use of worldly goods

The parable of the clever steward
Lk 16, 1-15

1 He also said to the disciples, "There was a rich man who had a steward, and charges were brought to him that this

* The second part of the parable shows to the Pharisees how even a person who has always remained in God's house may really be living far from him and, isolated in his own proud and wicked heart, unable to share in the Father's love and joy.

man was wasting his goods. ² And he called him and said to him, 'What is this that I hear about you? Turn in the account of your stewardship, for you *can no longer be steward.' ³ And the steward said to himself, 'What shall I do, since my master is taking the stewardship away from me? I am not strong enough to dig, and I am ashamed to beg. ⁴ I have decided what to do, so that people may receive me into their houses when I am put out of the stewardship.' ⁵ So, summoning his master's debtors one by one, he said to the first, 'How much do you owe my master?' ⁶ He said, 'A hundred measures of oil.' And he said to him, 'Take your bill, and sit down quickly and write fifty.' ⁷ Then he said to another, 'And how much do you owe?' He said, 'A hundred measures of wheat.' He said to him, 'Take your bill, and write eighty.' ⁸ The master commended the dishonest steward for his prudence; for the sons of this world are wiser in their own generation than the sons of light. ⁹ And I tell you, make friends for yourselves by means of unrighteous mammon, so that when it fails they may receive you into the eternal habitations.

¹⁰ "He who is faithful in a very little is faithful also in much; and he who is dishonest in a very little is dishonest also in much. ¹¹ If then you have not been faithful in the unrighteous mammon, who will entrust to you the true **riches? ¹² And if you have not been faithful in that which is another's, who

* The parable is certainly not intended to justify, or suggest as a model, the theft perpetrated by the steward: Jesus means rather: as the dishonest are cunning, especially in times of difficulty, so you are to be cunning in doing good, particularly in giving to the poor.

** The first condition of sharing in God's riches is to be faithful in the use of worldly goods, which in comparison are worth very little. Wealth must be used with a really free heart, for the good of others; otherwise it becomes an idol. The Jews of that time held that riches were a sign of God's blessing, and

will give you that which is your own? ¹³ No servant can serve two masters; for either he will hate the one and love the other, or he will be devoted to the one and despise the other. You cannot serve God and mammon." ¹⁴ The Pharisees, who were lovers of money, heard all this, and they scoffed at him. ¹⁵ But he said to them, "You are those who justify yourselves before men, but God knows your hearts; for what is exalted among men is an abomination in the sight of God."

The Law and the Kingdom of God
Lk 16, 16-17 (Mt 11, 12-15)

* ¹⁶ "The law and the prophets were until John; since then the good news of the kingdom of God is preached, and every one enters it violently. ¹⁷ But it is easier for heaven and earth to pass away, than for one dot of the law to become void."

Parable of the poor Lazarus and the rascally rich man
Lk 16, 19-31

¹⁹ "There was a rich man, who was clothed in purple and fine linen and who feasted sumptuously every day. ²⁰ And at his gate lay a poor man named Lazarus, full of sores, ²¹ who desired to be fed with what fell from the rich man's table; moreover the dogs came and licked his sores. ²² The poor man died and was carried by the angels to Abraham's bosom. The rich man also died and was buried; ²³ and in Hades,

the richer the Pharisees were the surer they were that they were righteous. Jesus strongly criticized their ideas and their behaviour.

* The Old Testament ended with John the Baptist. The age of the New Covenant between God and man began with Jesus. Entry into it however requires effort and a firm choice.

237

Jenin. The mosque. According to tradition, this may have been the village, on the borders of Galilee and Samaria, where the ten lepers were cured (Lk. 17, 11-19).

* being in torment, he lifted up his eyes, and saw Abraham far off and Lazarus in his bosom. 24 And he called out, 'Father Abraham, have mercy upon me, and send Lazarus to dip the end of his finger in water and cool my tongue; for I am in anguish in this flame.' 25 But Abraham said, 'Son, remember that you in your lifetime received your good things, and Lazarus in like manner evil things, but now he is comforted here, and you are in anguish. 26 And besides all this, between us and you a great chasm has been fixed, in order that those who would pass from here to you may not be able, and none may cross from there to us.' 27 And he said, 'Then I beg you, father, to send him to my father's house, 28 for I have five brothers, so that he may warn them, lest they also come into this place of torment.' 29 But Abraham said, 'They have Moses and the prophets; let them hear them.' 30 And he said, 'No, father Abraham; but if some one goes to them from the dead, they will repent.' 31 He said to him, 'If they do not hear Moses and the prophets, neither will they be convinced if some one should rise from the dead.' "

The position of the disciple

"Increase our faith"
Lk 17, 5-6

5 The apostles said to the Lord, "In-
** crease our faith!" 6 And the Lord said, "If you had faith as a grain of mustard

*   The two pictures are contrasted with one another; the rich man is now unhappy, the poor is blessed. God overturns human value-judgments as we have seen in Luke's beatitudes. The parable is intended to give prominence to the danger of wealth, which makes a man selfish, blind to the poverty of others and deaf to the claims of God.

**   Faith must increase in strength and depth. With such a faith, things which are humanly speaking, impossible will be obtained from God, as is expressed in a concrete and enigmatic manner by the illustration of the tree uprooted and planted in the sea.

239

seed, you could say to this sycamine tree, 'Be rooted up, and be planted in the sea,' and it would obey you."

"We are unworthy servants..."
Lk 17, 7-10

⁷ "Will any one of you, who has a servant ploughing or keeping sheep, say to him when he has come in from the field, 'Come at once and sit down at table'? ⁸ Willl he not rather say to him, 'Prepare supper for me, and gird yourself and serve me, till I eat and drink; and afterward you shall eat and drink'? ⁹ Does he thank the servant because he did what was commanded? ¹⁰ So you also, when you have done all that is commanded you, say, 'We are unworthy servants; we have only done what was * our duty.' "

Jesus heals ten lepers: only one is grateful
Lk 17, 11-19

¹¹ On the way to Jerusalem he was passing along between Samaria and Galilee. ¹² And as he entered a village, he was met by ten lepers, who stood at a distance ¹³ and lifted up their voices and said, "Jesus, Master, have mercy on us." ¹⁴ When he saw them he said to them, "Go and show yourselves to the priests." And as they went they were cleansed. ¹⁵ Then one of them, when he saw that he was healed, turned back, praising God with a loud voice; ¹⁶ and he fell on his face at Jesus' feet, giving him thanks.

* Contrary to the thought of the Pharisees, Jesus teaches that a man must fulfil his own task humbly, without boasting or claiming rights in the sight of God.

Now he was a Samaritan. ¹⁷ Then said Jesus, "Were not ten cleansed? Where are the nine? ¹⁸ Was no one found to return and give praise to God except this foreigner?" ¹⁹ And he said to him, "Rise and go your way; your faith has made you well."

Samaria
Sichem
Fara
Jordan

*

Jesus speaks of his second coming
Lk 17, 20-37 (Mt 24, 23-28; 37-41   Mk 13, 21-23)

** ²⁰ Being asked by the Pharisees when the kingdom of God was coming, he answered them, "The kingdom of God is not coming with signs to be observed; ²¹ nor will they say, 'Lo, here it is!' or 'There!' for behold, the kingdom of God is in the midst of you."

²² And he said to the disciples, "The days are coming when you will desire to see one of the days of the Son of man, and you will not see it. ²³ And they will say to you, 'Lo, there!' or 'Lo, here!' Do not go, do not follow them. ²⁴ For as the lightning flashes and lights up the sky from one side to the other, so will the Son of man be in his day. ²⁵ But first he must suffer many things and be rejected by this generation. ²⁶ As it was in the days of Noah, so will it be in the days of the Son of man. ²⁷ They ate, they drank, they married, they were given in marriage, until the day when Noah entered the ark, and the flood came and destroyed them all. ²⁸ Likewise as it was in the days of Lot—they ate, they drank, they bought, they sold, they planted, they built, ²⁹ but on the day when Lot went out from Sodom fire

* The despised Samaritan is the only one to give thanks to Jesus. He is now not only "cured," but also "saved."

** The Kingdom of God is realized in two stages; it is already present now, if not in an obvious way, and demands resolution and zeal. It will be fully realized when Jesus, after his sufferings, returns in glory "in his own day." It will be a coming unexpected by men, who are thoughtless and concerned with worldly wealth; it will be perdition for those who have wanted to "save" their lives and salvation for those who have known how to "lose" them.

Hand mill for grinding cereals, of Jesus' time. A stick pushed through the central hole made an axis, and one put in the whole at the side made a guide. This work was usually done by women (cf. Lk. 17, 35).

and brimstone rained from heaven and destroyed them all—³⁰ so will it be on the day when the Son of man is revealed. ³¹ On that day, let him who is on the housetop, with his goods in the house, not come down to take them away; and likewise let him who is in the field not turn back. ³² Remember Lot's wife. ³³ Whoever seeks to gain his life will lose it, but whoever loses his life will preserve it. ³⁴ I tell you, in that night there will be two men in one bed; one will be taken and the other left. ³⁵ There will be two women grinding together; one will be taken and the other left." * ³⁷ And they said to him, "Where, Lord?" He said to them, "Where the body is, there the eagles will be gathered together."

Parable of the importunate widow
Lk 18, 1-8

¹ And he told them a parable, to the ** effect that they ought always to pray and not lose heart. ² He said, "In a certain city there was a judge who neither feared God nor regarded man; ³ and there was a widow in that city who kept coming to him and saying, 'Vindicate me against my adversary.' ⁴ For a while he refused; but afterward he said to himself, 'Though I neither fear God nor regard man, ⁵ yet because this widow bothers me, I will vindicate her, or she will wear me out by her continual coming.' " ⁶ And the Lord said, "Hear what the unrighteous judge says. ⁷ And will not God vindicate his elect,

* The apostles asked where all this would happen. Jesus replied by means of a parable: wherever men are found.

** The parable exhorts to persevering prayer, made with the certainty of being heard, and above all with a lively faith and hope.

243

Valley of the Jordan about 20 km. north of Jericho. On the hill to the left rise the ruins of the "Alexandrion", a fortress-prison bound up with the story of Herod the Great.

who cry to him day and night? Will he delay long over them? ⁸ I tell you, he will vindicate them speedily. Nevertheless, when the Son of man comes, will he find faith on earth?"

The Pharisee and the tax collector
Lk 18, 9-14

⁹ He also told this parable to some who trusted in themselves that they * were righteous and despised others: ¹⁰ "Two men went up into the temple to pray, one a Pharisee and the other a tax collector. ¹¹ The Pharisee stood and prayed thus with himself, 'God, I thank thee that I am not like other men, extortioners, unjust, adulterers, or even like this tax collector. ¹² I fast twice a week, I give tithes of all that I get.' ¹³ But the tax collector, standing far off, would not even lift up his eyes to heaven, but beat his breast, saying, 'God, be merciful to me a sinner!' ¹⁴ I tell you, this man went down to his house justified rather than the other; for every one who exalts himself will be humbled, but he who humbles himself will be exalted."

Teaching on the East bank of the Jordan

Marriage is indissoluble
Mt 19, 3-12 (Mk 10, 2-12)

³ And Pharisees came up to him and ** tested him by asking, "Is it lawful to

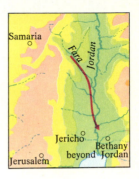

* "Some" here were probably Pharisees Jesus wished to teach that humility is an essential characteristic of prayer.

** Moses tolerated divorce as a lesser evil. Since only men had the right to repudiate their wives (and not vice versa) he prescribed a certificate of divorce in order to limit the practice and eliminate abuses (Deut. 24, 1). It was essentially a defence of the woman. Jesus goes beyond the provisional law and declares that God's real wish, expressed in Gen. 2, 24, is for marriage to be indissoluble.

245

Children playing in the water of the fountain at Nazareth called "the Spring of the Virgin". Jesus wanted the children near him so as to bless them (Mt. 19, 13-15).

divorce one's wife for any cause?" [4] He answered, "Have you not read that he who made them from the beginning made them male and female, [5] and said, 'For this reason a man shall leave his father and mother and be joined to his wife, and the two shall become one'? [6] So they are no longer two but one. What therefore God has joined together, let no man put asunder." [7] They said to him, "Why then did Moses command one to give a certificate of divorce, and to put her away? [8] He said to them, "For your hardness of heart Moses allowed you to divorce your wives, but from the beginning it was not so. [9] And I say to you: whoever divorces his wife, except for unchastity, and marries another, commits adultery; and he who marries a divorced woman commits adultery."

[10] The disciples said to him, "If such is the case of a man with his wife, it is not expedient to marry." [11] But he said to them, "Not all men can receive this precept, but only those to whom it is given. [12] For there are eunuchs who have been so from birth, and there are eunuchs who have been made eunuchs by men, and there are eunuchs who have made themselves eunuchs for the sake of the kingdom of heaven. He who is
* able to receive this, let him receive it."

"Let the children come to me"
Mt 19,13-15 (Mk 10, 13-16   Lk 18, 15-17)

[13] Then children were brought to him that he might lay his hands on them

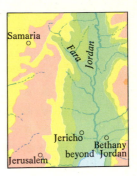

* If there are some people who must renounce marriage because of a defect or natural disposition, or for various circumstances in life, there is also a third sort of person — said Jesus — who freely remains celibate "for the sake of the Kingdom of heaven" i.e. for the love of God and the preaching of the Gospel. But that requires a special gift from God.

and pray. The disciples rebuked the people; 14 but Jesus said, "Let the children come to me, and do not hinder them; for to such belongs the kingdom of heaven." 15 And he laid his hands on them and went away.

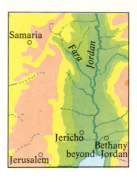

The rich young man: a missed vocation
Mt 19, 16-26 (Mk 10, 17-27 Lk 18, 18-27)

16 And behold, one came up to him, saying, "Teacher, what good deed must I do, to have eternal life?" 17 And he said to him, "Why do you ask me about what * is good? One there is who is good. If you would enter life, keep the commandments." 18 He said to him, "Which?" And Jesus said, "You shall not kill, You shall not commit adultery, You shall not steal, You shall not bear false witness, 19 Honour your father and mother, and, You shall love your neighbour as yourself." 20 The young man said to him, "All these I have observed; what do I still lack?" 21 Jesus said to him, "If you would be perfect, go, sell what you possess and give to the poor, and you will have treasure in heaven; and come, follow ** me." 22 When the young man heard this he went away sorrowful; for he had great possessions.

23 And Jesus said to his disciples, "Truly, I say to you, it will be hard for a rich man to enter the kingdom of heaven. 24 Again I tell you, it is easier for a camel to go through the eye of a needle than for a rich man to enter the *** kingdom of God." 25 When the disciples heard this they were greatly astonished,

* Goodness does not consist of things which are good to do, but in imitating God who alone is good.

** All are called to perfection and therefore it is not enough just to keep the commandments; it is necessary to follow Jesus. For the rich young man that meant, in practice, giving his wealth to the poor.

*** With a striking illustration Jesus puts us seriously on guard against the great difficulty of being saved, for any one who possesses so much material wealth. He ends by no longer being able to do without it.

248

saying, "Who then can be saved?" 26 But Jesus looked at them and said to them, "With men this is impossible, but with God all things are possible."

The reward for those who leave all for Jesus
Mt 19, 27-30 (Mk 10, 28-31 Lk 18, 28-30)

27 Then Peter said in reply, "Lo, we have left everything and followed you. What then shall we have?" 28 Jesus said to them, "Truly, I say to you, in the new world, when the Son of man shall sit on his glorious throne, you who have followed me will also sit on twelve thrones, judging the twelve tribes of Israel. 29 And every one who has left houses or brothers or sisters or father or mother or children or lands, for my name's sake, will receive a hundredfold, and inherit eternal life. 30 But many that are first will be last, and the last first."

Parable of the labourers in the vineyard
Mt 20, 1-16

1 "For the kingdom of heaven is like a householder who went out early in the morning to hire labourers for his vineyard. 2 After agreeing with the labourers for a denarius a day, he sent them into his vineyard. 3 And going out about the third hour he saw others standing idle in the market place; 4 and to them he said, 'You go into the vineyard too, and whatever is right I will give you.' So they went. 5 Going out again about the sixth hour and the ninth hour, he did

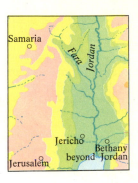

* The parable is drawn from the custom of the time: when an employer wanted workmen, he called them from the market-place, where the unemployed were wont to pass their days, and agreed a wage with them.

249

the same. ⁶ And about the eleventh hour he went out and found others standing; and he said to them, 'Why do you stand here idle all day?' ⁷ They said to him, 'Because no one has hired us.' He said to them, 'You go into the vineyard too.' ⁸ And when evening came, the owner of the vineyard said to his steward, 'Call the labourers and pay them their wages, beginning with the last, up to the first.' ⁹ And when those hired about the eleventh hour came, each of them received a denarius. ¹⁰ Now when the first came, they thought they would receive more; but each of them also received a denarius. ¹¹ And on receiving it they grumbled at the householder, ¹² saying, 'These last worked only one hour, and you have made them equal to us who have borne the burden of the day and the scorching heat.' ¹³ But he replied to one of them, 'Friend, I am doing you no wrong; did you not agree with me for a denarius? ¹⁴ Take what belongs to you, and go; I choose to give to this last as I give to you. ¹⁵ Am I not allowed to do what I choose with what belongs to me? Or do

* you begrudge my generosity?' ¹⁶ So the last will be first, and the first last."

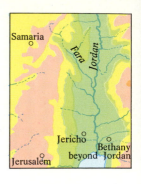

For the third time
Jesus predicts his passion
Mt 20, 17-19 (Mk 10, 32-34 Lk 18, 31-34)

¹⁷ And as Jesus was going up to Jerusalem, he took the twelve disciples aside, and on the way he said to them, ¹⁸ "Behold, we are going up to Jerusalem; and the Son of man will be delivered to the

* The teaching of the parable is that the kindness and generosity of God go beyond the works that we do: they are a gift rather than a reward.

chief priests and scribes, and they will condemn him to death, ¹⁹ and deliver him to the Gentiles to be mocked and scourged and crucified, and he will be raised on the third day."

Against the ambition of the disciples Jesus sets humility and service
Mt 20, 20-28 (Mk 10, 35-45)

²⁰ Then the mother of the sons of Zebedee came up to him, with her sons, and kneeling before him she asked him for something. ²¹ And he said to her, "What do you want?" She said to him, "Command that these two sons of mine may sit, one at your right hand and one at your left, in your kingdom." ²² But Jesus answered, "You do not know what you are asking. Are you able to drink the cup that I am to drink?" They said to him, "We are able." ²³ He * said to them, "You will drink my cup, but to sit at my right hand and at my left is not mine to grant, but it is for those for whom it has been prepared by my Father." ²⁴ And when the ten heard it, they were indignant at the two brothers. ²⁵ But Jesus called them to him and said, "You know that the rulers of the Gentiles lord it over them, and their great men exercise authority over them. ²⁶ It shall not be so among you; but whoever would be great among you must be your servant, ²⁷ and whoever would be first among you must be your slave; ²⁸ even as the Son of man came not to be served but to serve, and to ** give his life as a ransom for many."

* The reference is to the "cup" of suffering. Jesus predicts to the two apostles that they too will suffer martyrdom.

** Actually the other ten shared the same ambition as the sons of Zebedee, and were looking for a career and power in an earthly kingdom. But in the company of Jesus' disciples a very different law was in force: the greatest made himself a slave, authority was exercized as service. The model was Jesus himself who had not come to rule, but to serve to the point of giving his life to expiate men's sins.

The site of the "Herodian" Jericho, the town which existed in Jesus' time (Lk. 18, 35-19, 10). It is not to be confused either with ancient or with present day Jericho.

Jesus heals a blind man at Jericho
Lk 18, 35-43 (Mt 20, 29-34 Mk 10, 46-52)

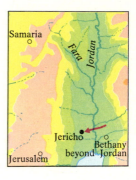

35 As he drew near to Jericho, a blind man was sitting by the roadside begging; 36 and hearing a multitude going by, he inquired what this meant. 37 They told him, "Jesus of Nazareth is passing by." 38 And he cried, "Jesus, Son of David, have mercy on me!" 39 And those who were in front rebuked him, telling him to be silent; but he cried out all the more, "Son of David, have mercy on me!" 40 And Jesus stopped, and commanded him to be brought to him; and when he came near, he asked him, 41 "What do you want me to do for you?" He said, "Lord, let me receive my sight." 42 And Jesus said to him, "Receive your sight; your faith has made you well." 43 And immediately he received his sight and followed him, glorifying God; and all the people, when they saw it, gave praise to God.

Jesus and Zacchaeus:
a moment of salvation
Lk 19, 1-10

1 He entered Jericho and was passing through. 2 And there was a man named * Zacchaeus; he was a chief tax collector, and rich. 3 And he sought to see who Jesus was, but could not, on account of the crowd, because he was small of stature. 4 So he ran on ahead and climbed up into a sycamore tree to see him, for he was to pass that way. 5 And when Jesus came to the place, he looked

* In a rich city, Jericho, Zacchaeus was chief of the tax collectors. Jesus made him invite him to his house. The reply to the grumbling of the people is precisely the conversion of the rich sinner. In this account we find Luke's typical themes; with Jesus has arrived the moment of salvation ("today"), the love of God goes out to sinners, and conversion leads to indifference to wealth and to charity through joy.

253

Panorama of Jericho. In the middle of the picture are the oasis and the present town, in the foreground the site where the Jericho of Jesus' day stood, and on the left in the background, the site of ancient Jericho.

up and said to him, "Zacchaeus, make haste and come down; for I must stay at your house today." ⁶ So he made haste and came down, and received him joyfully. ⁷ And when they saw it they all murmured, "He has gone in to be the guest of a man who is a sinner." ⁸ And Zacchaeus stood and said to the Lord, "Behold, Lord, the half of my goods I give to the poor; and if I have defrauded any one of anything, I restore it fourfold." ⁹ And Jesus said to him, "Today salvation has come to this house, since he also is a son of Abraham. ¹⁰ For the Son of man came to seek and to save the lost."

Parable of the king who entrusts his money to servants
Lk 19, 11-28

¹¹ As they heard these things, he proceeded to tell a parable, because he was near to Jerusalem, and because they supposed that the kingdom of God was
* to appear immediately. ¹² He said therefore, "A nobleman went into a far country to receive kingly power and then return. ¹³ Calling ten of his servants,
** he gave them ten pounds, and said to them, 'Trade with these till I come.' ¹⁴ But his citizens hated him and sent an embassy after him, saying, 'We do not want this man to reign over us.' ¹⁵ When he returned, having received the kingly power, he commanded these servants, to whom he had given the money, to be called to him, that he might

* The purpose of the parable has been made clear. The glorious manifestation of the Kingdom of God is at hand. Before it happens, Jesus must go away; he will ascend into heaven for his coronation as king. Finally he will return in glory as Judge. Meanwhile his disciples will await him with a feeling of responsibility, active in well-doing, and full of confidence.

** The "pound" approximated to a half-kilo of silver and was the equivalent of a hundred denarii, i.e. a hundred days' pay.

255

know what they had gained by trading. [16] The first came before him, saying, 'Lord, your pound has made ten pounds more.' [17] And he said to him, 'Well done, good servant! Because you have been faithful in a very little, you shall have authority over ten cities.' [18] And the second came, saying, 'Lord, your pound has made five pounds.' [19] And he said to him, 'And you are to be over five cities.' [20] Then another came, saying, 'Lord, here is your pound, which I kept laid away in a napkin; [21] for I was afraid *of you, because you are a severe man; you take up what you did not lay down, and reap what you did not sow.' [22] He said to him, 'I will condemn you out of your own mouth, you wicked servant! You knew that I was a severe man, taking up what I did not lay down and reaping what I did not sow? [23] Why then did you not put my money into the bank, and at my coming I should have collected it with interest?' [24] And he said to those who stood by, 'Take the pound from him, and give it to him who has the ten pounds.' [25] (And they said to him, 'Lord, he has ten pounds!') [26] 'I tell you, that to every one who has will more be given; but from him who has not, even what he has will be taken away. [27] But as for these enemies of mine, who did not want me to reign over them, bring them here and slay them before me.' "

[28] And when he had said this, he went on ahead, going up to Jerusalem.

* Relations with God must not be based on fear but should be expressed in active, faithful love.

256

VI - ACTIVITY IN JERUSALEM AND ITS SURROUNDINGS

This section tells the story of Jesus' decisive confrontation with the inhabitants of Jerusalem and particularly with the religious leaders of the nation.

According to the account in Matthew, Mark and Luke, Jesus was enthusiastically greeted as Messiah by the people, when he entered Jerusalem; but the controversies which followed demonstrated his final rejection by the authorities.

John, following a different line, speaks of Jesus' journey to Jerusalem on the occasion of the Feast of Tabernacles and refers to his activity in the holy city then; Jesus revealed himself to the Jews and obliged them to make a clear choice about him. After the raising of Lazarus came the Messianic entry into Jerusalem, but by that time Jesus saw that his "hour" was drawing near.

Jerusalem seen from the west. On these walls stood the house of Caiaphas the high priest and the citadel of Herod the Great.

Jesus chooses the battle-ground

Jesus at Jerusalem for the feast of Tabernacles
Jn 7, 2-13

² Now the Jews' feast of Tabernacles was at hand. ³ So his brethren said to him, "Leave here and go to Judea, that your disciples may see the works you are doing. ⁴ For no man works in secret if he seeks to be known openly. If you do these things, show yourself to the world." ⁵ For even his brethren did not believe in him. ⁶ Jesus said to them, " My time has not yet come, but your time is always here. ⁷ The world cannot hate you, but it hates me because I testify of it that its works are evil. ⁸ Go to the feast yourselves; I am not going up to this feast, for my time has not yet fully come." ⁹ So saying, he remained in Galilee.

¹⁰ But after his brethren had gone up to the feast, then he also went up, not * publicly but in private. ¹¹ The Jews were looking for him at the feast, and saying, "Where is he?" ¹² And there was much muttering about him among the people. While some said, "He is a good man," others said, "No, he is leading the people astray." ¹³ Yet for fear of the Jews no one spoke openly of him.

*   The argument about Jesus is the central question of these chapters: people's opinions were divided. The discussion was first of all about where he came from: "whence he comes and whither he goes." The Jews spoke of his human beginnings but Jesus made ever stronger and more disturbing affirmations about his divine origin.

Jesus declares:
it is God who has sent me
Jn 7, 14-29

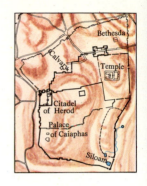

14 About the middle of the feast Jesus went up into the temple and taught. 15 The Jews marvelled at it, saying, "How is it that this man has learning, when he has never studied?" 16 So Jesus answered them, "My teaching is not mine, but his who sent me; 17 if any man's will is to do his will, he shall know whether the teaching is from God or whether I am speaking on my own authority. 18 He who speaks on his own authority seeks his own glory; but he who seeks the glory of him who sent him is true, and in him there is no falsehood. 19 Did not Moses give you the law? Yet none of you keeps the law. Why do you seek to kill me?" 20 The people answered, "You have a demon! * Who is seeking to kill you?" 21 Jesus answered them, "I did one deed, and you all marvel at it. 22 Moses gave you circumcision (not that it is from Moses, but from the fathers), and you circumcise a man upon the sabbath. 23 If on the sabbath a man receives circumcision, so that the law of Moses may not be broken, are you angry with me because on the sabbath I made a man's whole body well? 24 Do not judge by appearances, but judge with right judgment."

25 Some of the people of Jerusalem therefore said, "Is not this the man whom they seek to kill? 26 And here he is, speaking openly, and they say nothing

* Jesus was referring to the miracle he worked on his last visit to Jerusalem (the healing of the paralytic at the Pool of Bethesda). From that time the Jews had begun to persecute him, accusing him of blasphemy and sabbath-breaking.

to him! Can it be that the authorities really know that this is the Christ? 27 Yet we know where this man comes from; and when the Christ appears, no one * will know where he comes from." 28 So Jesus proclaimed, as he taught in the temple, "You know me, and you know where I come from? But I have not come of my own accord; he who sent me is true, and him you do not know. 29 I know him, for I come from him, and he sent me."

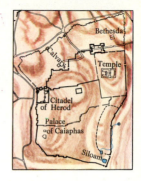

The Jews send police to arrest Jesus
Jn 7, 30-36

30 So they sought to arrest him; but no one laid hands on him, because his hour had not yet come. 31 Yet many of the people believed in him; they said, "When the Christ appears, will he do more signs than this man has done?"

32 The Pharisees heard the crowd thus muttering about him, and the chief priests and Pharisees sent officers to arrest him. 33 Jesus then said, "I shall be with you a little longer, and then I go to him who sent me; 34 you will seek ** me and you will not find me; where I am you cannot come." 35 The Jews said to one another, "Where does this man intend to go that we shall not find him? Does he intend to go to the Dispersion among the Greeks and teach the Greeks? 36 What does he mean by saying, 'You will seek me and you will not find me,' and 'Where I am you cannot come'?"

* The Jews are here referring to the popular belief that the Messiah will appear unexpectedly after spending his youth in an unknown place.

** This is the first time at Jerusalem that Jesus spoke of his death. "To seek God and not to find him" was one of the most severe threats in the Bible to the faithless people.

Water from a spring in the oasis of Engeddi, near the Dead Sea. "Living water" was seen by Jesus as a symbol of the Spirit which he would give to believers (cf. Jn. 7, 37-39).

Jesus promises the Holy Spirit to those who believe
Jn 7, 37-39

* ³⁷ On the last day of the feast, the great day, Jesus stood up and proclaimed, "If any one thirst, let him come to me and drink. ³⁸ He who believes in me, as the scripture has said, 'Out of his heart shall flow rivers of living water.' " ³⁹ Now this he said about the Spirit, which those who believed in him were to receive; for as yet the Spirit had not been given, because Jesus was not yet glorified.

The people are divided about Jesus
Jn 7, 40-44

⁴⁰ When they heard these words, some of the people said, "This is really the prophet." ⁴¹ Others said, "This is the Christ." But some said, "Is the Christ to come from Galilee? ⁴² Has not the scripture said that the Christ is descended from David, and comes from Bethlehem, the village where David was?" ⁴³ So ** there was a division among the people over him. ⁴⁴ Some of them wanted to arrest him, but no one laid hands on him.

The Sanhedrin also is divided about Jesus
Jn 7, 45-53

⁴⁵ The officers then went back to the chief priests and Pharisees, who said to them, "Why did you not bring him?"

* During the feast there was a ceremony of water; it was drawn from the Pool of Siloam and solemnly poured out outside the walls of the city, as a sign of overflowing salvation. Jesus declared that he was himself salvation and gave living water.

** Jesus was of the house of David and was really born at Bethlehem. But this last detail was not known to the great mass of the people, who believed him to be a native of Nazareth, and thus of the despised Galilee.

263

The entrance to the esplanade of the Temple as it is today. In the temple Jesus taught the people and disputed with the Jewish leaders (Jn. 8).

⁴⁶ The officers answered, "No man ever spoke like this man!" ⁴⁷ The Pharisees answered them, "Are you led astray, you also? ⁴⁸ Have any of the authorities or of the Pharisees believed in him? ⁴⁹ But this crowd, who do not know the law, are accursed." ⁵⁰ Nicodemus, who had gone to him before, and who was one of them, said to them, ⁵¹ "Does our law judge a man without first giving him a hearing and learning what he does?" ⁵² They replied, "Are you from Galilee too? Search and you will see that no prophet is to rise from Galilee." ⁵³ They went each to his own house...

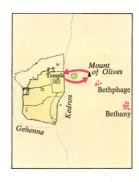

Jesus pardons the adultress: "Go and do not sin again" Jn 8, 1-11

¹ But Jesus went to the Mount of Olives.

² Early in the morning he came again to the temple; all the people came to him, and he sat down and taught them. ³ The scribes and the Pharisees brought a woman who had been caught in adultery, and placing her in the midst ⁴ they said to him, "Teacher, this woman has been caught in the act of adultery. ⁵ Now in the law Moses commanded us to stone such. What do you say about her?" ⁶ This they said to test him, that they might have some charge to bring against him. Jesus bent down and wrote with his finger on the ground. ⁷ And as they continued to ask him, he stood up and

* The leaders and the Pharisees contemptuously called the simple folk, not instructed like themselves and so not as meticulous in the observance of the Law, "people of the earth." In fact those people with their simplicity and rectitude were nearest to the truth.

said to them, "Let him who is without sin among you be the first to throw a stone at her." 8 And once more he bent down and wrote with his finger on the ground. 9 But when they heard it, they went away, one by one, beginning with the eldest, and Jesus was left alone with the woman standing before him. 10 Jesus looked up and said to her, "Woman, where are they? Has no one condemned you?" 11 She said, "No one, Lord." And * Jesus said, "Neither do I condemn you; go, and do not sin again."

"I am the light of the world"
Jn 8, 12-20

** 12 Again Jesus spoke to them, saying, "I am the light of the world; he who follows me will not walk in darkness, but will have the light of life." 13 The Pharisees then said to him, "You are bearing witness to yourself; your testimony is not true." 14 Jesus answered, "Even if I do bear witness to myself, my testimony is true, for I know whence I have come and whither I am going, but you do not know whence I come or whither I am going. 15 You judge according to the flesh, I judge no one. 16 Yet even if I do judge, my judgment is true, for it is not I alone that judge, but I and he who sent me. 17 In your law it is written that the testimony of two men is true; 18 I bear witness to myself, and the Father who sent me bears witness to me." 19 They said to him therefore, "Where is your Father?" Jesus answered,

* Only Jesus, who was guiltless, could condemn. But he had come to save and to summon to repentance.

** Jesus took his cue from the festival illuminations to say that he is the light of the world which shows God to us and which shines for all mankind. The Old Testament foretold that the light would shine with the coming of the Messiah. E.g. Isa. 49, 6: I will give you as a light to the nations, that my salvation may reach to the ends of the earth.

"You know neither me nor my Father; if you knew me, you would know my Father also." 20 These words he spoke in the treasury, as he taught in the temple; but no one arrested him, because his hour had not yet come.

"You will die in your sins unless you believe"
Jn 8, 21-29

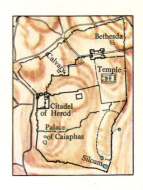

21 Again he said to them, "I go away, and you will seek me and die in your sin; where I am going, you cannot come." 22 Then said the Jews "Will he kill himself, since he says, 'Where I am going, you cannot come'?" 23 He said to them, "You are from below, I am from above; you are of this world, I am not of this world. 24 I told you that you would die in your sins, for you will die in your * sins unless you believe that I am he." 25 They said to him, "Who are you?" Jesus said to them, "Even what I have told you from the beginning. 26 I have much to say about you and much to judge; but he who sent me is true, and I declare to the world what I have heard from him." 27 They did not understand that he spoke to them of the Father. 28 So Jesus said, "When you have lifted up the Son of man, then you will know that I am he, and that I do nothing on my own authority but speak thus as the Father taught me. 29 And he who sent me is with me; he has not left me alone, for I always do what is pleasing to him."

* In the Old Testament "I am" is the name of God (Ex. 3, 14; Isa. 43, 10) and means that he is always near to his people, with a mysterious, saving presence. Jesus, taking this name to himself, claims implicitly to be God, coming into history to save men. This will be clearer than ever when he is "raised up" i.e. crucified and risen.

267

Mamre. Abraham's Well. The great Old Testament figure was the occasion of a hot dispute between Jesus and the Jewish leaders (Jn. 8, 31-59).

"The truth will make you free"
Jn 8, 30-36

³⁰ As he spoke thus, many believed in him.

³¹ Jesus then said to the Jews who had believed in him, "If you continue in my word, you are truly my disciples, ³² and you will know the truth, and the truth will make you free." ³³ They answered him, "We are descendants of Abraham, and have never been in bondage to any one. How is it that you say, 'You will be made free'?"

³⁴ Jesus answered them, "Truly, truly, I say to you, every one who commits sin is a slave to sin. ³⁵ The slave does not continue in the house for ever; the son * continues for ever. ³⁶ So if the Son makes you free, you will be free indeed."

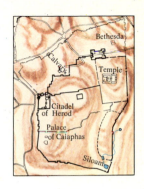

The unbelieving Jews are not true children of Abraham
Jn 8, 37-47

³⁷ "I know that you are descendants of Abraham; yet you seek to kill me, because my word finds no place in you. ³⁸ I speak of what I have seen with my Father, and you do what you have heard from your father."

³⁹ They answered him, "Abraham is our father." Jesus said to them, "If you were Abraham's children, you would do what Abraham did, ⁴⁰ but now you seek to kill me, a man who has told you the truth which I heard from God; this is not what Abraham did. ⁴¹ You do what your father did." They said to him, "We

* Jesus is the Son, always in communion with the Father, and perfectly free. He can bring real freedom to men, slaves of sin as they are, if they believe in him and are faithful to his word.

A view of the stupendous Mosque of Omar, built over the "sacred rock" of the ancient Hebrew Temple. On that rock Abraham may have prepared the altar for the sacrifice of his son Isaac.

were not born of fornication; we have
one Father, even God." ⁴² Jesus said to
them "If God were your Father, you
would love me, for I proceeded and
came forth from God; I came not of
my own accord, but he sent me. ⁴³ Why
do you not understand what I say? It
is because you cannot bear to hear my
word. ⁴⁴ You are of your father the devil,
and your will is to do your father's
desires. He was a murderer from the
beginning, and has nothing to do with
the truth, because there is no truth in
him. When he lies, he speaks according
to his own nature, for he is a liar and
the father of lies. ⁴⁵ But, because I tell
the truth, you do not believe me. ⁴⁶ Which
of you convicts me of sin? If I tell the
truth, why do you not believe me? ⁴⁷ He
who is of God hears the words of God;
the reason why you do not hear them
is that you are not of God."

Jesus affirms his eternal existence
Jn 8, 48-59

⁴⁸ The Jews answered him, "Are we
not right in saying that you are a Samaritan and have a demon?" ⁴⁹ Jesus answered, "I have not a demon; but I
honour my Father, and you dishonour
me. ⁵⁰ Yet I do not seek my own glory;
there is One who seeks it and he will
be the judge. ⁵¹ Truly, truly, I say to
you, if any one keeps my word, he will
never see death." ⁵² The Jews said to
him, "Now we know that you have a
demon. Abraham died, as did the prophets; and you say, 'If any one keeps

* To be "Abraham's
children" by physical
descent is worth no-
thing, if hearts are not
opened to God as was
Abraham's. For people
to call themselves "A-
braham's children" is
a lie, if they are un-
willing to hear from
Jesus the truth that he
is God's messenger. To
his hypocritical and
violent opponents Jes-
us said: You are "de-
vil's children" for he
has always, from the
beginnings of mankind,
been the father of
death and the father
of falsehood.

271

Jerusalem, the road which leads to the Pool of Siloam (cf. Jn. 9, 7). The rock in the centre of the photograph is the southern cliff of Ophel, the hill on which was built the very ancient heart of the city.

my word, he will never taste death.'
⁵³ Are you greater than our father Abraham, who died? And the prophets died! Who do you claim to be?" ⁵⁴ Jesus answered, "If I glorify myself, my glory is nothing; it is my Father who glorifies me, of whom you say that he is your God. ⁵⁵ But you have not known him; I know him. If I said, I do not know him, I should be a liar like you; but I do know him and I keep his word. ⁵⁶ Your father Abraham rejoiced that he was to see my day; he saw it and was glad." ⁵⁷ The Jews then said to him, "You are not yet fifty years old, and have you seen Abraham?" ⁵⁸ Jesus said to them, "Truly, truly, I say to you, before Abra-
* ham was, I am." ⁵⁹ So they took up stones to throw at him; but Jesus hid himself, and went out of the temple.

Jesus cures a man born blind
Jn 9, 1-41

¹ As he passed by, he saw a man blind from his birth. ² And his disciples asked him, "Rabbi, who sinned, this man or his parents, that he was born blind?" ³ Jesus answered, "It was not that this man sinned, or his parents, but that the
** works of God might be made manifest in him. ⁴ We must work the works of him who sent me, while it is day; night comes, when no one can work. ⁵ As long as I am in the world, I am the light of the world." ⁶ As he said this, he spat on the ground and made clay of the spittle and anointed the man's eyes with the clay, ⁷ saying to him, "Go, wash in the

* Jesus clearly affirmed that he was not only the Messiah for whom Abraham looked hopefully and joyfully, but also that he was truly the Son of God, existing eternally like the Father, even before Abraham's day. For this the Jews wished to stone Jesus, accusing him of blasphemy.

** Jesus corrected the ideas of his disciples. The latter thought that suffering was always God's punishment; Jesus said that it is included in God's plan, with the aim of salvation. He then completed the miracle, which aroused different reactions about his person. The story is told vividly and with a touch of irony.

273

Jerusalem. The entrance to the spring of Gihon. From this source water flowed to the Pool of Siloam by way of a subterranean channel cut in the rock by Hezekiah (about 700 B.C.).

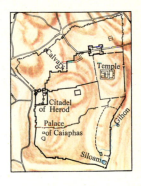

* pool of Siloam" (which means Sent). So he went and washed and came back seeing. 8 The neighbours and those who had seen him before as a beggar, said, "Is not this the man who used to sit and beg?" 9 Some said, "It is he"; others said, "No, but he is like him." He said, "I am the man." 10 They said to him, "Then how were your eyes opened?" 11 He answered, "The man called Jesus made clay and anointed my eyes and said to me, 'Go to Siloam and wash'; so I went and washed and received my sight." 12 They said to him, "Where is he?" He said, "I do not know."

13 They brought to the Pharisees the man who had formerly been blind. 14 Now it was a sabbath day when Jesus made the clay and opened his eyes. 15 The Pharisees again asked him how he had received his sight. And he said to them, "He put clay on my eyes, and I washed, and I see." 16 Some of the Pharisees said, "This man is not from God, for he does not keep the sabbath." But others said, "How can a man who is a sinner do such signs?" There was a division among them. 17 So they again said to the blind man, "What do you say about him, since he has opened your eyes?" He said, "He is a prophet."

18 The Jews did not believe that he had been blind and had received his sight, until they called the parents of the man who had received his sight, 19 and asked them, "Is this your son, who you say was born blind? How then does he now see?" 20 His parents answer-

* John notes how the name of the Pool may be symbolically taken, if applied to Christ who is truly "sent" by God. Those who come to him with faith find light.

275

Jerusalem. The Pool of Siloam as it is today. Water comes there from the spring of Gihon; it was here that the man born blind received sight.

ed, "We know that this is our son, and that he was born blind; 21 but how he now sees we do not know, nor do we know who opened his eyes. Ask him; he is of age, he will speak for himself." 22 His parents said this because they feared the Jews, for the Jews had already agreed that if any one should confess him to be Christ, he was to be * put out of the synagogue. 23 Therefore his parents said, "He is of age, ask him."

24 So for the second time they called the man who had been blind, and said to him, "Give God the praise; we know that this man is a sinner." 25 He answered, "Whether he is a sinner, I do not know; one thing I know, that though I was blind, now I see." 26 They said to him, "What did he do to you? How did he open your eyes?" 27 He answered them, "I have told you already, and you would not listen. Why do you want to hear it again? Do you too want to become his disciples?" 28 And they reviled him, saying, "You are his disciple, but we are disciples of Moses. 29 We know that God has spoken to Moses, but as for this man, we do not know where he comes from." 30 The man answered, "Why, this is a marvel! You do not know where he comes from, and yet he opened my eyes. 31 We know that God does not listen to sinners, but if any one is a worshipper of God and does his will, God listens to him. 32 Never since the world began has it been heard that any one opened the eyes of a man born blind. 33 If this man were not from God,

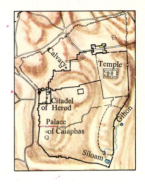

* The Jewish leaders tried to isolate Jesus by threatening those who became his disciples with the maximum civil-religious penalty, i.e. excommunication.

277

he could do nothing." ³⁴ They answered him, "You were born in utter sin, and would you teach us?" And they cast him out.

³⁵ Jesus heard that they had cast him out, and having found him he said, "Do you believe in the Son of man?" ³⁶ He answered, "And who is he, sir, that I may believe in him?" ³⁷ Jesus said to him, "You have seen him, and it is he who speaks to you." ³⁸ He said, "Lord, * I believe"; and he worshipped him. ³⁹ Jesus said, "For judgment I came into this world, that those who do not see may see, and that those who see may become blind." ⁴⁰ Some of the Pharisees near him heard this, and they said to him, "Are we also blind?" ⁴¹ Jesus said to them, "If you were blind, you would have no guilt; but now that you say, 'We see,' your guilt remains."

Jesus speaks of himself as "the door of the sheep and the good shepherd"
Jn 10, 1-21

** ¹ "Truly, truly, I say to you, he who does not enter the sheepfold by the door but climbs in by another way, that man is a thief and a robber; ² but he who enters by the door is the shepherd of the sheep. ³ To him the gatekeeper opens; the sheep hear his voice, and he calls his own sheep by name and leads them out. ⁴ When he has brought out all his own, he goes before them, and the sheep follow him, for they know his voice. ⁵ A stranger they will not follow,

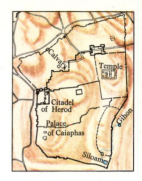

* The blind man not only received sight but also reached faith from his meeting with Christ, the light of the world. The Jews, on the other hand, believing themselves to see clearly, were really blind.

** For these illustrations Jesus had in mind the customs of Jewish shepherds. These kept their flocks in the open and gathered them together in great enclosures when evening came. In the morning each shepherd entered the sheep fold and called his own flock; the sheep recognized him by his voice and followed him, and so he led them to pasture. Taking his inspiration from these pictures, Jesus taught with what love and care he looks upon his people.

278

but they will flee from him, for they do not know the voice of strangers." ⁶ This figure Jesus used with them, but they did not understand what he was saying to them.

⁷ So Jesus again said to them, "Truly, truly, I say to you, I am the door of the sheep. ⁸ All who came before me are thieves and robbers; but the sheep did ＊ not heed them. ⁹ I am the door; if any one enters by me, he will be saved, and will go in and out and find pasture. ¹⁰ The thief comes only to steal and kill and destroy; I came that they may have life, and have it abundantly. ¹¹ I am the ＊＊ good shepherd. The good shepherd lays down his life for the sheep. ¹² He who is a hireling and not a shepherd, whose own the sheep are not, sees the wolf coming and leaves the sheep and flees; and the wolf snatches them and scatters them. ¹³ He flees because he is a hireling and cares nothing for the sheep. ¹⁴ I am the good shepherd; I know my own and my own know me, ¹⁵ as the Father knows me and I know the Father; and I lay down my life for the sheep. ¹⁶ And I have other sheep, that are not of this fold; I must bring them also, and they will heed my voice. So there shall be one flock, one shepherd. ¹⁷ For this reason the Father loves me, because I lay down my life, that I may take it again. ¹⁸ No one takes it from me, but I lay it down of my own accord. I have power to lay it down, and I have power to take it again; this charge I have received from my Father."

＊ Jesus declared himself the true shepherd in argument with those who should have been guides of the people but instead effected their ruin while seeking their own interests.

＊＊ Jesus is the good shepherd because he offers his own life freely and lovingly for all men.

279

Jerusalem. The south-east corner of the Temple esplanade. Along the eastern side (foreshortened in the photograph) ran Solomon's Portico (Jn. 10, 23), along the southern (facing us) the Royal Portico. Where they meet is the "Pinnacle".

[19] There was again a division among the Jews because of these words. [20] Many of them said, "He has a demon, and he is mad; why listen to him?" [21] Others said, "These are not the sayings of one who has a demon. Can a demon open the eyes of the blind?"

Jesus solemnly affirms his divinity
Jn 10, 22-39

* [22] It was the feast of the Dedication at Jerusalem; [23] it was winter, and Jesus was walking in the temple, in the portico of Solomon. [24] So the Jews gathered round him and said to him, "How long will you keep us in suspense? If you are the Christ, tell us plainly." [25] Jesus answered them, "I told you, and you do not believe. The works that I do in my Father's name, they bear witness to me; [26] but you do not believe, because you ** do not belong to my sheep. [27] My sheep hear my voice, and I know them, and they follow me; [28] and I give them eternal life, and they shall never perish, and no one shall snatch them out of my hand. [29] My Father, who has given them to me, is greater than all, and no one is able to snatch them out of the Father's hand. [30] I and the Father are one." [31] The Jews took up stones again to stone him. [32] Jesus answered them, "I have shown you many good works from the Father; for which of these do you stone me?" [33] The Jews answered him, "We stone you for no good work but for blasphemy; because you, being a man, make yourself God." [34] Jesus answered

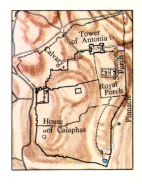

* The Feast of the Dedication commemorates the reconsecration of the Temple in 164 B.C. after its profanation by king Anthiochus IV.

** Jesus repeated some themes of his last discourse, but, above all affirmed his profound union with the Father. The Jews understood what that meant and wanted to stone him as a blasphemer.

them, "Is it not written in your law, 'I said, you are gods'? [35] If he called them gods to whom the word of God came (and scripture cannot be broken), [36] do you say of him whom the Father consecrated and sent into the world, 'You are blaspheming,' because I said, 'I am the Son of God?' [37] If I am not doing the works of my Father, then do not believe me; [38] but if I do them, even though you do not believe me, believe the works, that you may know and understand that the Father is in me and *I am in the Father" [39] Again they tried to arrest him, but he escaped from their hands.

Jesus withdraws beyond the Jordan
Jn 10, 40-42

[40] He went away again across the Jordan to the place where John at first baptized, and there he remained. [41] And many came to him; and they said, "John did no sign, but everything that John said about this man was true." [42] And many believed in him there.

The raising of Lazarus

Lazarus is taken ill and dies
Jn 11, 1-16

[1] Now a certain man was ill, Lazarus of Bethany, the village of Mary and her sister Martha. [2] It was Mary who anointed the Lord with ointment and wiped his feet with her hair, whose brother Lazarus was ill. [3] So the sisters sent to

* Jesus replied to this accusation by arguing from Scripture, as was the custom of the rabbis: if the Psalm (82, 6) called "gods" those who hold some office among the people, how much rather can Jesus, sent by the Father to save the world, be called Son of God. But a more obvious answer was given by his miracles; the Father would not have carried out such works through him if he were a blasphemer.

him, saying, "Lord, he whom you love is ill." [4] But when Jesus heard it he said, "This illness is not unto death; it is for the glory of God, so that the Son of
*God may be glorified by means of it."

[5] Now Jesus loved Martha and her sister and Lazarus. [6] So when he heard that he was ill, he stayed two days longer in the place where he was. [7] Then after this he said to the disciples, "Let us go into Judea again." [8] The disciples said to him, "Rabbi, the Jews were but now seeking to stone you, and are you going there again?" [9] Jesus answered,
**"Are there not twelve hours in the day? If any one walks in the day, he does not stumble, because he sees the light of this world. [10] But if any one walks in the night, he stumbles, because the light is not in him." [11] Thus he spoke, and then he said to them, "Our friend Lazarus has fallen asleep, but I go to awake him out of sleep. [12] The disciples said to him, "Lord, if he has fallen asleep, he will recover." [13] Now Jesus had spoken of his death, but they thought that he meant taking rest in sleep. [14] Then Jesus told them plainly, "Lazarus is dead; [15] and for your sake I am glad that I was not there, so that you may believe. But let us go to him." [16] Thomas, called the Twin, said to his fellow disciples, "Let us also go, that we may die with him."

"I am the resurrection and the life"
Jn 11, 17-37

[17] Now when Jesus came, he found

Ephraim

Jericho   Bethany
          beyond
          Jordan
Jerusalem

Bethany

Dead Sea

* Jesus knew what was going to happen; the death to follow would not be final but would be the occasion of an extraordinary sign.

** Jesus compared his life to a day's journey (12 hours). Since he had still to finish the work entrusted to him by God, he could not be in danger from his enemies. On the other hand, when he had finished everything, it would be as though night had fallen, with all its dangers; then the enemies would be able to bring about his death.

Bethany. The present entrance to "Lazarus tomb", opened in its rear wall. Here happened the great miracle fully described in Jn. 11.

that Lazarus had already been in the tomb four days. [18] Bethany was near Jerusalem, about two miles off, [19] and many of the Jews had come to Martha and Mary to console them concerning their brother. [20] When Martha heard that Jesus was coming, she went and met him, while Mary sat in the house. [21] Martha said to Jesus, "Lord, if you had been here, my brother would not have died. [22] And even now I know that whatever you ask from God, God will give you." [23] Jesus said to her, "Your brother will rise again." [24] Martha said to him, "I know that he will rise again

* in the resurrection at the last day." [25] Jesus said to her, "I am the resurrection and the life; he who believes in me, though he die, yet shall he live, [26] and whoever lives and believes in me shall never die. Do you believe this?" [27] She said to him, "Yes, Lord; I believe that you are the Christ, the Son of God, he who is coming into the world."

[28] When she had said this, she went and called her sister Mary, saying quietly, "The Teacher is here and is calling for you." [29] And when she heard it, she rose quickly and went to him. [30] Now Jesus had not yet come to the village, but was still in the place where Martha had met him. [31] When the Jews who were with her in the house, consoling her, saw Mary rise quickly and go out, they followed her, supposing that she was going to the tomb to weep there. [32] Then Mary, when she came where Jesus was and saw him, fell at his feet,

* Martha believed in Jesus, even if he did not reply in the way she had expected. Jesus made a solemn declaration to her: he is the resurrection and eternal life for all men who believe in him.

285

saying to him, "Lord, if you had been here, my brother would not have died." 33 When Jesus saw her weeping, and the Jews who came with her also weeping, he was deeply moved in spirit and troubled; 34 and he said, "Where have you laid him?" They said to him, "Lord, *come and see." 35 Jesus wept. 36 So the Jews said, "See how he loved him!" 37 But some of them said, "Could not he who opened the eyes of the blind man have kept this man from dying?"

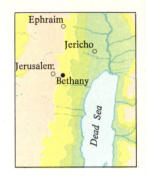

Jesus raises Lazarus from the dead
Jn 11, 38-44

38 Then Jesus, deeply moved again, came to the tomb; it was a cave, and a stone lay upon it. 39 Jesus said, "Take away the stone." Martha, the sister of the dead man, said to him, "Lord, by this time there will be an odour, for he has been dead four days." 40 Jesus said to her, "Did I not tell you that if you would believe you would see the glory of God?" 41 So they took away the stone. And Jesus lifted up his eyes and said, "Father, I thank thee that thou hast heard me. 42 I knew that thou hearest me always, but I have said this on account of the people standing by, that they may believe that thou didst send me." 43 When he had said this, he cried with a loud voice, "Lazarus, come out." 44 The dead man came out, his hands and feet bound with bandages, and his face wrapped with a cloth. Jesus said to them, "Unbind him, and let him go."

* Jesus felt friendship and shared intensely in human suffering, to the point of being deeply moved.

286

The Jewish leaders decide to kill Jesus
Jn 11, 45-53

45 Many of the Jews therefore, who had come with Mary and had seen what he did, believed in him; 46 but some of them went to the Pharisees and told them what Jesus had done. 47 So the * chief priests and the Pharisees gathered the council, and said, "What are we to do? For this man performs many signs. 48 If we let him go on thus, every one will believe in him, and the Romans will come and destroy both our holy place and our nation." 49 But one of them, Caiaphas, who was high priest that year, said to them, "You know nothing at all; 50 you do not understand that it is expedient for you that one man should die for the people, and that the ** whole nation should not perish." 51 He did not say this of his own accord, but being high priest that year he prophesied that Jesus shoul die for the nation, 52 and not for the nation only, but to gather into one the children of God who are scattered abroad. 53 So from that day on they took counsel how to put him to death.

Jesus withdraws to Ephraim
Jn 11, 54-57

54 Jesus therefore no longer went about openly among the Jews, but went from there to the country near the wilderness, to a town called Ephraim; and there he stayed with the disciples.
55 Now the Passover of the Jews was

* The miracle Jesus had wrought should have brought belief in him as the messenger sent by the Father; instead, it became for his enemies an incentive for hatred and vengeance. Jesus had rebuked them many times for their bad faith in closing their eyes so as not to see.

** John, with a flash of irony, observes that this was a true prophecy, even though he who made it did not understand its real meaning. In reality, God can, in his plan of salvation, make use even of the plans of wicked men.

287

Bethphage, the little village on the Mount of Olives, between Bethany and Jerusalem. To it Jesus sent to fetch the foal for his Messianic entry into Jerusalem.

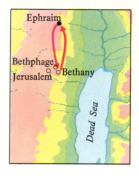

at hand, and many went up from the country to Jerusalem before the Passover, to purify themselves. ⁵⁶ They were looking for Jesus and saying to one another as they stood in the temple, "What do you think? That he will not come to the feast?" ⁵⁷ Now the chief priests and the Pharisees had given orders that if any one knew where he was, he should let them know, so that they might arrest him.

The entry of the Messiah into Jerusalem

**Entering Jerusalem,
Jesus is acclaimed as Messiah-King
Lk 19, 29-40 (Mt 21, 1-11   Mk 11, 1-10
Jn 12, 12-19)**

²⁹ When he drew near to Bethphage and Bethany, at the mount that is called Olivet, he sent two of the disciples, ³⁰ saying, "Go into the village opposite, where on entering you will find a colt tied, on which no one has ever yet sat; untie it and bring it here. ³¹ If any one asks you, 'Why are you untying it?' you shall say this, 'The Lord has need of it.'" ³² So those who were sent went away and found it as he had told them. ³³ And as they were untying the colt, its owners said to them, "Why are you untying the colt?" ³⁴ And they said, "The Lord has need of it." ³⁵ And they brought it to Jesus, and throwing their garments on the colt they set Jesus upon it. ³⁶ And as he rode along, they spread their

*   This is a sort of symbolic action, undertaken by Jesus: he is conscious of being the Messiah. Matthew sees the fulfilment of Zechariah's prophecy: "This took place to fulfil what was spoken by the prophet, saying, 'Tell the daughter of Zion, behold, your king is coming to you, humble, and mounted on an ass, and on a colt, the foal of an ass' " (Mt. 21, 4-5).

289

A fine panoramic view of Jerusalem from the Mount of Olives. Here has been built a chapel, called "Dominus flevit" (The Lord wept) in memory of Jesus' lament (Lk. 19, 41).

garments on the road. ³⁷ As he was now drawing near, at the descent of the Mount of Olives, the whole multitude of the disciples began to rejoice and praise God with a loud voice for all the mighty works that they had seen, ³⁸ saying, "Blessed is the King who comes in the name of the Lord! Peace in heaven and glory in the highest!" ³⁹ And some of the Pharisees in the multitude said to him, "Teacher, rebuke your disciples." ⁴⁰ He answered, "I tell you, if these were silent, the very stones would cry out."

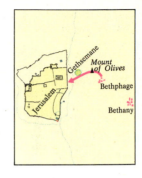

At the sight of Jerusalem Jesus weeps
Lk 19, 41-44

⁴¹ And when he drew near and saw the city he wept over it, ⁴² saying, "Would that even today you knew the things that make for peace! But now they are hid from your eyes. ⁴³ For the days shall come upon you, when your enemies will cast up a bank about you and surround you, and hem you in on every side, ⁴⁴ and dash you to the ground, you and your children within you, and they will not leave one stone upon another in you; because you did not know the time of your visitation."

The rejection by Israel

Jesus curses the unfruitful fig-tree
Mk 11, 11-14 (Mt 21, 18-19)

¹¹ And he entered Jerusalem, and went into the temple; and when he had looked

* The crowd of disciples too has recognized in Jesus the expected Messiah and enthusiastically acclaims him, unlike the suspicious and jealous Pharisees. Matthew (21, 15-16) notes that the latter were annoyed by the cries of the children; but Jesus defends his small supporters.

** Jesus weeps because he loves the holy city, which he loves, in rejecting him, rejects its own salvation. This is a last appeal for repentance. After this there remains nothing but the warning of ruin.

291

round at everything, as it was already late, he went out to Bethany with the twelve.

¹² On the following day, when they came from Bethany, he was hungry. ¹³ And seeing in the distance a fig tree in leaf, he went to see if he could find anything on it. When he came to it, he found nothing but leaves, for it was not the season for figs. ¹⁴ And he said *to it, "May no one ever eat fruit from you again." And his disciples heard it.

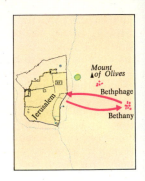

"A house of prayer for all nations"
Mk 11, 15-19 (Mt 21, 12-17 Lk 19, 45-48)

¹⁵ And they came to Jerusalem. And **he entered the temple and began to drive out those who sold and those who bought in the temple, and he overturned the tables of the money-changers and the seats of those who sold pigeons; ¹⁶ and he would not allow any one to carry anything through the temple. ¹⁷ And he taught, and said to them, "Is it not written, 'My house shall be called a house of prayer for all the nations'? But you have made it a den of robbers." ¹⁸ And the chief priests and the scribes heard it and sought a way to destroy him; for they feared him, because all the multitude was astonished at his teaching. ¹⁹ And when evening came they went out of the city.

"Have faith in God"
Mk 11, 20-25 (Mt 21, 20-22)

²⁰ As they passed by in the morning,

*   The cursing of the fig tree is a symbolic action, such as the biblical prophets sometimes used. It is like a parable which is acted as well as spoken. By it Jesus intends to show the severity with which God will judge the Israelites and all who disappoint his expectations, seeing that they are barren of good works.

**   Mark, Matthew and Luke, unlike John, record the visit of Jesus to the Temple at this moment, before the passion. The house of prayer for the people of Israel is cleansed and opened to all peoples.

they saw the fig tree withered away to its roots. 21 And Peter remembered and said to him, "Master, look! The fig tree *which you cursed has withered." 22 And Jesus answered them, "Have faith in God. 23 Truly, I say to you, whoever says to this mountain, 'Be taken up and cast into the sea,' and does not doubt in his heart, but believes that what he says will come to pass, it will be done for him. 24 Therefore I tell you, whatever you ask in prayer, believe that you receive it, and you will. 25 And whenever you stand praying, forgive, if you have anything against any one; so that your Father also who is in heaven may forgive you your trespasses."

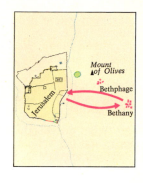

Dispute about and rejection of Jesus' authority
Mt 21, 23-27 (Mk 11, 27-33 Lk 20, 1-8)

** 23 And when he entered the temple, the chief priests and the elders of the people came up to him as he was teaching, and said, "By what authority are you doing these things, and who gave you this authority?" 24 Jesus answered them, "I also will ask you a question; and if you tell me the answer, then I also will tell you by what authority I do these things. 25 The baptism of John, whence was it? From heaven or from men?" And they argued with one another, "If we say, 'From heaven,' he will say to us, 'Why then did you not believe him?' 26 But if we say, 'From men,' we are afraid of the multitude; for all hold

* The confirmation of the efficacy of Jesus' word is followed by a short instruction on prayer, which must be made with faith in God and in a state of peace with all men.

** Now begins a series of controversies between Jesus and his adversaries, the teachers of the Law and the Pharisees, who are joined by the chief priests and the elders of the people. This is the decisive conflict which will lead up to Jesus' condemnation to death.

293

that John was a prophet." ²⁷ So they answered Jesus, "We do not know." And he said to them, "Neither will I tell you by what authority I do these things."

The parable
of the two sons sent to work
Mt 21, 28-32

²⁸ "What do you think? A man had two sons; and he went to the first and said, 'Son, go and work in the vineyard today.' ²⁹ And he answered, 'I will not'; but afterward he repented and went. ³⁰ And he went to the second and said the same; and he answered, 'I go, sir,' but did not go. ³¹ Which of the two did the will of his father?" They said, "The first." Jesus said to them, "Truly, I say to you, the tax collectors and the harlots go into the kingdom of God before you. * ³² For John came to you in the way of righteousness, and you did not believe him, but the tax collectors and the harlots believed him; and even when you saw it, you did not afterward repent and believe him."

The parable
of the murderous vine-dressers
Mt 21, 33-46 (Mk 12, 1-12 Lk 20, 9-19)

** ³³ "Hear another parable. There was a householder who planted a vineyard, and set a hedge around it, and dug a wine press in it, and built a tower, and let it out to tenants, and went into another country. ³⁴ When the season of fruit drew near, he sent his servants to

* Here is the explanation of the parable. Sinners, both men and women, even though they had in the first instance said No to the Father, have repented and fulfilled his wishes; on the contrary, the Pharisees and chiefs of the people who have obeyed in word, have repudiated God by their deeds.

** The same illustration of the vineyard was used by the prophet Isaiah (5, 1-7) in a similar situation: God's love for his people being met with a lack of response. In the parable Jesus, in addition to condemning the wickedness and bad faith of the religious rulers, implicitly declares himself to be the Son of God.

the tenants, to get his fruit; ³⁵ and the tenants took his servants and beat one, killed another, and stoned another. ³⁶ Again he sent other servants, more than the first; and they did the same to them. ³⁷ Afterward he sent his son to them, saying, 'They will respect my son.' ³⁸ But when the tenants saw the son, they said to themselves, 'This is the heir; come, let us kill him and have his inheritance.' ³⁹ And they took him and cast him out of the vineyard, and killed him. ⁴⁰ When therefore the owner of the vineyard comes, what will he do to those tenants?" ⁴¹ They said to him, "He will put those wretches to a miserable death, and let out the vineyard to other tenants who will give him the fruits in their seasons."

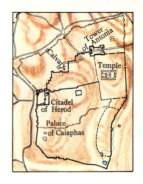

⁴² Jesus said to them, "Have you never read in the scriptures:

* 'The very stone which
the builders rejected
has become the head of the corner;
this was the Lord's doing,
and it is marvellous in our eyes'?

⁴³ Therefore I tell you, the kingdom of God will be taken away from you and given to a nation producing the fruits of it. ⁴⁴ And he who falls on this stone will be broken to pieces; but when it falls on any one, it will crush him."

⁴⁵ When the chief priests and the Pharisees heard his parables, they perceived that he was speaking about them. ⁴⁶ But when they tried to arrest him, they feared the multitudes, because they held him to be a prophet.

* The quotation is from Psalm 118, 22-23. Jesus himself is the stone rejected by the Jews and, instead, made by God the keystone of the whole building.

295

Vineyards in the neighbourhood of Ramallah, a dozen kilometres norfh of Jerusalem. In the centre is a round tower, where the press could be located and which served as a storehouse.

The parable of the banquet and the wedding garment
Mt 22, 1-14

[1] And again Jesus spoke to them in
* parables, saying, [2] "The kingdom of heav-
en may be compared to a king who gave
a marriage feast for his son, [3] and sent
his servants to call those who were
invited to the marriage feast; but they
would not come. [4] Again he sent other
servants, saying, 'Tell those who are
invited, Behold, I have made ready my
dinner, my oxen and my fat calves are
killed, and everything is ready; come
to the marriage feast.' [5] But they made
light of it and went off, one to his farm,
another to his business, [6] while the rest
seized his servants, treated them shame-
fully, and killed them. [7] The king was
angry, and he sent his troops and destroyed those murderers and burned their
city. [8] Then he said to his servants, 'The
wedding is ready, but those invited were
not worthy. [9] Go therefore to the tho-
roughfares, and invite to the marriage
feast as many as you find.' [10] And those
servants went out into the streets and
gathered all whom they found, both
bad and good; so the wedding hall was
filled with guests.

** [11] But when the king came in to look
at the guests, he saw there a man who
had no wedding garment; [12] and he said
to him, 'Friend, how did you get in here
without a wedding garment?' And he
was speechless. [13] Then the king said to
the attendants, 'Bind him hand and foot,
and cast him into the outer darkness;

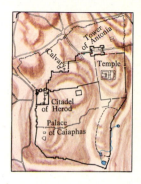

* The meaning of
this parable is similar
to that of the preced-
ing one. The Hebrews,
the first guests invited
to share in the King-
dom of God, have re-
fused the invitation,
i.e. they have not be-
lieved in Jesus. In add-
ition they will kill him
as they have killed the
prophets. Therefore
their city will be given
to the flames, and their
place will be allotted
to others, sinners and
Gentiles.

** The second part of
the parable, reported
by Matthew only, is a
lesson for the new
guests: to enter into
salvation it is not
enough just to say Yes,
they must pay regard
to the conditions, and
faithfully carry out
God's will.

297

This is the silver denarius (magnified four times) with the image and the name of Tiberius Caesar Augustus. Probably one of these coins was at the centre of the controversy mentioned in Mt. 22, 15-22.

there men will weep and gnash their teeth.' ¹⁴ For many are called, but few are chosen."

"Render to Caesar the things that are Caesar's and to God the things that are God's"
Mt 22, 15-22 (Mk 12, 3-17   Lk 20, 20-26)

¹⁵ Then the Pharisees went and took counsel how to entangle him in his talk. ¹⁶ And they sent their disciples to him, along with the Herodians, saying, "Teacher, we know that you are true, and teach the way of God truthfully, and care for no man; for you do not regard the position of men. ¹⁷ Tell us, then, what you think. Is it lawful to pay taxes to Caesar, or not?" ¹⁸ But Jesus, aware of their malice, said, "Why put me to the test, you hypocrites? ¹⁹ Show me the money for the tax." And they brought him a coin. ²⁰ And Jesus said to them, "Whose likeness and inscription is this?" ²¹ They said, "Caesar's." Then he said to * them, "Render therefore to Caesar the things that are Caesar's, and to God the things that are God's." ²² When they heard it, they marvelled; and they left him and went away.

Jesus confirms the final resurrection
Mt 22, 23-33 (Mk 12, 18-27   Lk 20, 27-40)

²³ The same day Sadducees came to him, who say that there is no resurrection; and they asked him a question, ** ²⁴ saying, "Teacher, Moses said, 'If a man dies, having no children, his brother

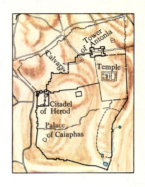

*   Since the Jews used the coinage of Caesar, also drawing advantages from doing so, they did in practice recognize his authority and it was right for them to pay tribute. But Jesus adds that God alone is Absolute and to him alone is due the total loyalty of the heart. The political authority is recognized but revalued. Recognition of the Father is the foundation of equality and of the liberty of all men.

**   The purpose of this law (Deut. 25, 5-6) was to secure the continuity of the family and the stability of hereditary possessions.

299

must marry the widow, and raise up children for his brother.' ²⁵ Now there were seven brothers among us; the first married, and died, and having no children left his wife to his brother. ²⁶ So too the second and third, down to the seventh. ²⁷ After them all, the woman died. ²⁸ In the resurrection, therefore, to which of the seven will she be wife? For they all had her."

²⁹ But Jesus answered them, "You are wrong, because you know neither the scriptures nor the power of God. ³⁰ For in the resurrection they neither marry nor are given in marriage, but are like angels in heaven. ³¹ And as for the resurrection of the dead, have you not read what was said to you by God, ³² 'I am the God of Abraham, and the God of Isaac, and the God of Jacob'? He is not

* God of the dead, but of the living." ³³ And when the crowd heard it, they were astonished at his teaching.

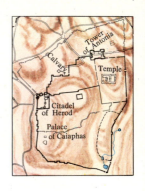

Jesus teaches the greatest commandment
Mt 22, 34-40 (Mk 12, 28-34)

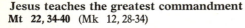

³⁴ But when the Pharisees heard that he had silenced the Sadducees, they came together. ³⁵ And one of them, a lawyer, asked him a question, to test him. ³⁶ "Teacher, which is the great commandment in the law?" ³⁷ And he said to him, "You shall love the Lord your God with all your heart, and with all your soul, and with all your mind. ³⁸ This is the great and first commandment. ³⁹ And a second is like it, You

* Jesus confirms the truth of the resurrection of the dead, which will be wrought by the power of God, even though it is impossible to give details of the new world, because life will be completely different. By the quotation from Exod. 3, 6 Jesus means that Abraham, Isaac and Jacob are alive in God's presence and their bodies await the resurrection. God is the God of life; his love and his covenant will survive our death.

300

shall love your neighbour as yourself. 40 On these two commandments depend all the law and the prophets."

*

Jesus, David's son, is greater than David
Mt 22, 41-46 (Mk 12, 35-37 Lk 20, 41-44)

41 Now while the Pharisees were gathered together, Jesus asked them a question, 42 saying, "What do you think of the Christ? Whose son is he?" They said to him, "The son of David." 43 He said to them, "How is it then that David, inspired by the Spirit, calls him Lord, saying,

44 'The Lord said to my Lord,

Sit at my right hand,

till I put thy enemies under thy feet'?
45 If David thus calls him Lord, how is he his son?" 46 And no one was able to answer him a word, nor from that day did any one dare to ask him any more questions.

**

Jesus denounces the pride of the scribes and Pharisees
Mt 23, 1-12 (Mk 12, 38-40 Lk 20, 45-47)

1 Then said Jesus to the crowds and to his disciples, 2 "The scribes and the Pharisees sit on Moses' seat; 3 so practise and observe whatever they tell you, but not what they do; for they preach, but do not practise. 4 They bind heavy burdens, hard to bear, and lay them on men's shoulders; but they themselves will not move them with their finger. 5 They do all their deeds to be seen by men; for they make their phylacteries

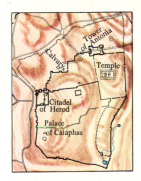

* With the quotation of Deut. 6, 5 — according to Jesus — the answer is not complete. Together with the commandment to love God it is necessary to place the equally important one to love one's neighbour. The former is the motive of the latter, and the latter the confirmation of the former. Together they summarize God's whole will.

** Everyone knew that the Messiah had to be a son of David. But Jesus, with an argument typical of the rabbis, invites them to take notice that the Messiah is greater than his ancestor, David. In fact David (Psalm 110, 1), saying that the Lord invites the Messiah to sit at his own right hand, calls the latter "my Lord."

301

A Hebrew father teaching his son to pray. The picture (by Krestin) shows clearly the philacteries, bound to the left arm of the old man, and the tassels, hanging from the child's shawl (cf. Mt. 23, 5).

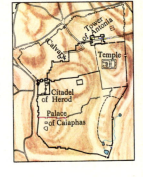

* broad and their fringes long, ⁶ and they love the place of honour at feasts and the best seats in the synagogues, ⁷ and salutations in the market places, and being called rabbi by men. ⁸ But you are not to be called rabbi, for you have one teacher, and you are all brethren. ⁹ And call no man your father on earth, for you have one Father, who is in heaven. ¹⁰ Neither be called masters, for you have one master, the Christ. ¹¹ He who is greatest among you shall be your servant; ¹² whoever exalts himself will be humbled, and whoever humbles himself will be exalted."

"Woe to you, hypocrites"
Mt 23, 13-39 (Lk 11, 49-51; 13, 34-35)

¹³ "But woe to you, scribes and Pharisees, hypocrites! because you shut the kingdom of heaven against men; for you neither enter yourselves, nor allow those who would enter to go in. ¹⁵ Woe to you, scribes and Pharisees, hypocrites! for you traverse sea and land to make a single proselyte, and when he becomes a proselyte, you make him twice as much a child of hell as yourselves.

¹⁶ Woe to you, blind guides, who say, 'If any one swears by the temple, it is nothing; but if any one swears by the gold of the temple, he is bound by his oath.' ¹⁷ You blind fools! For which is greater, the gold or the temple that has made the gold sacred? ¹⁸ And you say, 'If any one swears by the altar, it is nothing; but if any one swears by the gift that is on the altar, he is bound by

* The Jews, taking Deut. 6, 8 literally, wore, bound to their arms or hanging from their foreheads, little leather pouches (philacteries) containing passages from the Bible. The Pharisees wore bigger ones than other people, to draw attention to their zeal.

his oath.' ¹⁹ You blind men! For which is greater, the gift or the altar that makes the gift sacred? ²⁰ So he who swears by the altar, swears by it and by everything on it; ²¹ and he who swears by the temple, swears by it and by him who dwells in it; ²² and he who swears by heaven, swears by the throne of God and by him who sits upon it.

²³ Woe to you, scribes and Pharisees, hypocrites! for you tithe mint and dill and cummin, and have neglected the weightier matters of the law, justice and mercy and faith; these you ought to have done, without neglecting the others. ²⁴ You blind guides, straining out a gnat and swallowing a camel!

²⁵ Woe to you, scribes and Pharisees, hypocrites! for you cleanse the outside of the cup and of the plate, but inside they are full of extortion and rapacity. ²⁶ You blind Pharisee! first cleanse the inside of the cup and of the plate, that the outside also may be clean.

* ²⁷ Woe to you, scribes and Pharisees, hypocrites! for you are like whitewashed tombs, which outwardly appear beautiful, but within they are full of dead men's bones and all uncleanness. ²⁸ So you also outwardly appear righteous to men, but within you are full of hypocrisy and iniquity.

²⁹ Woe to you, scribes and Pharisees, hypocrites! for you build the tombs of the prophets and adorn the monuments of the righteous, ³⁰ saying, 'If we had lived in the days of our fathers, we would not have taken part with them

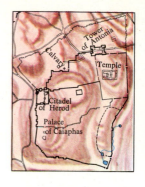

* The conflict between Jesus and the scribes and Pharisees here reaches its height in severity of tone and denunciation. Jesus does not challenge their doctrinal principles, but their behaviour and their twisted, distorted religiosity: inconsistency, different standards for themselves and for others, an observance of the law which was rigid but merely external and made them feel in place, and indeed in their rightful place, before God, and better than other people. The "pharisaic" spirit is an always present temptation, and this page is a very severe warning for Christians also.

in shedding the blood of the prophets.'
³¹ Thus you witness against yourselves,
that you are sons of those who murdered
* the prophets. ³² Fill up, then, the measure of your fathers. ³³ You serpents, you
brood of vipers, how are you to escape
being sentenced to hell? ³⁴ Therefore I
send you prophets and wise men and
scribes, some of whom you will kill and
crucify, and some you will scourge in
your synagogues and persecute from
town to town, ³⁵ that upon you may come
all the righteous blood shed on earth,
from the blood of innocent Abel to the
blood of Zechariah the son of Barachiah,
whom you murdered between the sanc-
tuary and the altar. ³⁶ Truly, I say to you,
all this will come upon this generation."

** ³⁷ "O Jerusalem, Jerusalem, killing the
prophets and stoning those who are sent
to you! How often would I have gathered your children together as a hen gathers her brood under her wings, and
you would not! ³⁸ Behold, your house is
forsaken and desolate. ³⁹ For I tell you,
you will not see me again, until you
say, 'Blessed is he who comes in the
name of the Lord.' "

The sayings about the end of Jerusalem and of the world

Jesus praises the generosity of a poor widow
Lk 21, 1-4 (Mk 12, 41-44)

¹ He looked up and saw the rich put-
ting their gifts into the treasury; ² and

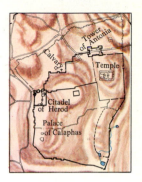

* These men, since
they built the tombs of
the murdered prophets,
considered themselves
better than their fa-
thers. In reality they
were "filling up the
measure" of their fa-
thers, for they were
making their prepara-
tions for murdering
Christ, the greatest of
the prophets.

** Invective has be-
come sorrowful lament.
Yet at the end is the
announcement of the
day when Christ will
return in glory, ack-
nowledged and acclaim-
ed as Messiah by all.

305

The "pinnacle" gives an idea of the tremendous size of Herod's temple. Compare the height of the people with the enormous blocks of stone. The Jews thought of their temple with pride (cf. Lk. 21, 5).

he saw a poor widow put in two copper coins. ³ And he said, "Truly I tell you, this poor widow has put in more than all of them; ⁴ for they all contributed out of their abundance, but she out of her poverty put in all the living that she had."

The ruin of the temple at Jerusalem
Lk 21, 5-7 (Mt 24, 1-3   Mk 13, 1-4)

* ⁵ And as some spoke of the temple, how it was adorned with noble stones and offerings, he said, ⁶ "As for these things which you see, the days will come when there shall not be left here one stone upon another that will not be thrown down." ⁷ And they asked him, "Teacher, when will this be, and what will be the sign when this is about to take place?"

The age of the Church: persecutions and witness
Lk 21, 8-19 (Mt 24, 4-14   Mk 13, 5-13)

⁸ And he said, "Take heed that you are not led astray; for many will come in my name, saying, 'I am he!' and, 'The time is at hand!' Do not go after them. ⁹ And when you hear of wars and tumults, do not be terrified; for this must first take place, but the end will not be at once."

¹⁰ Then he said to them, "Nation will rise against nation, and kingdom against kingdom; ¹¹ there will be great earthquakes, and in various places famines and pestilences; and there will be terrors

* For this discourse of Jesus, Luke takes the material passed down to him, and presents it in a short and clear form, making more distinct what it is which refers to the destruction of Jerusalem, and what to the end of the world, and above all paying due attention to the time between, i.e. the age of the Church.

Tiles found at Jerusalem with the name of the Roman 10th Legion and its symbol, the wild boar. It was one of the legions which, under the orders of Titus, destroyed Jerusalem in A.D. 70.

and great signs from heaven. ¹² But before all this they will lay their hands on you and persecute you, delivering you up to the synagogues and prisons, and you will be brought before kings and governors for my name's sake. ¹³ This
* will be a time for you to bear testimony. ¹⁴ Settle it therefore in your minds, not to meditate beforehand how to answer; ¹⁵ for I will give you a mouth and wisdom, which none of your adversaries will be able to withstand or contradict. ¹⁶ You will be delivered up even by parents and brothers and kinsmen and friends, and some of you they will put to death; ¹⁷ you will be hated by all for my name's sake. ¹⁸ But not a hair of your head will perish. ¹⁹ By your endurance you will gain your lives."

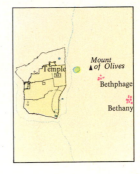

** The destruction of Jerusalem, a foreshadowing of the end of the world
Lk 21, 20-24 (Mt 24, 15-22 Mk 13, 14-20)

²⁰ "But when you see Jerusalem surrounded by armies, then know that its desolation has come near. ²¹ Then let those who are in Judea flee to the mountains, and let those who are inside the city depart, and let not those who are out in the country enter it; ²² for these are days of vengeance, to fulfil all that is written. ²³ Alas for those who are with child and for those who give suck in those days! For great distress shall be upon the earth and wrath upon this people; ²⁴ they will fall by the edge of the sword, and be led captive among

* It is impossible to work out the date or foresee the manner of the coming of the Kingdom in its fullness. Even wars and disasters are not signs of the imminence of the end. The Kingdom is already present and the important thing is to live calmly, zealously and courageously through the present time, though it be marked with difficulties and persecutions. Besides, all this is an opportunity for witnessing to Christ.

** The destruction of Jerusalem came about through the efforts of the Roman legions commanded by Titus in A.D. 70 after a long and terrifying siege.

309

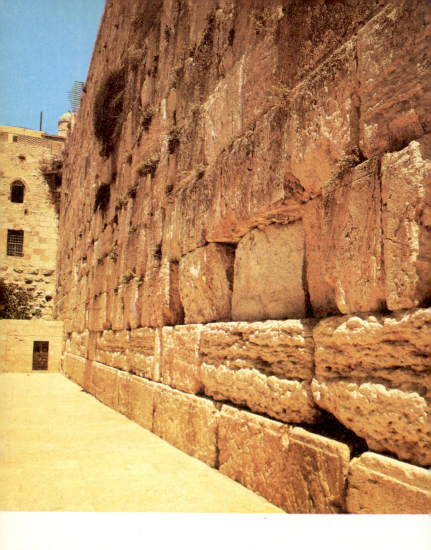

Jerusalem. The "wailing wall" is all that remains of the wall of the western side of Herod's temple. The Jews assemble there to bewail its destruction and to pray.

all nations; and Jerusalem will be trodden down by the Gentiles, until the times of the Gentiles are fulfilled."

The coming, sure and soon, of the Son of Man
Lk 21, 25-33 (Mt 24, 29-36 Mk 13, 24-32)

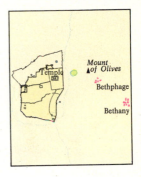

* ²⁵ "And there will be signs in sun and moon and stars, and upon the earth distress of nations in perplexity at the roaring of the sea and the waves, ²⁶ men fainting with fear and with foreboding of what is coming on the world; for the powers of the heavens will be shaken. ²⁷ And then they will see the Son of man coming in a cloud with power and great glory. ²⁸ Now when these things begin to take place, look up and raise your heads, because your redemption is drawing near."

²⁹ And he told them a parable: "Look at the fig tree, and all the trees; ³⁰ as soon as they come out in leaf, you see for yourselves and know that the summer is already near. ³¹ So also, when you see these things taking place, you know that the kingdom of God is near. ³² Truly, I say to you, this generation will not ** pass away till all has taken place. ³³ Heaven and earth will pass away, but my words will not pass away.

Live in the present with an alert mind
Lk 21, 34-38

³⁴ "But take heed to yourselves lest your hearts be weighed down with dissipation and drunkenness and cares of

* Jewish writers of this period, when speaking of God's final intervention in the world, always used this strong, imaginative language called "apocalyptic." The whole world is shaken by the power of God, who comes to judge and to resolve the anomalies of history. Jesus says that he himself, the Son of man, will be the divine Judge. Then there will be complete liberation.

** The end of Jerusalem will come to pass within the course of a generation, whereas Jesus was unwilling to reveal the date of the end of the world. At this point Mark adds: "But of that day or that hour no one knows, not even the angels, nor the Son, but only the Father" (Mk. 13, 32).

Oil lamps of Jesus' time, with their pitchers. In the centre is a lantern. In nuptial processions it was usual to have candelabra of a larger sort, in the shape of torches and always fed with oil (cf. Mt. 25, 3-4).

this life, and that day come upon you suddenly like a snare; ³⁵ for it will come upon all who dwell upon the face of the whole earth. ³⁶ But watch at all times, praying that you may have strength to escape all these things that will take place, and to stand before the Son of man."

³⁷ And every day he was teaching in the temple, but at night he went out and lodged on the mount called Olivet. ³⁸ And early in the morning all the people came to him in the temple to hear him.

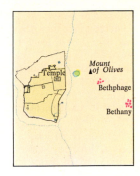

Parable of the ten young women at the wedding procession
Mt 25, 1-13

** ¹ "Then the kingdom of heaven shall be compared to ten maidens who took their lamps and went to meet the bridegroom. ² Five of them were foolish, and five were wise. ³ For when the foolish took their lamps, they took no oil with them; ⁴ but the wise took flasks of oil with their lamps. ⁵ As the bridegroom was delayed, they all slumbered and slept. ⁶ But at midnight there was a cry, 'Behold, the bridegroom! Come out to meet him.' ⁷ Then all those maidens rose and trimmed their lamps. ⁸ And the foolish said to the wise, 'Give us some of your oil, for our lamps are going out.' ⁹ But the wise replied, 'Perhaps there will not be enough for us and for you; go rather to the dealers and buy for yourselves.' ¹⁰ And while they went to buy, the bridegroom came, and those who were ready went in with him to the

* The future sheds its light on the present moment and makes it important for salvation. The Christian lives in hope and loyalty.

** This discourse of Jesus ends in Matthew's gospel with two parables which exhort to Christian vigilance, to being watchful and active. For the first parable Jesus takes his starting point from contemporary customs for the marriage ceremony: towards evening the bride waited with her friends for the arrival of the bridegroom, and then went in procession to his house. Even if the bridegroom is late, says Jesus, it is wise to be ready at any moment.

313

marriage feast; and the door was shut. [11] Afterward the other maidens came also, saying, 'Lord, lord, open to us.' [12] But he replied, 'Truly, I say to you, I do not know you.' [13] Watch therefore, for you know neither the day nor the hour."

Parable of the talents
Mt 25, 14-30

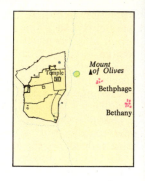

* [14] "For it will be as when a man going on a journey called his servants and entrusted to them his property; [15] to one he gave five talents, to another two, to another one, to each according to his ability. Then he went away. [16] He who had received the five talents went at once and traded with them; and he made five talents more. [17] So also, he who had the two talents made two talents more. [18] But he who had received the one talent went and dug in the ground and hid his master's money. [19] Now after a long time the master of those servants came and settled accounts with them. [20] And he who had received the five talents came forward, bringing five talents more, saying, 'Master, you delivered to me five talents; here I have made five talents more.' [21] His master said to him, 'Well done, good and faithful servant; you have been faithful over a little, I will set you over much; enter into the joy of your master.' [22] And he also who had the two talents came forward, saying, 'Master, you delivered to me two talents; here I have made two talents more.' [23] His master said to him, 'Well done, good and faithful servant;

* Watchfulness is not a negative attitude, but requires zeal and loyalty in order to make the gifts received from God bear fruit for the benefit of one's neighbour: natural endowments, a good education, climate, material wealth, etc... At the day of reckoning the idle servant will be cast out like a sinner.

314

you have been faithful over a little, I will set you over much; enter into the joy of your master.' ²⁴ He also who had received the one talent came forward, saying, 'Master, I knew you to be a hard man, reaping where you did not sow, and gathering where you did not winnow; ²⁵ so I was afraid, and I went and hid your talent in the ground. Here you have what is yours.' ²⁶ But his master answered him, 'You wicked and slothful servant! You knew that I reap where I have not sowed, and gather where I have not winnowed? ²⁷ Then you ought to have invested my money with the bankers, and at my coming I should have received what was my own with interest. ²⁸ So take the talent from him, and give it to him who has the ten talents. ²⁹ For to every one who has will more be given, and he will have abundance; but from him who has not, even what he has will be taken away. ³⁰ And cast the worthless servant into the outer darkness; there men will weep and gnash their teeth.' "

Mount of Olives

Temple

Bethphage

Bethany

The principle of the last judgment
Mt 25, 31-46

* ³¹ "When the Son of man comes in his glory, and all the angels with him, then he will sit on his glorious throne. ³² Before him will be gathered all the nations, and he will separate them one from another as a shepherd separates the sheep from the goats, ³³ and he will place the sheep at his right hand, but the goats at the left. ³⁴ Then the King

*   From the impressive and poetic scene which Jesus describes, it is evident that the fundamental principle of the last judgment, which awaits all men, will be charity towards their neighbour, service to the most neglected and needy brethren. They are Jesus' "brothers," for he made himself one with them: therefore help given or withheld from them is given or withheld from Jesus himself.

Jerusalem. The majestic "Golden gate", facing east. It is a Byzantine-Arabic erection on the foundation of the Herodian gate. The Muslims walled up its double gateway, and they think that it will be re-opened only on the day of judgment.

will say to those at his right hand, 'Come, O blessed of my Father, inherit the kingdom prepared for you from the foundation of the world; 35 for I was hungry and you gave me food, I was thirsty and you gave me drink, I was a stranger and you welcomed me, 36 I was naked and you clothed me, I was sick and you visited me, I was in prison and you came to me.' 37 Then the righteous will answer him, 'Lord, when did we see thee hungry and feed thee, or thirsty and give thee drink? 38 And when did we see thee a stranger and welcome thee, or naked and clothe thee? 39 And when did we see thee sick or in prison and visit thee? 40 And the King will answer them, 'Truly I say to you, as you did it to one of the least of these my brethren, you did it to me.' 41 Then he will say to those at his left hand, 'Depart from me, you cursed, into the eternal fire prepared for the devil and his angels; 42 for I was hungry and you gave me no food, I was thirsty and you gave me no drink, 43 I was a stranger and you did not welcome me, naked and you did not clothe me, sick and in prison and you did not visit me.' 44 Then they also will answer, 'Lord, when did we see thee hungry or thirsty or a stranger or naked or sick or in prison, and did not minister to thee?' 45 Then he will answer them, 'Truly, I say to you, as you did it not to one of the least of these, you did it not to me.' 46 And they will go away into eternal punishment, but the righteous into eternal life."

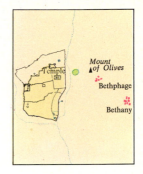

Phials of irridescent glass of Jesus' day, found at Bethany. They were used to hold precious ointments (cf. Mt. 26, 6-7).

The passion approaches

The Sanhedrin's plot against Jesus
Mt 26, 1-5 (Mk 14, 1-2 Lk 22, 1-2)

* ¹ When Jesus had finished all these sayings, he said to his disciples, ² "You know that after two days the Passover is coming, and the Son of man will be delivered up to be crucified."

³ Then the chief priests and the elders of the people gathered in the palace of the high priest, who was called Caiaphas, ⁴ and took counsel together in order to arrest Jesus by stealth and kill him. ⁵ But they said, "Not during the feast, lest there be a tumult among the people."

The fragrant ointment on Jesus' head foretells his burial
Mt 26, 6-13 (Mk 14, 3-9 Jn 12, 1-11)

⁶ Now when Jesus was at Bethany in the house of Simon the leper, ⁷ a woman came up to him with an alabaster jar of very expensive ointment, and she poured it on his head, as he sat at table. ⁸ But when the disciples saw it, they were indignant, saying, "Why this waste? ⁹ For this ointment might have been sold for a large sum, and given to the poor." ¹⁰ But Jesus, aware of this, said to them, "Why do you trouble the woman? For she has done a beautiful thing to me. ¹¹ For you always have the poor with

** you, but you will not always have me. ¹² In pouring this ointment on my body she has done it to prepare me for burial.

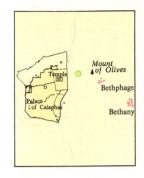

Mount of Olives
Temple
Bethphage
Palace of Caiaphas
Bethany

*   Matthew emphasizes Jesus' foreknowledge of his imminent passion. The death on the Cross is not for him a tragic fatality but the culminating act of his mission.

** Jesus says to his disciples that in practice they will have other opportunities of helping the poor, whereas the deed of this woman is a thoughtful and generously loving act towards himself as he is about to die: an anticipation, as it were, of his burial.

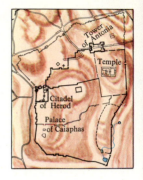

¹³ Truly, I say to you, wherever this gospel is preached in the whole world, what she has done will be told in memory of her."

Judas betrays Jesus for money
Mt 26, 14-16 (Mk 14, 10-11 Lk 22, 3-6)

¹⁴ Then one of the twelve, who was called Judas Iscariot, went to the chief priests ¹⁵ and said, "What will you give me if I deliver him to you?" And they
* paid him thirty pieces of silver. ¹⁶ And from that moment he sought an opportunity to betray him.

Jesus speaks of his 'hour':
the cross and glory
Jn 12, 20-36

²⁰Now among those who went up to worship at the feast were some Greeks. ²¹ So these came to Philip, who was from Bethsaida in Galilee, and said to him, "Sir, we wish to see Jesus." ²² Philip went and told Andrew; Andrew went with Philip and they told Jesus. ²³ And Jesus answered them, "The hour has
** come for the Son of man to be glorified. ²⁴ Truly, truly, I say to you, unless a grain of wheat falls into the earth and dies, it remains alone; but if it dies, it bears much fruit. ²⁵ He who loves his life loses it, and he who hates his life in this world will keep it for eternal life. ²⁶ If any one serves me, he must follow me; and where I am, there shall my servant be also; if any one serves me, the Father will honour him.

* The figure corresponds to the value of a slave. In fact the Mosaic law condemned anyone who had accidentally killed a slave to a fine of thirty silver coins.

** In these Gentiles who wished to meet him, Jesus sees an anticipation of the fruits of his death. Facing it he is deeply disturbed, but he accepts it through loyalty to his Father and through love. The "hour of glorification" is for the evangelist the hour of Jesus' death and resurrection. He is the grain of wheat which by dying will bear much fruit. And whoever wishes to follow him will pass along the same road to death and resurrection.

²⁷ Now is my soul troubled. And what shall I say? 'Father, save me from this hour'? No, for this purpose I have come to this hour. ²⁸ Father, glorify thy name." Then a voice came from heaven, "I have glorified it, and I will glorify it again." ²⁹ The crowd standing by heard it and said that it had thundered. Others said, "An angel has spoken to him." ³⁰ Jesus answered, "This voice has come for your sake, not for mine. ³¹ Now is the judgment of this world, now shall the ruler of this world be cast out; ³² and I, when
*I am lifted up from the earth, will draw all men to myself." ³³ He said this to show by what death he was to die. ³⁴ The crowd answered him, "We have heard from the law that the Christ remains for ever. How can you say that the Son of man must be lifted up? Who is this Son of man?" ³⁵ Jesus said to them, "The light is with you for a little longer. Walk while you have the light, lest the darkness overtake you; he who walks in the darkness does not know where he goes. ³⁶ While you have the light, believe in the light, that you may become sons of light."

When Jesus had said this, he departed and hid himself from them.

* Judgment will take place before the cross of Jesus, the sign of God's love: defeat and condemnation for Satan, who was controlling the world, and salvation for men. All will be drawn to Christ, crucified and glorious: around him will be built unity among men.

** At the end of Jesus' public activity, John draws up a sort of final balance-sheet. Most people, in spite of the signs, have not believed. This may be explained by two quotations taken from the prophet Isaiah (53, 1 and 6, 9-10); unbelief was foreseen in God's plan, even though it remains the fruit of man's evil will.

The mystery of unbelief
Jn 12, 37-50

* ³⁷ Though he had done so many signs before them, yet they did not believe in him; ³⁸ it was that the word spoken by the prophet Isaiah might be fulfilled:

"Lord, who has believed our report,
and to whom has the arm
of the Lord been revealed?"
³⁹ Therefore they could not believe. For
Isaiah again said,
⁴⁰ "He has blinded their eyes
and hardened their heart,
lest they should see with their eyes
and perceive with their heart,
and turn for me to heal them."
⁴¹ Isaiah said this because he saw his
* glory and spoke of him. ⁴² Nevertheless
many even of the authorities believed in
him, but for fear of the Pharisees they
did not confess it, lest they should be
put out of the synagogue: ⁴³ for they
loved the praise of men more than the
praise of God.

⁴⁴ And Jesus cried out and said, "He
who believes in me, believes not in me,
but in him who sent me. ⁴⁵ And he who
sees me sees him who sent me. ⁴⁶ I have
come as light into the world, that whoever believes in me may not remain in
darkness. ⁴⁷ If any one hears my sayings
and does not keep them, I do not judge
him; for I did not come to judge the
world but to save the world. ⁴⁸ He who
rejects me and does not receive my
sayings has a judge; the word that I
have spoken will be his judge on the
last day. ⁴⁹ For I have not spoken on
my own authority; the Father who sent
me has himself given me commandment
** what to say and what to speak. ⁵⁰ And
I know that his commandment is eternal
life. What I say, therefore, I say as the
Father has bidden me."

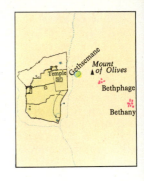

* For the evangelist
Jesus is the centre of
and the key to the
interpretation of the
whole of the Bible.

** This is Jesus' last
public utterance and
his last appeal, as he
re-affirms before the
unbelieving and doubt-
ful his mission as Mes-
siah Son of God.

322

VII - THE PASSION AND RESURRECTION

The last events in the life of Jesus were the first to be gathered together and narrated in the early Church.

At the last supper Jesus instituted the Eucharist, the sacrament of his life given and offered in sacrifice for the salvation of men; in the same intimate setting John records Jesus' farewell sayings, his spiritual testament as it were. Then all the evangelists give ample space to the account of the passion and death. But the defeat is only in appearance. The Easter news discloses this: Jesus of Nazareth, crucified, has arisen and is alive again! The empty tomb and, above all, the appearances of the risen Christ confirm this.

From that moment the death and resurrection of Christ are proclaimed to all men. They are the centre of the Christian faith.

The ancient stony road which leads down from the Mount of Olives to the Valley of the Kedron and the city of Jerusalem, passing close to the garden of Gethsemane. Jesus used this road many times.

The Last Supper

Jesus institutes the Eucharist
Lk 22, 7-20 (Mt 26, 17-20; 26-29 Mk 14, 12-17)

* ⁷ Then came the day of Unleavened Bread, on which the passover lamb had to be sacrificed. ⁸ So Jesus sent Peter and John, saying, "Go and prepare the passover for us, that we may eat it." ⁹ They said to him, "Where will you have us prepare it?" ¹⁰ He said to them, "Behold, when you have entered the city, a man carrying a jar of water will meet you; follow him into the house which he enters, ¹¹ and tell the householder, 'The Teacher says to you, Where is the guest room, where I am to eat the passover with my disciples?' ¹² And he will show you a large upper room furnished; there make ready." ¹³ And they went, and found it as he had told them; and they prepared the passover.

¹⁴ And when the hour came, he sat at table, and the apostles with him. ¹⁵ And he said to them, "I have earnestly desired to eat this passover with you before I suffer; ¹⁶ for I tell you I shall not eat it until it is fulfilled in the

** kingdom of God." ¹⁷ And he took a cup, and when he had given thanks he said, "Take this, and divide it among yourselves; ¹⁸ for I tell you that from now on I shall not drink of the fruit of the vine until the kingdom of God comes." ¹⁹ And he took bread, and when he had given thanks he broke it and gave it to them, saying, "This is my body which is given

* The days of Unleavened Bread were so called because the Mosaic Law laid down the use of nothing but bread without yeast (unleavened) during those days. Jesus' last Supper thus took place in the context of the Jewish Passover.

** These words refer to the preliminary blessing of the paschal meal. Jesu knows that these are the last hours which he will spend with his apostles.

325

Jerusalem. The present entrance to the Cenacle. The room of the last Supper is on the upper floor. After Easter the Cenacle became the centre of the life of the first Christian community.

* for you. Do this in remembrance of me."
²⁰ And likewise the cup after supper, saying, "This cup which is poured out for you is the new covenant in my
** blood."

Jesus speaks of the traitor
Lk 22, 21-23 (Mt 26, 21-25 Mk 14, 18-21)

²¹ "But behold the hand of him who betrays me is with me on the table. ²² For the Son of man goes as it has been determined; but woe to that man by whom he is betrayed!" ²³ And they began to question one another, which of them it was that would do this.

Jesus teaches humility and promises the kingdom
Lk 22, 24-30

²⁴ A dispute also arose among them, which of them was to be regarded as the greatest. ²⁵ And he said to them, "The kings of the Gentiles exercise lordship over them; and those in authority over them are called benefactors. ²⁶ But not so with you; rather let the greatest among you become as the youngest, and the leader as one who serves. ²⁷ For which is the greater, one who sits at table, or one who serves? Is it not the one who sits at table? But I am among you as one who serves.

²⁸ You are those who have continued with me in my trials; ²⁹ as my Father appointed a kingdom for me, so do I appoint for you ³⁰ that you may eat and drink at my table in my kingdom, and

*   At the last Supper Jesus transformed the bread and wine, making his Body and Blood present through these signs, and offering them in sacrifice for the salvation of the world. From the beginning, the Christian community assembled to repeat and make actual this action of Jesus, in the "breaking of the bread."

**   The "New Covenant" between God and men, promised by Jeremiah (31, 31-34) and Ezekiel (36, 24-28) was to bring the forgiveness of sins and the gift of the Spirit, who changes man so that he really fulfils God's will. All this is realized by the death and resurrection of Christ, who is present in the Eucharist.

327

sit on thrones judging the twelve tribes of Israel."

"Simon, I have prayed for you..."
Lk 22, 31-38 (Mt 26, 30-35   Mk 14, 26-31)

* ³¹ "Simon, Simon, behold, Satan demanded to have you, that he might sift you like wheat, ³² but I have prayed for you that your faith may not fail; and when you have turned again, strengthen your brethren." ³³ And he said to him, "Lord, I am ready to go with you to prison and to death." ³⁴ He said, "I tell you, Peter, the cock will not crow this day, until you three times deny that you know me."

³⁵ And he said to them, "When I sent you out with no purse or bag or sandals, did you lack anything?" They said, "Nothing." ³⁶ He said to them, "But now, let him who has a purse take it, and likewise a bag. And let him who has no sword sell his mantle and buy one. ³⁷ For I tell you that this scripture must be fulfilled in me, 'And he was reckoned with transgressors'; for what is written about me has its fulfilment." ³⁸ And they said, "Look, Lord, here are two swords." ** And he said to them, "It is enough."

The farewell discourses according to John

Jesus washes the disciples' feet
Jn 13, 1-17

*** ¹ Now before the feast of the Passover, when Jesus knew that his hour had

*   Jesus wishes to prepare the disciples for the difficult trial to which their faith will be subjected when they see him condemned and crucified. (According to Mk. 14, 26 Jesus quoted the prophet Zechariah: "Strike the shepherd that the sheep may be scattered"). In particular he predicts Peter's denial, but lays precisely on him, once he has repented, the task of sustaining the faith of the community.

**   The illustration of the sword shows the strength with which they must be armed as they face the stern trial. But the disciples show that they have not understood its meaning.

*** Jesus begins with an action of profound love and humility,

come to depart out of this world to the Father, having loved his own who were in the world, he loved them to the end. [2] And during supper, when the devil had already put it into the heart of Judas Iscariot, Simon's son, to betray him, [3] Jesus, knowing that the Father had given all things into his hands, and that he had come from God and was going to God, [4] rose from supper, laid aside his garments, and girded himself with a towel. [5] Then he poured water into a basin, and began to wash the disciples' feet, and to wipe them with the towel with which he was girded.

* [6] He came to Simon Peter; and Peter said to him, "Lord, do you wash my feet?" [7] Jesus answered him, "What I am doing you do not know now, but afterward you will understand." [8] Peter said to him, "You shall never wash my feet." Jesus answered him, "If I do not wash you, you have no part in me." [9] Simon Peter said to him, "Lord, not my feet only but also my hands and my head!" [10] Jesus said to him, "He who has bathed does not need to wash, except for his feet, but he is clean all over; and you are clean, but not all of you." [11] For he knew who was to betray him; that was why he said, "You are not all clean."

[12] When he had washed their feet, and taken his garments, and resumed his place, he said to them, "Do you know what I have done to you? [13] You call me Teacher and Lord; and you are right, for so I am. [14] If I then, your Lord and

which is followed by a short dialogue; then he talks at length to the disciples and ends with a prayer to the Father. The atmosphere is one of great intimacy: these are the last lessons, recommendations and promises made by Jesus now that his "hour" has come. He is addressing the disciples there present, but also all the Christian communities of the future.

* At that time it was the custom, before the beginning of a meal, for the slaves to go from one guest to another washing their feet (they did not sit but reclined on divans). Jesus therefore performed a function reserved for slaves. It is easy to understand Peter's reaction.

329

Teacher, have washed your feet, you also ought to wash one another's feet. [15] For I have given you an example, that you also should do as I have done to you. [16] Truly, truly, I say to you, a servant is not greater than his master; nor is he who is sent greater than he * who sent him. [17] If you know these things, blessed are you if you do them."

Jesus tells who will betray him
Jn 13, 18-30

[18] "I am not speaking of you all; I know whom I have chosen; it is that the scripture may be fulfilled, 'He who ate my bread has lifted his heel against ** me.' [19] I tell you this now, before it takes place, that when it does take place you may believe that I am he. [20] Truly, truly, I say to you, he who receives any one whom I send receives me; and he who receives me receives him who sent me."

[21] When Jesus had thus spoken, he was troubled in spirit, and testified, "Truly, truly, I say to you, one of you will betray me." [22] The disciples looked at one another, uncertain of whom he spoke. [23] One of his disciples, whom Jesus *** loved, was lying close to the breast of Jesus; [24] so Simon Peter beckoned to him and said, "Tell us who it is of whom he speaks." [25] So lying thus, close to the breast of Jesus, he said to him, "Lord, who is it?" [26] Jesus answered, "It is he to whom I shall give this morsel when I have dipped it." So when he had dipped the morsel, he gave it to Judas, the son of Simon Iscariot. [27] Then after the

* The act of washing the disciples' feet summarizes symbolically the whole of Jesus' life, which consisted of humbling himself and giving himself "to the limit." The disciples will be blessed if they imitate him by humbly serving each other.

** This is a quotation from Psalm 41, 10 and means: My very dear friend, who has eaten with me, has betrayed me. The betrayal raises the love of Christ to an even higher level.

*** The "disciple whom Jesus loved" was in all probability John the evangelist and author of the fourth gospel himself. He was placed on a divan in front of Jesus.

morsel, Satan entered into him. Jesus said to him, "What you are going to do, do quickly." 28 Now no one at the table knew why he said this to him. 29 Some thought that, because Judas had the money box, Jesus was telling him, "Buy what we need for the feast"; or, that he should give something to the poor. 30 So, after receiving the morsel, he immediately went out; and it was night.

"I give you a new commandment"
Jn 13, 31-35

31 When he had gone out, Jesus said, "Now is the Son of man glorified, and * in him God is glorified; 32 if God is glorified in him, God will also glorify him in himself, and glorify him at once. 33 Little children, yet a little while I am with you. You will seek me; and as I said to the Jews so now I say to you, 'Where I am going you cannot come.' ** 34 A new commandment I give to you, that you love one another; even as I have loved you, that you also love one another. 35 By this all men will know that you are my disciples, if you have love for one another."

Jesus foretells Peter's denial
Jn 13, 36-38

36 Simon Peter said to him, "Lord, where are you going?" Jesus answered, "Where I am going you cannot follow me now; but you shall follow afterward." *** 37 Peter said to him, "Lord, why cannot I follow you now? I will lay

* Jesus considered that his passion was starting then. For the evangelist John the passion is already a "glorification," that is the supreme expression of God's glory, which is love. Jesus' resurrection is the Father's answer.

** The command of mutual love is "new" because it has in Jesus its pattern and its source: "Love one another as I have loved you," i.e. as far as to give your lives. Brotherly love is the badge of Christians.

*** Perhaps this is an allusion to Peter's future martyrdom.

331

Jerusalem. The "upper room" of the Cenacle where Jesus instituted the Eucharist, and gave his last reminders to his disciples. Here he appeared after the Resurrection and here also the events of Pentecost took place. The room was restored and decorated in the fourteenth century.

down my life for you." [38] Jesus answered, "Will you lay down your life for me? Truly, truly, I say to you, the cock will not crow, till you have denied me three times."

"I am the way and the truth and the life"
Jn 14, 1-14

[1] "Let not your hearts be troubled; believe in God, believe also in me. [2] In my Father's house are many rooms; if it were not so, would I have told you that I go to prepare a place for you? [3] And when I go and prepare a place for you, I will come again and will take you to myself, that where I am you may be also. [4] And you know the way where I am going."

[5] Thomas said to him, "Lord, we do not know where you are going; how can we know the way?" [6] Jesus said to
*him, "I am the way, and the truth, and the life; no one comes to the Father, but by me. [7] If you had known me, you would have known my Father also; henceforth you know him and have seen him."

[8] Philip said to him, "Lord, show us the Father, and we shall be satisfied." [9] Jesus said to him, "Have I been with you so long, and yet you do not know me, Philip? He who has seen me has seen the Father; how can you say, 'Show us the Father'? [10] Do you not believe that I am in the Father and the Father in me? The words that I say to

* Jesus states that he is the only "way" by which we can reach God; the very "truth" of God, his plan of salvation, revealed to men, and carried out; the "life" for anyone who comes to him with faith. In this well-known answer, Jesus declares himself the only mediator between God and men.

you I do not speak on my own authority; but the Father who dwells in me does his works. [11] Believe me that I am in the Father and the Father in me; or else believe me for the sake of the works themselves.

[12] Truly, truly, I say to you, he who believes in me will also do the works that I do; and greater works than these will he do, because I go to the Father. [13] Whatever you ask in my name, I will do it, that the Father may be glorified in the Son; [14] if you ask anything in my name, I will do it."

Jesus promises the Holy Spirit
Jn 14, 15-31

[15] "If you love me, you will keep my commandments. [16] And I will pray the Father, and he will give you another Counsellor, to be with you for ever, [17] even the Spirit of truth, whom the world cannot receive, because it neither sees him nor knows him; you know him, for he dwells with you, and will be in you.

* [18] I will not leave you desolate; I will come to you. [19] Yet a little while, and the world will see me no more, but you will see me; because I live, you will live also. [20] In that day you will know that I am in my Father, and you in me, and I ** in you. [21] He who has my commandments and keeps them, he it is who loves me; and he who loves me will be loved by my Father, and I will love him and manifest myself to him." [22] Judas (not Iscariot) said to him, "Lord, how is it

* Jesus must go away and will no longer by physically present with his people. But he will not leave them "orphans" in a situation in which they will experience persecution, doubt and discouragement. He "will come" again, not only at the end of history, but soon, when he sends the Holy Spirit. The word translated "Counsellor" means at the same time advocate, help, defender and protector.

** God's love awaits the answering love of man; this consists in welcoming and definitely observing the word of Jesus. Then Jesus Christ and the Father himself will show themselves and give themselves more and more profoundly and intimately.

that you will manifest yourself to us, and not to the world?" 23 Jesus answered him, "If a man loves me, he will keep my word, and my Father will love him, and we will come to him and make our home with him. 24 He who does not love me does not keep my words; and the word which you hear is not mine but the Father's who sent me.

25 These things I have spoken to you, while I am still with you. 26 But the Counsellor, the Holy Spirit, whom the Father will send in my name, he will teach you all things, and bring to your

* remembrance all that I have said to you. 27 Peace I leave with you; my peace I give to you; not as the world gives do I give to you. Let not your hearts be troubled, neither let them be afraid. 28 You heard me say to you, 'I go away, and I will come to you.' If you loved me, you would have rejoiced, because I

** go to the Father; for the Father is greater than I. 29 And now I have told you before it takes place, so that when it does take place, you may believe. 30 I will no longer talk much with you, for the ruler of this world is coming. He has no power over me; 31 but I do as the Father has commanded me, so that the

** world may know that I love the Father. Rise, let us go hence."

"I am the vine, you are the branches"
Jn 15, 1-11

1 "I am the true vine, and my Father is the vinedresser. 2 Every branch of mine that bears no fruit, he takes away,

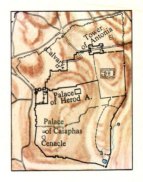

* This is the way the Holy Spirit works: by interior, personal teaching which makes us remember, understand and appreciate the word of Jesus. Its effect is strength and peace which overcome all fear and uncertainty.

** Jesus, in that he is Son of God, is equal to the Father; in that he is man, he is inferior to him.

*** Jesus now faces the passion, which seems to be the triumph of Satan "the prince of this world." Not that he is more powerful than Jesus, but Jesus submits to the cross freely, for love and in obedience to the Father.

This Jewish-Christian tomb of the second century A.D. already displays the symbolism of the vine and the branches, used by Jesus when he spoke of the profound mystery of our communion with him (Jn. 15, 1-11).

and every branch that does bear fruit he prunes that it way bear more fruit. ³ You are already made clean by the word which I have spoken to you. ⁴ Abide in me, and I in you. As the branch cannot bear fruit by itself, unless it abides in the vine, neither can you, unless you abide in me. ⁵ I am the vine, you are the branches. He who abides in me, and I in him, he it is that bears much fruit, for apart from me you can do nothing. ⁶ If a man does not abide in me, he is cast forth as a branch and withers; and the branches are gathered, thrown into the fire and burned. ⁷ If you abide in me, and my words abide in you, ask whatever you will, and it shall be done for you. ⁸ By this my Father is glorified, that you bear much fruit, and so prove to be my disciples. ⁹ As the Father has loved me, so have I loved you; abide in my love. ¹⁰ If you keep my commandments, you will abide in my love, just as I have kept my Father's commandments and abide in his love. ¹¹ These things I have spoken to you, that my joy may be in you, and that your joy may be full."

"This is my commandment: love one another"
Jn 15, 12-17

¹² "This is my commandment, that you love one another as I have loved you. ¹³ Greater love has no man than this, that a man lay down his life for his friends. ¹⁴ You are my friends if you do what I command you. ¹⁵ No longer do I

* With the illustration of the vine and the branches, Jesus makes us see the profound, inward communion which unites all his disciples to him. The two key expressions are "abide in" Christ who is the vine, and, consequently, "bear fruit." Grafted in Christ, we must remain united with him, welcome his word and keep his commandments, in that love which springs from the Father and the Son. It is the divine life which Christ communicates to us, the life of grace. The branch which is separated from the vine dries up and cannot bear any fruit which is of value in God's sight.

337

Jerusalem. The garden, down in the valley of the Kedron, which is the traditional site of St. Stephen's martyrdom. In his last utterances Jesus forewarned his disciples of persecution (Jn. 15, 20).

call you servants, for the servant does not know what his master is doing; but I have called you friends, for all that I have heard from my Father I have made known to you. ¹⁶ You did not choose me, but I chose you and appointed you *that you should go and bear fruit and that your fruit should abide; so that whatever you ask the Father in my name, he may give it to you. ¹⁷ This I command you, to love one another."

"If they persecuted me, they will persecute you too"
Jn 15, 18-27; 16, 1-4

¹⁸ "If the world hates you, know that it has hated me before it hated you. ¹⁹ If you were of the world, the world would love its own; but because you are not of the world, but I chose you out of the world, therefore the world hates you. ²⁰ Remember the word that I said to you, 'A servant is not greater than his master.' If they persecuted me, they will persecute you; if they kept my word, they will keep yours also. ²¹ But all this they will do to you on my account, because they do not know him who sent me. ²² If I had not come and spoken to them, they would not have sin; but now they have no excuse for their sin. ²³ He who hates me hates my Father also. ²⁴ If I had not done among them the works which no one else did, they would not have sin; but now they have seen and hated both me and my Father. ²⁵ It is to fulfil the word that is written in their law, 'They hated me

* The fruit which God wants is mutual love: a love like that of Jesus which goes so far as to be able to suffer and die for those he loves.

** In the fourth gospel, the word "world" has two fundamental meanings, different from one another: positively, it is the whole of mankind whom God so loved that he sent his Son to save them (3, 16); negatively, it represents the whole mass of the forces opposed to God and his plan of salvation, in pursuit of a philosophy of selfishness. In these farewell utterances the negative meaning prevails. But, with the help of the Spirit, proceeding from the Father, the disciples will bear witness to Christ.

339

without a cause.' 26 But when the Counsellor comes, whom I shall send to you from the Father, even the Spirit of truth, who proceeds from the Father, he will bear witness to me; 27 and you also are witnesses, because you have been with me from the beginning.

1 I have said all this to you to keep you from falling away. 2 They will put you out of the synagogues; indeed, the hour is coming when whoever kills you will think he is offering service to God. 3 And they will do this because they have not known the Father, nor me. 4 But I have said these things to you, that when their hour comes you may remember that I told you of them.

I did not say these things to you from the beginning, because I was with you."

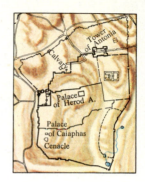

Jesus explains the action of the Holy Spirit
Jn 16, 5-15

5 "But now I am going to him who sent me; yet none of you asks me, 'Where are you going?' 6 But because I have said these things to you, sorrow has filled your hearts. 7 Nevertheless I tell you the truth: it is to your advantage that I go away, for if I do not go away, the Counsellor will not come to you; but if I go, I will send him to you. 8 And when he comes, he will convince the world of sin and of righteousness *and of judgment: 9 of sin, because they do not believe in me; 10 of righteousness, because I go to the Father, and you will

* The Spirit will make it clear that not to believe in Jesus means opposition to God and is man's ruin ("sin"); that Christ's resurrection and ascension are a sign of the victory of crucified love ("righteousness"); that the world which opposes God is already condemned to defeat ("judgment"). Being convinced of this, the disciples will have interior peace and liberty.

see me no more; [11] of judgment, because the ruler of this world is judged.

[12] I have yet many things to say to you, but you cannot bear them now. [13] When the Spirit of truth comes, he
* will guide you into all the truth; for he will not speak on his own authority, but whatever he hears he will speak, and he will declare to you the things that are to come. [14] He will glorify me, for he will take what is mine and declare it to you. [15] All that the Father has is mine; therefore I said that he will take what is mine and declare it to you."

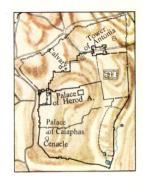

Jesus will soon return and turn sadness into joy
Jn 16, 16-24

** [16] "A little while, and you will see me no more; again a little while, and you will see me." [17] Some of his disciples said to one another, "What is this that he says to us, 'A little while, and you will not see me, and again a little while, and you will see me'; and, 'because I go to the Father'?" [18] They said, "What does he mean by 'a little while'? We do not know what he means." [19] Jesus knew that they wanted to ask him; so he said to them, "Is this what you are asking yourselves, what I meant by saying, 'A little while, and you will not see me, and again a little while, and you will see me'? [20] Truly, truly, I say to you, you will weep and lament, but the world will rejoice; you will be sorrowful, but your sorrow will turn into joy. [21] When a woman is in travail she has sorrow,

* The Spirit is the teacher of the soul, who makes us understand Jesus and leads us to know all truth profoundly.

** For a little time the disciples will be distressed by the death of Jesus, but shortly afterwards they will be full of joy, when they see him risen from the dead.

341

because her hour has come; but when she is delivered of the child, she no longer remembers the anguish, for joy that a child is born into the world. 22 So you have sorrow now, but I will see you again and your hearts will rejoice, and *no one will take your joy from you. 23 In that day you will ask nothing of me. Truly, truly, I say to you, if you ask anything of the Father, he will give it to you in my name. 24 Hitherto you have asked nothing in my name; ask, and you will receive, that your joy may be full."

"Be of good cheer:
I have overcome the world!"
Jn 16, 25-33

25 "I have said this to you in figures; the hour is coming when I shall no longer speak to you in figures but tell you plainly of the Father. 26 In that day you will ask in my name; and I do not say to you that I shall pray the Father for you; 27 for the Father himself loves you, because you have loved me and have believed that I came from the **Father. 28 I came from the Father and have come into the world; again, I am leaving the world and going to the Father."

29 His disciples said, "Ah, now you are speaking plainly, not in any figure! 30 Now we know that you know all things, and need none to question you; by this we believe that you came from God." 31 Jesus answered them, "Do you now believe? 32 The hour is coming, indeed it

* The joy of the disciples is the joy of gratitude and of confidence in the Father, and it is the joy of selflessness which sees beyond affliction the growth of new life. Such joy has its deepest roots in faith, in hope and in mutual love.

** A summary of Jesus' mission; having come from the Father to reveal him to men and to save them, he now returns to the Father and remains the "way" by which all mankind may approach God.

342

has come, when you will be scattered, every man to his home, and will leave me alone; yet I am not alone, for the Father is with me. ³³ I have said this to you, that in me you may have peace. In the world you have tribulation; but be of good cheer, I have overcome the world."

Jesus prays for himself
Jn 17, 1-5

* ¹ When Jesus had spoken these words, he lifted up his eyes to heaven and said, "Father, the hour has come; glorify thy Son that the Son may glorify thee, ² since thou hast given him power over all flesh, to give eternal life to all whom thou hast given him. ³ And this is eternal **life, that they know thee the only true God, and Jesus Christ whom thou hast sent. ⁴ I glorified thee on earth, having accomplished the work which thou gavest me to do; ⁵ and now, Father, glorify thou me in thy own presence with the glory which I had with thee before the world was made."

Jesus prays for his disciples
Jn 17, 6-19

⁶ "I have manifested thy name to the men whom thou gavest me out of the world; thine they were, and thou gavest them to me, and they have kept thy word. ⁷ Now they know that everything that thou hast given me is from thee; ⁸ for I have given them the words which thou gavest me, and they have received them and know in truth that I came

* The final prayer with which the discourse ends is called Jesus' "High Priestly prayer" and is one of the finest and most profound passages of the gospel. It is a long outpouring of the Son to the Father, and at the same time the loftiest revelation of himself that Jesus makes.

** "To know" in the Bible is not merely "to have knowledge of with the mind" but also means the living experience that one has of a person. Therefore, to know God the Father and Jesus Christ means to understand, to love, to obey and to imitate.

Jerusalem. The ancient pathway with steps, which descends from the neighbourhood of the Cenacle to the Pool of Siloam and thence to the Kedron. It was in all probability the path which Jesus used on the night of Maundy Thursday.

from thee; and they have believed that thou didst send me. ⁹ I am praying for them; I am not praying for the world but for those whom thou hast given me, for they are thine; ¹⁰ all mine are thine, and thine are mine, and I am glorified in them. ¹¹ And now I am no more in the world, but they are in the world, and I am coming to thee. Holy Father, keep them in thy name, which thou hast given me, that they may be one, even as we are one. ¹² While I was with them, I kept them in thy name, which thou hast given me; I have guarded them, and none of them is lost but the son of
* perdition, that the scripture might be fulfilled. ¹³ But now I am coming to thee; and these things I speak in the world, that they may have my joy fulfilled in themselves. ¹⁴ I have given them thy word; and the world has hated them because they are not of the world, even as I am not of the world. ¹⁵ I do not pray that thou shouldst take them out of the world, but that thou shouldst keep them from the evil one. ¹⁶ They are not of the world, even as I am not of the world. ¹⁷ Sanctify them in the truth; thy word is truth. ¹⁸ As thou didst send me into the world, so I have sent
** them into the world. ¹⁹ And for their sake I consecrate myself, that they also may be consecrated in truth."

Jesus prays for the Church
Jn 17, 20-26

²⁰ "I do not pray for these only, but also for those who believe in me through

* The reference is to Judas Iscariot who betrayed him. The expression "son of perdition" is a way of saying in Hebrew: "he who would have lost himself," but it does not contain that element of fatality which is in error given to the phrase. The reference to Scripture is to Psalm 41, 10.

** For his disciples Jesus asks "that they may be one" and that the Father "will keep them from the evil one, and sanctify them in the truth." Their situation is to be noted: they are plunged into the "world" which is hostile to God, but they do not belong to the "world"; they are however sent into it to carry on Jesus' mission of bringing the knowledge of God, and salvation, to men.

345

Jerusalem, the Garden of Gethsemane at the foot of the Mount of Olives. On the left is the basilica which commemorates Jesus' agony (Mk. 14, 32-42).

their word, 21 that they may all be one; even as thou, Father, art in me, and I in thee, that they also may be in us, so that the world may believe that thou hast sent me. 22 The glory which thou hast given me I have given to them, that they may be one even as we are one, 23 I in them and thou in me, that they may become perfectly one, so that the world may know that thou hast sent me and hast loved them even as thou hast * loved me. 24 Father, I desire that they also, whom thou hast given me, may be with me where I am, to behold my glory which thou hast given me in thy love for me before the foundation of the world. 25 O righteous Father, the world has not known thee, but I have known thee; and these know that thou hast sent me. 26 I made known to them thy name, and I will make it known, that the love with which thou hast loved me may be in them, and I in them."

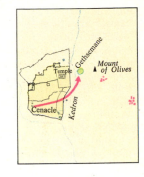

The night in which he was betrayed

At Gethsemane, Jesus is arrested
Mk 14, 32-52 (Mt 26, 36-56 Lk 22, 39-53)

32 And they went to a place which was ** called Gethsemane; and he said to his disciples, "Sit here, while I pray." 33 And he took with him Peter and James and John, and began to be greatly distressed and troubled. 34 And he said to them, "My soul is very sorrowful, even to death; remain here, and watch." 35 And

* The last petition of Jesus' prayer is that all who will in future believe in him (the Christians) may always remain united in the love of God. For this reason this last part is generally called the "prayer for unity."

** Gethsemane means olive-press. It was therefore an olive-grove. Luke says that Jesus was wont to spend nights there.

going a little farther, he fell on the ground and prayed that, if it were possible, the hour might pass from him. ³⁶ And he said, "Abba, Father, all things are possible to thee; remove this cup from me; yet not what I will, but what thou wilt." ³⁷ And he came and found them sleeping, and he said to Peter, "Simon, are you asleep? Could you not watch one hour? ³⁸ Watch and pray that you may not enter into temptation; the spirit indeed is willing, but the flesh is weak." ³⁹ And again he went away and
* prayed, saying the same words. ⁴⁰ And again he came and found them sleeping, for their eyes were very heavy; and they did not know what to answer him. ⁴¹ And he came the third time, and said to them, "Are you still sleeping and taking your rest? It is enough; the hour has come; the Son of man is betrayed into the hands of sinners. ⁴² Rise, let us be going; see, my betrayer is at hand."

⁴³ And immediately, while he was still speaking, Judas came, one of the twelve, and with him a crowd with swords and clubs, from the chief priests and the scribes and the elders. ⁴⁴ Now the betrayer had given them a sign, saying, "The one I shall kiss is the man; seize him and lead him away safely." ⁴⁵ And when he came, he went up to him at once, and said, "Master!" And he kissed him. ⁴⁶ And they laid hands on him and seized him. ⁴⁷ But one of those who stood by drew his sword, and struck the slave of the hight priest and cut off his ear. ⁴⁸ And Jesus said to them, "Have you

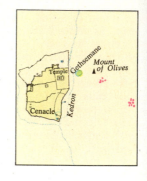

* Mark brings into prominence the anguish and even the fear of Jesus at this moment. He is completely man as he faces imminent death. But he prays: he turns to the Father, trustfully calling him Abba, and asks if it be possible to escape such suffering, but in the end he consents to and chooses the Father's plan. He will die with men and for men. Luke adds (22, 43-44): "There appeared unto him an angel from heaven, strengthening him. And being in an agony he prayed more earnestly; and his sweat became like great drops of blood falling down upon the ground."

come out as against a robber, with swords and clubs to capture me? ⁴⁹ Day after day I was with you in the temple teaching, and you did not seize me. But let the scriptures be fulfilled." ⁵⁰ And
* they all forsook him, and fled.

⁵¹ And a young man followed him, with nothing but a linen cloth about his body; and they seized him, ⁵² but he left the linen cloth and ran away naked.

Peter's denial and an officer's blow
Jn 18, 12-27 (Mt 26, 57-58; 69-75
Mk 14, 53-54; 66-72 Lk 22, 54-62)

¹² So the band of soldiers and their captain and the officers of the Jews seized Jesus and bound him. ¹³ First they led him to Annas; for he was the father-in-law of Caiaphas, who was high priest that year. ¹⁴ It was Caiaphas who had given counsel to the Jews that it was expedient that one man should die for the people.

¹⁵ Simon Peter followed Jesus, and so did another disciple. As this disciple was known to the high priest, he entered the court of the high priest along with Jesus, ¹⁶ while Peter stood outside at the door. So the other disciple, who was known to the high priest, went out and spoke to the maid who kept the door, and brought Peter in. ¹⁷ The maid who kept the door said to Peter, "Are not you also one of this man's disciples?" He said, "I am not." ¹⁸ Now the servants and officers had made a charcoal fire, because it was cold, and they were standing and warming themselves;

* In his whole account of the passion, Mark mentions the incidents in a concise way, without comment or explanation. Here he has no more than an implicit protest against the wickedness of the rulers. There follows the desertion by everybody. In Matthew on the other hand Jesus explains why he does not resist. To the man who struck with a sword he says: "Put your sword back into its place; for all who take the sword will perish by the sword. Do you think that I cannot appeal to my Father, and he will at once send me more than twelve legions of angels? But how then should the scriptures be fulfilled, that it must be so?" (Mt. 26, 52-54).

Jerusalem. Underground caves found near the church of St. Peter in Gallicantu (which recalls Peter's weeping at the crowing of a cock). Caves like this may have been used as prisons.

Peter also was with them, standing and warming himself.

¹⁹ The high priest then questioned Jesus about his disciples and his teaching. ²⁰ Jesus answered him, "I have spoken openly to the world; I have always taught in synagogues and in the temple, where all Jews come together; I have said nothing secretly. ²¹ Why do you ask me? Ask those who have heard me, what I said to them; they know what I said." ²² When he had said this, one of the officers standing by struck Jesus with his hand, saying, "Is that how you answer the high priest?" ²³ Jesus answered him, "If I have spoken wrongly, bear witness to the wrong; but if I have spoken rightly, why do you strike me?" ²⁴ Annas then sent him bound to Caiaphas the high priest.

²⁵ Now Simon Peter was standing and warming himself. They said to him, "Are not you also one of his disciples?" He denied it and said, "I am not." ²⁶ One of the servants of the high priest, a kinsman of the man whose ear Peter had cut off, asked, "Did I not see you in * the garden with him? ²⁷ Peter again denied it; and at once the cock crowed.

Jesus is insulted and slapped
Lk 22, 63-65 (Mt 26, 67-68 Mk 14, 65)

⁶³ Now the men who were holding Jesus mocked him and beat him; ⁶⁴ they also blindfolded him and asked him, "Prophesy! Who is it that struck you?" ⁶⁵ And they spoke many other words against him, reviling him.

* The account of Peter's denial is set against the background of Jesus' interrogation. This results in a sharp contrast: on the one hand is the courage, the majesty and the love of Jesus, on the other fear, cowardice and betrayal. The fact of the denial by the chief of the apostles is attested by all four evangelists, even though with differing details. Luke ends his account by saying: "The Lord turned and looked at Peter. And Peter remembered the word of the Lord, how he said to him 'Before the cock crows today, you will deny me three times', and he went out and wept bitterly" (Lk. 22, 61-62).

The Jewish trial

Jesus before the Sanhedrin
Lk 22, 66-71 (Mt 26, 59-66   Mk 14, 55-64)

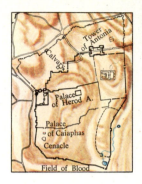

66 When day came, the assembly of the elders of the people gathered together, both chief priests and scribes; and they led him away to their council, and they said, 67 "If you are the Christ, tell us." But he said to them, "If I tell you, you will not believe; 68 and if I ask you, you will not answer. 69 But from now on the *Son of man shall be seated at the right hand of the power of God." 70 And they **all said, "Are you the Son of God, then?" And he said to them, "You say that I am." 71 And they said, "What further testimony do we need? We have heard it ourselves from his own lips."

Judas' suicide
Mt 27, 3-10

3 When Judas, his betrayer, saw that he was condemned, he repented and brought back the thirty pieces of silver to the chief priests and the elders, 4 saying, "I have sinned in betraying innocent blood." They said, "What is that to us? See to it yourself." 5 And throwing down the pieces of silver in the temple, he departed; and he went and hanged himself. 6 But the chief priests, taking the pieces of silver, said, "It is not lawful to put them into the treasury, since they are blood money." 7 So they took counsel, and bought with them the potter's field, to bury strangers

* Jesus, bound and a prisoner, replies clearly that he is the expected Messiah, who is to be enthroned near God (Psalm 110, 1) and appointed king and judge of history (Son of man: Dan. 7, 13-14).

** The members of the Sanhedrin understand that Jesus has gone beyond the question and has said implicitly that he is a divine Messiah. So they ask him for a precise reply on this point. And Jesus clearly affirms that he is truly the Son of God, which to them is blasphemy.

in. ⁸ Therefore that field has been called the Field of Blood to this day. ⁹ Then was fulfilled what had been spoken by
* the prophet Jeremiah, saying, "And they took the thirty pieces of silver, the price of him on whom a price had been set by some of the sons of Israel, ¹⁰ and they gave them for the potter's field, as the Lord directed me."

The Roman trial

Jesus before Pilate and Herod
Lk 23, 1-12 (Mt 27, 1-2; 11-14 Mk 15, 1-5
Jn 18, 28)

** ¹ Then the whole company of them arose, and brought him before Pilate. ² And they began to accuse him, saying, "We found this man perverting our nation, and saying that he himself is Christ a king." ³ And Pilate asked him, "Are you the King of the Jews?" And he answered him, "You have said so." ⁴ And Pilate said to the chief priests and the multitudes, "I find no crime in this man." ⁵ But they were urgent, saying, "He stirs up the people, teaching throughout all Judea, from Galilee even to this place."

⁶ When Pilate heard this, he asked whether the man was a Galilean. ⁷ And when he learned that he belonged to Herod's jurisdiction, he sent him over to Herod, who was himself in Jerusalem at that time. ⁸ When Herod saw Jesus, he was very glad, for he had long desired to see him, because he had heard about him, and he was hoping to see some

* Matthew emphasizes the fulfilment of the Scriptures. Two texts are put together in the quotation; Zech. 11, 12-13 and Jer. 32, 6-9.

** The Roman authority had taken away from the Sanhedrin the right of inflicting the death penalty. The Sanhedrin wants Jesus' death because he has blasphemed in declaring himself Son of God. But, knowing that Pilate, being a Gentile, will not be acquainted with the gravity of such a charge, the chiefs of the Jews bring their suit on the political plane, declaring that Jesus has made himself out to be a king. John (18, 28) notes that "they did not enter the praetorium, so that they might not be defiled but might eat the Passover."

Jerusalem. The site of the fortress of Antonia, seen from the Temple esplanade. It was here that Pilate probably set up his praetorium during the Passover festivals.

sign done by him. ⁹ So he questioned him at some length; but he made no answer. ¹⁰ The chief priests and the scribes stood by, vehemently accusing him. ¹¹ And Herod with his soldiers treated him with contempt and mocked him; then, arraying him in gorgeous apparel, he sent him back to Pilate. ¹² And Herod and Pilate became friends with each other that very day, for before this they had been at enmity with each other.

"I will chastise him and release him"
Lk 23, 13-16

¹³ Pilate then called together the chief priests and the rulers and the people, ¹⁴ and said to them, "You brought me this man as one who was perverting the people; and after examining him before you, behold, I did not find this man guilty of any of your charges against him; ¹⁵ neither did Herod, for he sent him back to us. Behold, nothing deserv- *ing death has been done by him; ¹⁶ I will therefore chastise him and release him."

Pilate questions Jesus
Jn 18, 29-38

** ²⁹ So Pilate went out to them and said, "What accusation do you bring against this man?" ³⁰ They answered him, "If this man were not an evildoer, we would not have handed him over." ³¹ Pilate said to them, "Take him yourselves and judge him by your own law." The Jews said to him, "It is not lawful for us to

* Luke emphasizes that from the political point of view Jesus is innocent; he is accused, but unjustly. Pilate, from that moment, starts a series of attempts to free Jesus by a compromise, but does not wish to face risks of unpopularity.

** John gives an extraordinarily full account of the trial before Pilate. He reads its course on two levels: outwardly Jesus is judged by men, and there is a sharp contrast between his powerlessness and his claim to be king; in reality he is truly men's king, majestic and glorious, and it is he who will be judge: before Christ men must make their choice.

355

put any man to death." [32] This was to fulfil the word which Jesus had spoken to show by what death he was to die.

[33] Pilate entered the praetorium again and called Jesus, and said to him, "Are you the King of the Jews?" [34] Jesus answered, "Do you say this of your own accord, or did others say it to you about me?" [35] Pilate answered, "Am I a Jew? Your own nation and the chief priests have handed you over to me; what have you done?" [36] Jesus answered, "My kingship is not of this world; if my kingship were of this world, my servants would fight, that I might not be handed over to the Jews; but my kingship is not from the world." [37] Pilate said to him, "So you are a king?" Jesus answered, "You say that I am a king. For this I was born, and for this I have come into the world, to bear witness to the
* truth. Every one who is of the truth hears my voice." [38] Pilate said to him, "What is truth?" After he had said this, he went out to the Jews again, and told them, "I find no crime in him."

Barabbas is preferred to Jesus
Mt 27, 15-23 (Mk 15, 6-14 Lk 23, 17-23 Jn 18, 39-40)

** [15] Now at the feast the governor was accustomed to release for the crowd any one prisoner whom they wanted. [16] And they had then a notorious prisoner, called Barabbas. [17] So when they had gathered, Pilate said to them, "Whom do you want me to release for you, Barabbas or Jesus who is called Christ?" [18] For he

* Jesus is king inasmuch as he bears witness to the truth, and this will appear particularly on the cross, which will be the throne of love. Whoever hears Jesus' word and allows himself to be drawn to him "when he is lifted up from the earth" (Jn. 12, 32) will belong to his kingdom.

** Matthew develops this episode more than do the others, and stresses the fact that Jesus is innocent and that the people of Israel, taken as a whole, oppose a clear refusal to their Messiah.

knew that it was out of envy that they had delivered him up. [19] Besides, while he was sitting on the judgment seat, his wife sent word to him, "Have nothing to do with that righteous man, for I have suffered much over him today in a dream." [20] Now the chief priests and the elders persuaded the people to ask for Barabbas and destroy Jesus. [21] The governor again said to them, "Which of the two do you want me to release for you?" And they said, "Barabbas." [22] Pilate said to them, "Then what shall I do with Jesus who is called Christ?" They all said, "Let him be crucified." [23] And he said, "Why, what evil has he done?" But they shouted all the more, "Let him be crucified."

Jesus is condemned to death
Mt 27, 24-26 (Mk 15, 15   Lk 23, 24-25)

[24] So when Pilate saw that he was gaining nothing, but rather that a riot was beginning, he took water and washed his hands before the crowd, saying, "I am innocent of this righteous man's
*blood; see to it yourselves." [25] And all the people answered, "His blood be on us and on our children!" [26] Then he released for them Barabbas, and having scourged Jesus, delivered him to be crucified.

Jesus is crowned with thorns
Mt 27, 27-30 (Mk 15, 16-19 Jn 19, 1-3)

[27] Then the soldiers of the governor took Jesus into the praetorium, and

*   Pilate abjures his responsibility with a typically oriental, symbolic gesture. In reality his blame is not entirely taken away thus. All the same it is emphasized, even more, that it is the people who are responsible for the killing of Jesus: this is the complete rupture between Israel and the Messiah. Matthew does not justify anti-semitism; he is merely convinced that from that time forward Israel as such is no longer "the people of salvation": it is replaced by the Church, the new community of converted individuals who are drawn without distinction from all peoples.

Jerusalem. The so-called Arch of the "Ecce homo". It is approximately on the site of the Gospel incident, but the Roman arch is a century later.

they gathered the whole battalion before him. [28] And they stripped him and put a scarlet robe upon him, [29] and plaiting a crown of thorns they put it on his head, and put a reed in his right hand. And kneeling before him they mocked him, saying, "Hail, King of the Jews!" [30] And they spat upon him, and took the reed and struck him on the head.

"Here is the man!"
Jn 19, 4-7

[4] Pilate went out again, and said to them, "Behold, I am bringing him out to you, that you may know that I find no crime in him." [5] So Jesus came out, wearing the crown of thorns and the purple robe. Pilate said to them, "Here is the man!" [6] When the chief priests and the officers saw him, they cried out, "Crucify him, crucify him!" Pilate said to them, "Take him yourselves and crucify him, for I find no crime in him." [7] The Jews answered him, "We have a law, and by that law he ought to die, because he has made himself the Son of God."

Pilate questions Jesus for the last time
Jn 19, 8-11

[8] When Pilate heard these words, he was the more afraid; [9] he entered the praetorium again and said to Jesus, "Where are you from?" But Jesus gave no answer. [10] Pilate therefore said to him, "You will not speak to me? Do you not know that I have power to release

* For John, the crowning with thorns, which historically was intended to be mocking and derisory, assumes a symbolical meaning: in the humiliation of the passion Jesus truly becomes king. So the words of Pilate, seeking to arouse compassion for Jesus, and those of the Jews, desiring his death, are involuntarily an authentic description of Christ: he is Man and at the same time Son of God, the real king of Israel and of all mankind. This is the deep sense of the latter part of the trial in John's detailed account.

359

Above: A view of the "Pavement", the flag-stones discovered to the west of the Antonia fortress. In all probability this is the place of which Jn. 19, 13 speaks.

Below: Detail of the stone which bears cut into it the "king's game" widely popular among the Roman soldiery.

you, and power to crucify you?" [11] Jesus answered him, "You would have no power over me unless it had been given you from above; therefore he who delivered me to you has the greater sin."

"Here is your king!"
Jn 19, 12-16

[12] Upon this Pilate sought to release him, but the Jews cried out, "If you release this man, you are not Caesar's friend; every one who makes himself a king sets himself against Caesar." [13] When Pilate heard these words, he brought Jesus out and sat down on the judgment seat at a place called The Pavement, and in Hebrew, Gabbatha. [14] Now it was the day of Preparation of the Passover; it was about the sixth hour. He said to the Jews, "Here is your King!" [15] They cried out, "Away with him, away with him, crucify him!" Pilate said to them, "Shall I crucify your King?" The chief priests answered, "We have no king but Caesar." [16] Then he handed him over to them to be crucified.

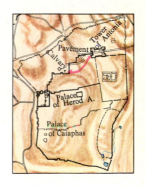

The crucifixion and death

The road to Calvary
Lk 23, 26-32 (Mt 27, 31-32 Mk 15, 20-21 Jn 19, 17)

[26] And as they led him away, they seized one Simon of Cyrene, who was coming in from the country, and laid on him the cross, to carry it behind Jesus. [27] And there followed him a great

* The Jews resort to blackmail, and in the face of their threats Pilate betrays justice.

** Probably, following the Roman custom, the "cross" carried by Jesus (and therefore by Simon the Cyrenian) was only the cross-beam called "patibulum", whereas the vertical stake was prepared at the place of torture.

361

Jerusalem. The present entrance to the Basilica of the Holy Sepulchre.
This basilica, with its well-built structure and design, is the most
precious of the Christian monuments in Jerusalem.

multitude of the people, and of women who bewailed and lamented him. ²⁸ But Jesus turning to them said, "Daughters of Jerusalem, do not weep for me, but weep for yourselves and for your children. ²⁹ For behold, the days are coming when they will say, 'Blessed are the barren, and the wombs that never bore, and the breasts that never gave suck!' ³⁰ Then they will begin to say to the mountains, 'Fall on us'; and to the hills, 'Cover us.' ³¹ For if they do this when the wood is green, what will happen when it is dry?"

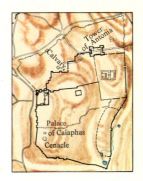

³²Two others also, who were criminals, were led away to be put to death with him.

Jesus is crucified
Lk 23, 33-38 (Mt 27, 33-34 Mk 15, 22-32 Jn 19, 18-24)

³³ And when they came to the place which is called The Skull, there they crucified him, and the criminals, one on the right and one on the left. ³⁴ And Jesus said, "Father, forgive them; for they know not what they do." And they cast lots to divide his garments. ³⁵ And the people stood by, watching; but the rulers scoffed at him, saying, "He saved others; let him save himself, if he is the Christ of God, his Chosen One!" ³⁶ The soldiers also mocked him, coming up and offering him vinegar, ³⁷ and saying, "If you are the King of the Jews, save yourself!" ³⁸ There was also an inscription over him, "This is the King of the Jews."

* To the women who show a certain compassion towards him, Jesus addresses a stern call to repentance, foretelling the dreadful days of the destruction of Jerusalem. The illustration of wood is a proverbial one; in this case it means: if an innocent man (green wood) is punished like this, what will be the punishment of the sinners (dry wood)? They will be consumed with the fire of the judgment of God.

** The spur of rock was called, because of its shape, "Cranium" (Greek) or "Calvary" (Latin) or "Golgotha" (Aramaic).

*** The first of Jesus' words from the cross is a word of pity and love for his enemies.

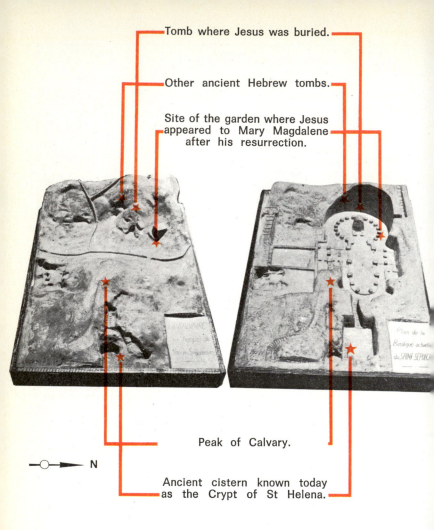

Tomb where Jesus was buried.

Other ancient Hebrew tombs.

Site of the garden where Jesus appeared to Mary Magdalene after his resurrection.

N

Peak of Calvary.

Ancient cistern known today as the Crypt of St Helena.

Two models of the area of Calvary: as it must have been in Jesus' day and as it is in our time. Their juxtaposition allows us to pick out the whereabouts of the holy places, today incorporated in the great and unique Basilica of the Holy Sepulchre.

"Today you will be with me in Paradise"
Lk 23, 39-43

³⁹ One of the criminals who were hanged railed at him, saying, "Are you not the Christ? Save yourself and us!" ⁴⁰ But the other rebuked him, saying, "Do you not fear God, since you are under the same sentence of condemnation? ⁴¹ And we indeed justly; for we are receiving the due reward of our deeds; but this man has done nothing wrong." ⁴² And he said, "Jesus, remember me when you come in your kingly power." ⁴³ And he said to him, "Truly, I say to you, today you will be with me in Paradise."

"My God, my God, why hast thou forsaken me?"
Mk 15, 33-36 (Mt 27, 45-49 Lk 23, 44-45)

³³ And when the sixth hour had come, there was darkness over the whole land until the ninth hour. ³⁴ And at the ninth hour Jesus cried with a loud voice, * "Eloi, Eloi, lama sabachthani?" which means, "My God, my God, why hast thou forsaken me?" ³⁵ And some of the bystanders hearing it said, "Behold, he is calling Elijah." ³⁶ And one ran and, filling ** a sponge full of vinegar, put it on a reed and gave it to him to drink, saying, "Wait, let us see whether Elijah will come to take him down."

Jesus gives his mother to us
Jn 19, 25-27

²⁵ So the soldiers did this. But stand-

* Mark, followed by Matthew, brings into prominence Jesus' loneliness and anguish on the cross. The phrase quoted in Aramaic is the beginning of Psalm 22. The psalm expresses with the greatest intensity the suffering of the persecuted righteous man, who feels himself abandoned even by God. In this desolation however the psalmist makes a heroic act of faith and loyalty to God, who will liberate him in the end.

** All the evangelists, though in different ways, record that, on the cross, Jesus was given vinegar (Ps. 69, 22) and that lots were cast for his clothes (Ps. 22, 19).

Jerusalem. Basilica of the Holy Sepulchre. The altar built on the rock of Calvary, which can still be touched through an opening made in the floor under the altar. The chapel is several metres above the level of the Basilica.

ing by the cross of Jesus were his mother, and his mother's sister, Mary the wife of Clopas, and Mary Magdalene. 26 When Jesus saw his mother, and the disciple whom he loved standing near,
* he said to his mother, "Woman, behold, your son!" 27 Then he said to the disciple, "Behold, your mother!" And from that hour the disciple took her to his own home.

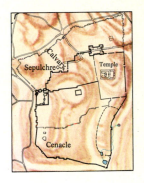

"It is finished!"
Jn 19, 28-30

28 After this Jesus, knowing that all was now finished, said (to fulfil the scripture), "I thirst." 29 A bowl full of vinegar stood there; so they put a sponge full of the vinegar on hyssop and held it to his mouth. 30 When Jesus had received the vinegar, he said, "It is finished."

Jesus dies
Lk 23, 45-46 (Mt 27, 50-51 Mk 15, 37-38 Jn 19, 30)

45 The curtain of the temple was torn
** in two. 46 Then Jesus, crying with a loud voice, said, "Father, into thy hands I commit my spirit!" And having said this he breathed his last.

After the death of Jesus
Lk 23, 47-49 (Mt 27, 51-56 Mk 15, 39-41)

47 Now when the centurion saw what had taken place, he praised God, and said, "Certainly this man was innocent!"

* This scene, recorded by John, as well as being an act of filial piety on Jesus' part, has a deeper meaning: at the foot of the cross the new community of faith and salvation is being formed. Mary represents the Church and becomes its mother, while the beloved disciple represents all believers.

** The veil separated the innermost part of the Temple from the rest, and prevented access to the place where God was present. In the tearing of this veil the evangelists see a symbolic meaning: with Jesus' death there is an end to the religious institution of the Old Testament, and henceforth all men can approach God.

367

⁴⁸ And all the multitudes who assembled to see the sight, when they saw what had taken place, returned home beating their breasts. ⁴⁹ And all his acquaintances and the women who had followed him from Galilee stood at a distance and saw these things.

His heart is pierced
Jn 19, 31-37

³¹ Since it was the day of Preparation, in order to prevent the bodies from remaining on the cross on the sabbath (for that sabbath was a high day), the Jews asked Pilate that their legs might be broken, and that they might be taken away. ³² So the soldiers came and broke the legs of the first, and of the other who had been crucified with him; ³³ but when they came to Jesus and saw that he was already dead, they did not break his legs. ³⁴ But one of the soldiers pierced his side with a spear, and at once there * came out blood and water. ³⁵ He who saw it has borne witness—his testimony is true, and he knows that he tells the truth—that you also may believe. ³⁶ For ** these things took place that the scripture might be fulfilled, "Not a bone of him shall be broken." ³⁷ And again another scripture says, "They shall look on him whom they have pierced."

Jesus is buried
Jn 19, 38-42 (Mt 27, 57-61   Mk 15, 42-47 Lk 23, 50-56)

³⁸ After this Joseph of Arimathea, who

* In this fact John sees not only the confirmation of Jesus' death, but, above all, a deep symbolic significance: from the Crucified flows salvation, grace and the gift of the Spirit, which brings the Church to birth.

** John first quotes Ex. 12, 46: Jesus is the true paschal Lamb, sacrificed to free us and to save us; and then Zech. 12, 10: he who looks to the Crucified with a penitent, believing heart, will share in the gift of "water" which purifies and gives life.

was a disciple of Jesus, but secretly, for fear of the Jews, asked Pilate that he might take away the body of Jesus, and Pilate gave him leave. So he came and took away his body. ³⁹ Nicodemus also, who had at first come to him by night, came bringing a mixture of myrrh and aloes, about a hundred pounds' weight. ⁴⁰ They took the body of Jesus, and bound it in linen cloths with the spices, as is the burial custom of the Jews. ⁴¹ Now in the place where he was crucified there was a garden, and in the garden a new tomb where no one had ever been laid. ⁴² So because of the Jewish day of Preparation, as the tomb was close at hand, they laid Jesus there.

The guard at the tomb
Mt 27, 62-66

⁶² Next day, that is, after the day of Preparation, the chief priests and the Pharisees gathered before Pilate ⁶³ and said, "Sir, we remember how that impostor said, while he was still alive, 'After three days I will rise again.' ⁶⁴ Therefore order the sepulchre to be made secure until the third day, lest his disciples go and steal him away, and tell the people, 'He has risen from the dead,' and the last fraud will be worse than the first." ⁶⁵ Pilate said to them, "You have a guard of soldiers; go, make it as secure as you can." ⁶⁶ So they went and made the sepulchre secure by sealing the stone and * setting a guard.

* This detail, added by Matthew, prepares the way for the later announcement of the resurrection. The power of God will not be stopped by men's seals.

369

Jerusalem, Basilica of the Holy Sepulchre. Exterior of the shrine built over Jesus' tomb. Inside it a sheet of marble covers the rock on which the body of Jesus was laid. It is a glorious tomb because of the mystery of the Resurrection.

The empty tomb
and the news of the Resurrection

The empty tomb
Lk 24, 1-12

* ¹ But on the first day of the week, at early dawn, they went to the tomb, taking the spices which they had prepared. ² And they found the stone rolled away from the tomb, ³ but when they went in they did not find the body. ⁴ While they were perplexed about this, behold, two men stood by them in dazzling apparel; ⁵ and as they were frightened and bowed their faces to the ground, the men said to them, "Why do you seek the living among the dead? He is not here, but has risen. ⁶ Remember how he told you, while he was still in Galilee, ⁷ that the Son of man must be delivered into the hands of sinful men, and be crucified, and on the third day rise." ⁸ And they remembered his words, ⁹ and returning from the tomb they told all this to the eleven and to all the rest. ¹⁰ Now it was Mary Magdalene and Joanna and Mary the mother of James and the other women with them who told this to the apostles; ¹¹ but these words seemed to them an idle tale, and they did not believe them. ¹² But Peter rose and ran to the tomb; stooping and looking in, he saw the linen cloths by themselves; and he went home wondering at what had happened.

* The day after the sabbath, specially in memory of Jesus' resurrection, has been named the "Lord's Day" and has become the feast day of Christians. On this first Lord's Day the tomb was found empty and this was also carefully checked by the chief of the apostles and the beloved disciple.

Jerusalem. Entrance to a tomb belonging to the Herod family and so contemporary with Jesus. A typical feature is the great round stone which, running in a groove, closed the entrance to the tomb.

The risen Jesus appears to Mary Magdalen
Jn 20, 11-18

11 But Mary stood weeping outside the tomb, and as she wept she stooped to look into the tomb; 12 and she saw two angels in white, sitting where the body of Jesus had lain, one at the head and one at the feet. 13 They said to her, "Woman, why are you weeping?" She said to them, "Because they have taken away my Lord, and I do not know * where they have laid him." 14 Saying this, she turned round and saw Jesus standing, but she did not know that it was Jesus. 15 Jesus said to her, "Woman, why are you weeping? Whom do you seek?" Supposing him to be the gardener, she said to him, "Sir, if you have carried him away, tell me where you have laid him, and I will take him away." 16 Jesus said to her, "Mary." She turned and said to him in Hebrew, "Rabboni!" (which means Teacher). 17 Jesus said to her, "Do not hold me, for I have not yet ** ascended to the Father; but go to my brethren and say to them, I am ascending to my Father and your Father, to my God and your God." 18 Mary Magdalene went and said to the disciples, "I have seen the Lord"; and she told them that he had said these things to her.

Jesus of Nazareth, who was crucified, has arisen
Mk 16, 1-8 (Mt 28, 1-8 Lk 24, 1-8)

1 And when the sabbath was past,

* Seeing the sign of the empty tomb is not in itself enough to induce belief in the resurrection. It is also necessary to see the risen Jesus and to meet him. Matthew mentions briefly a similar appearance (28, 9-10) but he says that Mary Magdalen was accompanied by "the other Mary", i.e. the mother of James.

** Jesus' resurrection is not a return to his former life, but the beginning of a new and different life. Because of this the relationship with him also cannot continue as it was before. Now he is "the Lord" and returns to the Father; communion with him is established in faith.

373

Mary Magdalene, and Mary the mother of James, and Salome, bought spices, so that they might go and anoint him. ² And very early on the first day of the week they went to the tomb when the sun had risen. ³ And they were saying to one another, "Who will roll away the stone for us from the door of the tomb?" ⁴ And looking up, they saw that the stone was rolled back; for it was very large. ⁵ And entering the tomb, they saw a young man sitting on the right side, dressed in a white robe; and they were amazed. ⁶ And he said to them, "Do not be amazed; you seek Jesus of Nazareth, * who was crucified. He has risen, he is not here; see the place where they laid him. ⁷ But go, tell his disciples and Peter that he is going before you to Galilee; there you will see him, as he told you." ⁸ And they went out and fled from the tomb; for trembling and astonishment had come upon them; and they said ** nothing to any one, for they were afraid.

False rumours
Mt 28, 11-15

¹¹ While they were going, behold, some of the guard went into the city and told the chief priests all that had taken place. ¹² And when they had assembled with the elders and taken counsel, they gave a sum of money to the soldiers ¹³ and said, "Tell people, 'His disciples came by night and stole him away while we were asleep.' ¹⁴ And if this comes to the governor's ears, we will satisfy him and keep you out of trouble." ¹⁵ So they

* This is the Easter message. The Risen Lord is the same Jesus of Nazareth who was crucified. Passion and resurrection are intimately joined together: the way of the cross has brought Christ to the glory of the resurrection. In this way God reveals the mystery of his Son.

** This behaviour of the women stresses the novelty and extraordinary grandeur of the divine message; before it a person stands confused and uncomprehending. Luke in his turn records a similar reaction from the apostles to the announcement of the women: "these words seemed to them an idle tale, and they did not believe them" (24, 11). But

took the money and did as they were directed; and this story has been spread among the Jews to this day.

Appearances of the risen Lord

The risen Jesus appears to two disciples on the road to Emmaus
Lk 24, 13-35

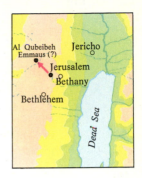

* ¹³ That very day two of them were going to a village named Emmaus, about seven miles from Jerusalem, ¹⁴ and talking with each other about all these things that had happened. ¹⁵ While they were talking and discussing together, Jesus himself drew near and went with them. ¹⁶ But their eyes were kept from recognizing him. ¹⁷ And he said to them, "What is this conversation which you are holding with each other as you walk?" And they stood still, looking sad. ¹⁸ Then one of them, named Cleopas, answered him, "Are you the only visitor to Jerusalem who does not know the things that have happened there in these days?" ¹⁹ And he said to them, "What things?" And they said to him, "Concerning Jesus of Nazareth, who was a prophet mighty in deed and word before God and all the people, ²⁰ and how our chief priests and rulers delivered him up to be condemned to death, and crucified him. ²¹ But we had hoped that he was the one to redeem Israel. Yes, and besides all this, it is now the third day since this happened. ²² Moreover, some women of our company amazed us. They were at the tomb early

the power of the risen Christ will overcome every doubt, misunderstanding and resistance.

* This is one of the most beautiful stories. The two disciples gradually come to recognize Jesus and so pass from grief to enthusiasm. In Luke's account we feel the atmosphere of the brotherly meetings of the early Christians as they read the Scriptures in the light of the risen Christ and then "broke bread" i.e. celebrated the Eucharist.

375

Al-Qubeibeh is probably the site of Emmaus. In the photograph is the "Roman road" which goes through the ancient village (cf. Lk. 24, 28-33).

in the morning, ²³ and did not find his body; and they came back saying that they had even seen a vision of angels, who said that he was alive. ²⁴ Some of those who were with us went to the tomb, and found it just as the women had said; but him they did not see." ²⁵ And he said to them, "O foolish men, and slow of heart to believe all that the prophets have spoken! ²⁶ Was it not necessary that the Christ should suffer these things and enter into his glory?" ²⁷ And beginning with Moses and all the prophets, he interpreted to them in all the scriptures the things concerning himself.

* ²⁸ So they drew near to the village to which they were going. He appeared to be going further, ²⁹ but they constrained him, saying, "Stay with us, for it is toward evening and the day is now far spent." So he went in to stay with them. ³⁰ When he was at table with them, he took the bread and blessed, and broke it, and gave it to them. ³¹ And their eyes were opened and they recognized him; and he vanished out of their sight. ³² They said to each other. "Did not our hearts burn within us while he talked to us on the road, while he opened to us the scriptures?" ³³ And they rose that same hour and returned to Jerusalem; and they found the eleven gathered together and those who were with them, ³⁴ who said, "The Lord has risen indeed, and has appeared to Simon!" ³⁵ Then they told what had happened on the road, and how he was known to them in the breaking of the bread.

*   When a person has had an experience of the resurrection, the Scriptures help him to understand Jesus' life, and also the scandal of his death on the cross, in a new light. The risen Jesus is the fulfilment and the key to the interpretation of the Scriptures. He shows the victory of God's love and is the foundation of hope.

377

The risen Jesus gives the apostles power to forgive sins
Jn 20, 19-23 (Lk 24, 36-43)

19 On the evening of that day, the first day of the week, the doors being shut where the disciples were, for fear of the Jews, Jesus came and stood among them and said to them, "Peace be with you." 20 When he had said this, he showed * them his hands and his side. Then the disciples were glad when they saw the Lord. 21 Jesus said to them again, "Peace be with you. As the Father has sent me, even so I send you." 22 And when he had said this, he breathed on them, and ** said to them, "Receive the Holy Spirit. 23 If you forgive the sins of any, they are forgiven; if you retain the sins of any, they are retained."

"Do not be faithless, but believing!"
Jn 20, 24-29

24 Now Thomas, one of the twelve, called the Twin, was not with them when Jesus came. 25 So the other disciples told him, "We have seen the Lord." But he said to them, "Unless I see in his hands the print of the nails, and place my finger in the mark of the nails, and place my hand in his side, I will not believe."

26 Eight days later, his disciples were again in the house, and Thomas was with them. The doors were shut, but Jesus came and stood among them, and said, "Peace be with you." 27 Then he said to Thomas, "Put your finger here,

* John emphasizes the reality of the risen Christ who is the same Jesus who suffered the passion and shows its marks. But we are concerned with a very different sort of existence: he enters through closed doors. The same thing is brought out strongly by Luke (24, 36-43): the risen Jesus is not a body-less phantom. He can be looked at and touched, and he can even eat with the disciples. These will have to be first hand witnesses of the resurrection.

** The risen Jesus keeps his promises: he gives peace and confers the Holy Spirit, sending the apostles on their mission and giving them the power to forgive sins. The Christian sacrament of penance has its origin here.

378

and see my hands; and put out your hand, and place it in my side; do not be
* faithless, but believing." 28 Thomas answered him, "My Lord and my God!"
29 Jesus said to him, "Have you believed because you have seen me? Blessed are those who have not seen and yet believe."

Epilogue of John the Evangelist
Jn 20, 30-31

30 Now Jesus did many other signs in the presence of the disciples, which are not written in this book; 31 but these are written that you may believe that Jesus is the Christ, the Son of God, and that believing you may have life in his name.

The risen Jesus appears to the disciples near the Lake of Galilee
Jn 21, 1-14

1 After this Jesus revealed himself again to the disciples by the Sea of Tiberias; and he revealed himself in this way. 2 Simon Peter, Thomas called the Twin, Nathanael of Cana in Galilee, the sons of Zebedee, and two others of his disciples were together. 3 Simon Peter said to them, "I am going fishing." They said to him, "We will go with you." They went out and got into the boat; but that night they caught nothing.

4 Just as day was breaking, Jesus stood on the beach; yet the disciples did not know that it was Jesus. 5 Jesus said to them, "Children, have you any fish?" They answered him, "No." 6 He said to

* The incredulous Thomas is reproved because he ought to have believed without needing to see. All the same the kindness of the Lord allowed him a confirmation. But from that time onwards Christ's disciples will have to believe on the testimony of the apostles, without claiming a direct and palpable knowledge of the facts. They will have experience of the risen Christ on the level of faith and for that reason they will be "blessed".

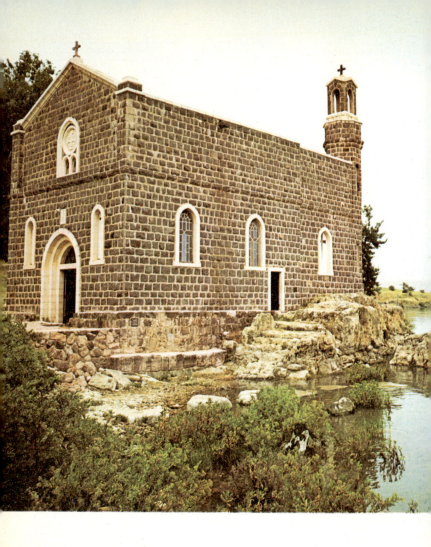

Tabgha, on the Lake of Gennesaret. The "Chapel of the primacy" (Jn. 21, 15-19) is built on the foundations of very ancient churches, a fact which speaks in favour of the authenticity of the site.

them, "Cast the net on the right side of the boat, and you will find some." So they cast it, and now they were not able to haul it in, for the quantity of * fish. 7 That disciple whom Jesus loved said to Peter, "It is the Lord!" When Simon Peter heard that it was the Lord, he put on his clothes, for he was stripped for work, and sprang into the sea. 8 But the other disciples came in the boat, dragging the net full of fish, for they were not far from the land, but about a hundred yards off.

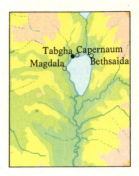

9 When they got out on land, they saw a charcoal fire there, with fish lying on it, and bread. 10 Jesus said to them, "Bring some of the fish that you have just caught." 11 So Simon Peter went aboard and hauled the net ashore, full of large fish, a hundred and fifty-three of them; and although there were so many, the net was not torn. 12 Jesus said to them, "Come and have breakfast." Now none of the disciples dared ask him, "Who are you?" They knew it was the Lord. 13 Jesus came and took the bread and gave it to them, and so with the fish. 14 This was now the third time that Jesus was revealed to the disciples after he was raised from the dead.

Jesus confers the primacy on Peter
Jn 21, 15-19

15 When they had finished breakfast, Jesus said to Simon Peter, "Simon, son of John, do you love me more than these?" He said to him, "Yes, Lord; you know that I love you." He said to him,

* This chapter seems to be an appendix added to John's gospel by one of his disciples, who collected in these pages other personal memories of the apostle. In an atmosphere of close fellowship the risen Jesus appears to his disciples. Among them Peter and "the disciple whom Jesus loved" receive special prominence.

"Feed my lambs." [16] A second time he said to him, "Simon, son of John, do you love me?" He said to him, "Yes, Lord; you know that I love you." He said to him, "Tend my sheep." [17] He said to him the third time, "Simon, son of John, do you love me?" Peter was griev- * ed because he said to him the third time, "Do you love me?" And he said to him, "Lord, you know everything; you know that I love you." Jesus said to him, "Feed my sheep. [18] Truly, truly, I say to you, when you were young, you girded yourself and walked where you would; but when you are old, you will stretch out your hands, and another will gird you and carry you where you do not wish to go." [19] (This he said to show by what death he was to glorify God.) And after this he said to him, "Follow me."

The destiny of the beloved disciple
Jn 21, 20-23

[20] Peter turned and saw following them the disciple whom Jesus loved, who had lain close to his breast at the supper and had said, "Lord, who is it that is going to betray you?" [21] When Peter saw him, he said to Jesus, "Lord, what about this man?" [22] Jesus said to him, "If it is my will that he remain until I come, what is that to you? Follow me!" [23] The saying spread abroad among the breth- ren that this disciple was not to die; yet Jesus did not say to him that he was not to die, but, "If it is my will ** that he remain until I come, what is ** that to you?"

Tabgha Capernaum
Magdala Bethsaida

* Jesus' question, re- peated three times, calls to mind Peter's triple denial during the passion. Now Peter re- affirms his love for the Master three times, and and Jesus gives him the task of directing the whole Church. He will be the visible represent- ative of Christ, the good shepherd.

** The verse is intend- ed to clear up a mis- understanding and to repudiate a saying which had spread ac- cording to which "this disciple" — probably John himself — would live until the Lord's return. That interpre- tation did not agree with the sense of the phrase which Jesus used. Perhaps Jesus

Epilogue of the disciples of John the Evangelist
Jn 21, 24-25

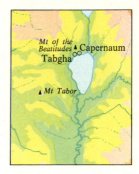

Mt of the Beatitudes ▲ Capernaum
Tabgha

▲ Mt Tabor

24 This is the disciple who is bearing witness to these things, and who has written these things; and we know that his testimony is true. 25 But there are also many other things which Jesus did; were every one of them to be written, I suppose that the world itself could not contain the books that would be written.

The Ascension

The risen Jesus confers on the disciples the apostolic mission
Mt 28, 16-20

16 Now the eleven disciples went to Galilee, to the mountain to which Jesus had directed them. 17 And when they saw him they worshipped him; but some doubted. 18 And Jesus came and said to them, "All authority in heaven and on earth has been given to me. 19 Go therefore and make disciples of all nations, baptizing them in the name of the Father and of the Son and of the Holy Spirit, 20 teaching them to observe all that I have commanded you; and lo, I am with you always, to the close of the
∗ age."

meant that it is possible to follow him not only through martyrdom, but with the loyalty of a life lived entirely in his love.

∗ The gospel of Matthew ends with these words. The Lord sends his disciples into all the world and promises that he will always be present in the community of those who believe in him.

383

Jerusalem, the Mount of Olives. This little building, now turned into a mosque, is built on the site of the last appearance of the risen Jesus and records his Ascension (Lk. 24, 50-51).

The apostles as witnesses of the risen Christ
Lk 24, 44-49

44 Then he said to them, "These are my words which I spoke to you, while I was still with you, that everything written about me in the law of Moses and the prophets and the psalms must be fulfilled." 45 Then he opened their minds to understand the scriptures, 46 and said to them, "Thus it is written, that the Christ should suffer and on the third day rise from the dead, 47 and that repentance and forgiveness of sins should be preached in his name to âll nations, beginning from Jerusalem. 48 You

* are witnesses of these things. 49 And behold, I send the promise of my Father upon you; but stay in the city, until you are clothed with power from on high."

The risen Jesus ascends to heaven
Lk 24, 50-53

50 Then he led them out as far as Bethany, and lifting up his hands he blessed them. 51 While he blessed them, he parted from them, and was carried up into heaven. 52 And they worshipped him, and returned to Jerusalem with great joy, 53 and were continually in the temple blessing God.

Mark's final summing up
Mk 16, 9-20

9 Now when he rose early on the first

* This recalls the fundamental theme of the preaching of the early Church: the proclamation that Jesus died and rose again, according to the divine plan for the salvation of mankind, and the invitation to repent and accept from God the forgiveness of sins and the gift of the Spirit. This joyful news and the new life which flows from it must, through the testimony of Christians, reach the whole world.

day of the week, he appeared first to Mary Magdalene, from whom he had cast out seven demons. 10 She went and told those who had been with him, as they mourned and wept. 11 But when they heard that he was alive and had been seen by her, they would not believe it.

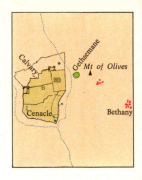

12 After this he appeared in another form to two of them, as they were walking into the country. 13 And they went back and told the rest, but they did not believe them.

14 Afterward he appeared to the eleven themselves as they sat at table; and he upbraided them for their unbelief and hardness of heart, because they had not believed those who saw him after he had risen. 15 And he said to them "Go into all the world and preach the gospel to the whole creation. 16 He who believes and is baptized will be saved; but he who does not believe will be condemned. 17 And these signs will accompany those who believe: in my name they will cast out demons; they will speak in new tongues; 18 they will pick up serpents, and if they drink any deadly thing, it will not hurt them; they will lay their hands on the sick, and they will recover."

19 So then the Lord Jesus, after he had spoken to them, was taken up into heaven, and sat down at the right hand of God. 20 And they went forth and preached everywhere, while the Lord worked with them and confirmed the message by the signs that attended it.

INDEX

Index of subjects

in the same series ▶

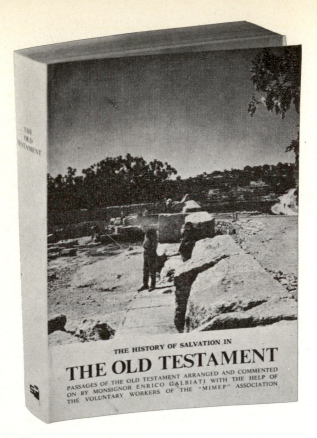

THE HISTORY OF SALVATION IN

THE OLD TESTAMENT

Passages from the various books of the Old Testament have been arranged in continuous narrative form. The introduction, commentary and notes will help the reader to understand both the themes of the Bible and its message of salvation. The colour photographs and other illustrations and maps, together with their captions, vividly bring home the places mentioned in the text. 466 pages.

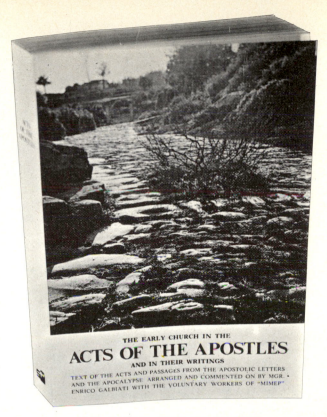

THE EARLY CHURCH IN THE
ACTS OF THE APOSTLES
AND IN THEIR WRITINGS
TEXT OF THE ACTS AND PASSAGES FROM THE APOSTOLIC LETTERS
AND THE APOCALYPSE ARRANGED AND COMMENTED ON BY MGR. •
ENRICO GALBIATI WITH THE VOLUNTARY WORKERS OF "MIMEP"

THE EARLY CHURCH IN THE

ACTS OF THE APOSTLES

AND IN THEIR WRITINGS

Here are to be found all the passages of theological importance which, when more or less co-ordinated, make up biblical theology in the New Testament. It makes known the history, life and teaching of the primitive Church and explains in their historical context the teachings of the Apostles which today are being offered once more to the faithful in the biblical readings of the liturgy. Illustrated throughout with photographs and maps. 450 pages.